Wissenschaftliche Untersuchungen zum Neuen Testament

Begründet von Joachim Jeremias und Otto Michel
Herausgegeben von
Martin Hengel und Otfried Hofius

27

The Parable of the Wicked Tenants

An Inquiry into Parable Interpretation

by
Klyne Snodgrass

WIPF & STOCK · Eugene, Oregon

Wipf and Stock Publishers
199 W 8th Ave, Suite 3
Eugene, OR 97401

The Parable of the Wicked Tenants
An Inquiry into Parable Interpretation
By Snodgrass, Klyne
Copyright©1983 Mohr Siebeck
ISBN 13: 978-1-61097-152-2
Publication date 5/1/2011
Previously published by Mohr Siebeck, 1983

This edition reprinted 2011 by Wipf and Stock
through special arrangement with J.C.B. Mohr (Paul Siebeck).
Copyright J.C.B. Mohr (Paul Siebeck) 1983.

To
Phyllis

Table of Contents

Preface VII

Abbreviations IX

Introduction 1

Chapter 1: Attempts to Interpret the Parable 3
    Adolf Jülicher 3
    The De-Allegorizing Approach 5
    Werner Georg Kümmel 8
    Novel Approaches 10

Chapter 2: What Methold Should be Used? 12
    Can a Parable be an Allegory? 13
    Other Methodological Considerations 26

Chapter 3: The Cultural Setting of the Parable 31

Chapter 4: An Analysis of the Parable and its Development ... 41
    Comparison of the Various Accounts 42
    The Development of the Tradition 52

Chapter 5: The Origin and Meaning of the Parable 72
    The Owner and his Vineyard 73
    The Tenants and the Servants 77
    The Son 80
    The Judgment Pronouncement 87
    The Stone 95
    The Parable as a Unit 106

Conclusions 111
Appendix: The Wordplay Between בן and אבן 113

Bibliography 119
    Monographs and Commentaries 119
    Articles 122
    Dissertations 126

Index of Passages Cited 127

Index of Persons 136

Preface

My fascination with the Parable of the Wicked Tenants originated with my doctoral studies in 1970, because of the relation of this parable to the stone testimonia. Any study that has extended over such a long time accumulates debts of gratitude to a variety of people. There are two people who should be mentioned, without whom this study would never have been done. Dr. Richard Longenecker is responsible for much of my interest in Biblical studies and has assisted me in a variety of ways over several years. In addition, he carefully read and commented in detail on this manuscript. Principal Matthew Black supervised my doctoral dissertation and made judicious comments, particularly with regard to my work on this parable. Professors Ernest Best and R. McL. Wilson also read my work and offered helpful suggestions.

Recently while I was on sabbatical at the University of Tübingen, I was privileged to be able to discuss my work with Professors Hengel, Betz, and Stuhlmacher, and I am grateful for their hospitality and encouragement. North Park Theological Seminary granted the sabbatical, and I would like to thank Dean Glenn Anderson for his constant support. The Association of Theological Schools provided an award to further my research, and several individuals in the Evangelical Covenant Church also provided financial assistance. I am extremely grateful to each of them. Several people in the North Park community provided help with languages that are not customary for Biblical studies, and our library staff graciously made available the resources needed for my research. Ms. Carol Nordstrom typed the final draft of the manuscript, and Mr. Rob Satterberg prepared the indexes. I am grateful to each of these persons.

My family has also provided encouragement at every level of my work, but I would particularly like to thank my wife, Phyllis, and our children, Nathan and Valerie, for the sacrifices that they have made. My wife has provided assistance in a variety of ways, including typing at several points. Most of all, however, she made life enjoyable even when it was not always easy to do so.

Finally, I would like to thank the editors and the people at Mohr-Siebeck for the expertise they bring to the publishing task. Herr Rudolf Pflug has been particularly helpful in seeing this book through to its final form.

Klyne Snodgrass
North Park Theological
Seminary
Chicago, Illinois

Abbreviations

BAG	W. Bauer, W. F. Arndt, & F. W. Gingrich, *A Greek English Lexicon of the New Testament*. 2d edition
BDB	F. Brown, S. R. Driver, & C. A. Briggs, *A Hebrew and English Lexicon of the Old Testament*
BGU	*Ägyptische Urkunden aus den königlichen Museen zu Berlin. Griechische Urkunden*
Bib	*Biblica*
BJRL	*Bulletin of the John Rylands Library*
BZ	*Biblische Zeitschrift*
CBQ	*Catholic Biblical Quarterly*
CTM	*Concordia Theological Monthly*
DtR	Midrash Rabbah on Deuteronomy
DJD	*Discoveries in the Judean Desert*
EcclR	Midrash Rabbah on Ecclesiastes
EsR	Midrash Rabbah on Esther
ET	*The Expository Times*
ETL	*Ephemerides Theologicae Lovanienses*
Flor.	Florilegium
HTR	*Harvard Theological Review*
HUCA	*Hebrew Union College Annual*
IEJ	*Israel Exploration Journal*
Interp	*Interpretation*
JAOS	*Journal of the American Oriental Society*
JBL	*Journal of Biblical Literature*
JTS	*The Journal of Theological Studies*
JTSns	*The Journal of Theological Studies*, new series
LvR	Midrash Rabbah on Leviticus
LmR	Midrash Rabbah on Lamentations
LSJ	H. G. Liddell and R. Scott, *A Greek-English Lexicon*. Revised by H. S. Jones and R. Mackenzie
M-M	J. H. Moulton and G. Milligan. *The Vocabulary of the Greek New Testament*
MPs	*The Midrash on Psalms*
NmR	Midrash Rabbah on Numbers
NovT	*Novum Testamentum*
NTS	*New Testament Studies*
PCZ	C. C. Edgar (ed.), *Catalogue général des antiquités égyptiennes du Musée du Caire: Zenon Papyri*

Pesiq. R	Pesiqta Rabbati
P. Oxy	*The Oxyrhynchus Papyri*
PRE	Pirqe de Rabbi Eliezer
RB	*Revue Biblique*
RQ	*Revue de Qumran*
S-B	H. Strack and P. Billerbeck, *Kommentar zum Neuen Testament*
SDt	Sifre Deuteronomy
SE	*Studia Evangelica*
SEA	*Svensk Exegetisk Arsbok*
SSR	Midrash Rabbah on the Song of Solomon
ST	*Studia Theologica*
Tanch	Midrash Tanchuma
TDNT	G. Kittel and G. Friedrich (eds.), *Theological Dictionary of the New Testament*
UBS	K. Aland, et al. (eds.), *The Greek New Testament*. United Bible Societies
VC	*Vigiliae Christianae*
W-H	B. F. Westcott and F. J. A. Hort. *The New Testament in Greek*
YJS	*Yale Judaica Studies*
ZAW	*Zeitschrift für die alttestamentliche Wissenschaft*
ZNW	*Zeitschrift für die neutestamentliche Wissenschaft*
ZST	*Zeitschrift für systematische Theologie*

Introduction

The parables of Jesus are powerful and dramatic expressions of his teaching. They are at the same time both "weapons of warfare" in his ministry and unparalleled works of art. Once encountered, they dominate our thinking and force us to reorient our existence. In both past and present, however, the parables have often been abused so that the message is diluted or trimmed away. The discussion of the interpretation of parables has been and continues to be a heated hermeneutical debate[1]. Both the power of Jesus' preaching and the contours of this debate are revealed when one focuses on the parable found in Matthew 21,33–45 (with parallels in Mark 12,1–12; Luke 20,9–19; and the Gospel of Thomas 65–67), which is usually known as the Parable of the Wicked Tenants (or Husbandmen). All the questions germane to parable interpretation and many that are crucial to an understanding of the New Testament are raised by this parable.

Despite its importance, however, the Parable of the Wicked Tenants has been an enigma to modern interpretation. The approaches to the parable have been quite varied. Some interpreters place this parable at the apex of the ministry of Jesus, while others assign little importance to it or virtually ignore it. In some cases the conclusions drawn have been unsatisfactory either because of presuppositions that are too rigid or that have been shown to be erroneous by recent developments. Any discussion of the parable is necessarily a complex one in that it involves the relation of the three Synoptic accounts, an assessment of the account in the Gospel of Thomas, the meaning of παραβολή, the religious and economic background in Palestine, the self-designation of Jesus, and the theological shaping of the parable by the tradition and the evangelists.

---

[1] See the account of the history of the interpretation of the parables in Geraint Vaughan Jones, *The Art and Truth of the Parables* (London: SPCK, 1964), pp. 3–54; or in Warren S. Kissinger, *The Parables of Jesus* (Meteuchen, N.J.: The Scarecrow Press, 1979), pp. 1–230. There is also a survey of the discussion since Joachim Jeremias' classic work in Norman Perrin, *Jesus and the Language of the Kingdom* (Philadelphia: Fortress Press, 1976), pp. 89–193.

Despite the fact that numerous studies of the parable have been done, few have dealt adequately with all these issues. The most comprehensive attempts are those by S. M. Gozzo in Latin[2] and M. Hubaut in French[3], but besides being inaccessible to many, the study by Gozzo does not treat several important issues, and both studies have taken positions that lack adequate support. Other valuable studies have been done[4], but most have focused on certain aspects of the investigation. Because of the importance of this parable as a possible key to understanding the ministry of Jesus, particularly since its relevance has often been minimized, this parable deserves closer analysis.

---

[2] Seraphinus M. Gozzo, *Disquisitio critico-exegetica in parabolam N. Testamenti de perfidis vinitoribus* (Romae: Pontificium Athenaeum Anatonianum, 1949).

[3] Michel Hubaut, *La parabole des vignerons homicides*. Cahiers de la *Revue Biblique* 16 (Paris: Gabalda, 1976).

[4] See especially Martin Hengel, "Das Gleichnis von den Weingärtnern Mc 12, 1–12 im Lichte der Zenonpapyri und der rabbinischen Gleichnisse," *ZNW*, LIX (1968), 1–39; and Xavier Léon-Dufour, "La parabole des vignerons homicides," *Sciences Ecclésiastiques*, XVII (1965), 365–396.

Chapter 1

Attempts to Interpret the Parable

Before analyzing the parable, a survey of representative approaches to it will be helpful. No attempt will be made here to comment on the validity of the line of argument taken, but inconsistencies in the approach of an individual will be noted.

The interpretation of this parable in the history of the church did not raise many questions. It was viewed consistently as a more or less allegorical representation of Israel's continual rejection of God's message and as climaxing in her rejection of Jesus[1]. Many scholars today would still take a position similar to this approach although they would, no doubt, use different language and make certain qualifications, and most would pay no attention to the details in the story. In the modern period, however, especially since the work of Adolf Jülicher, questions about the authenticity and meaning of the parable have been raised, and various approaches have appeared.

Adolf Jülicher

Regardless of how one estimates the positive thrust of Jülicher's work, its importance for parable research is undeniable in that he pointed out the fallacy of allegorizing the parables. Jülicher discredited

---

[1] E. g., Origen, *Commentaria in Evangelium secundum Matthaeum* (Migne, *Patrologia Graecae*, 13, 1488–1489) or Chrysostom, *Commentariorum in Matthaeum Homily* LXVIII (Migne, *Patrologia Graecae*, 58, 639f.).

Often, the details of the story were assigned allegorical significance. For example, Origen understood the tower in the vineyard as the temple, the wall as the care of God, the winepress as the place of the libations, and the absence of the owner as the time when God no longer appeared to the people.

For overviews of ancient interpretations of this parable, see Rafael Silva, "La párabola de los renteros homicidas," *Compostellanum*, XV (1970), 322–326; and Joachim Gnilka, *Das Evangelium nach Markus* (Zürich: Benzinger Verlag, 1979), II, 149–150.

this type of parable exegesis by saying that Jesus' parables were not allegories and did not have allegorical traits. Instead, they were simple comparisons which were self-evident and did not require interpretation. For him, with a parable there could be no question of several points of comparison between the imagery and the idea since a parable illustrates only one point of contact between the two. Where allegory or allegorical traits appear, the evangelists are to blame[2].

Despite this delimiting of the concept of parable, Jülicher gave a full discussion of the Parable of the Wicked Tenants because he felt that one could not prove that Jesus did not use unusual forms of speech on occasion[3]. Jülicher believed that the accounts in Matthew and Luke are both modifications of that in Mark, and that for all three, the story is an allegory of the sending of God's son to the leaders of his people. On his view the details of the story are unimportant and one can make sense of Mark 12,1-9 ‖ only if he follows the spirit and not the letter. The owner of the vineyard and the tenants are both impossible creations since no one would act as these did. There is nothing left of a story of everyday life; rather, the story has meaning only in the sphere of God and the history of Israel. Mark 12,10 is a later addition to the parable which directs attention to another point, the restoration of the rejected son. Matthew has added 21,43 to give the basic thought of the parable in discourse, but has not taken any consideration of the messianically interpreted citation. Due to the thought association with the messianic stone, Luke has added 20,18 to bring out the threatening character of the parable. Thus, the citation of Psalm 118,22 is out of place, secondary, and eliminated as a gloss although Jesus could have used the verse of his rejection on another occasion.

With these later additions out of the way, Jülicher admitted it is still possible that Mark 12,1-9 contain actual words of Jesus. Although none of the elements (including the reference to Jesus as Son) is out of keeping with Jesus' own ministry, Jülicher still suspected that the parable is a product of the first Christian generation since it is the view of history of an average man who experienced the crucifixion and yet believed in the Son of God. It lacks any original feature, psychological motivation for the characters, and poetic freshness. Jülicher granted that it is possible

---

[2] *Die Gleichnisreden Jesu* (Freiburg i. B.: Akademische Verlagsbuchhandlung von J. C. B. Mohr, Vol. I, 1888; Vol. II, 1889), I, 65-85.
[3] *Ibid.*, II, 385-406.

that there was an original Parable of the Wicked Tenants by Jesus, but felt it is impossible that it could be reconstructed since the Markan account is completely a product of early Christian theology.

To summarize, it was not so much any specific detail of the parable as its overall tone that convinced Jülicher that this parable is derived from the early Church. He did not appeal directly to the fact that this is an allegory except to the extent that this is implied in saying that it can only be understood spiritually and in references to the inferior quality of the story.

The de-allegorizing approach

Several scholars have refused to reject the parable completely since they felt that a genuine parable lies beneath the external allegorical covering. C. H. Dodd[4] and J. Jeremias[5] are the main proponents of this position. Both felt that in its main lines, the story is natural and realistic in the political and economic situation of first century Palestine. It is the story of an absentee landlord who was to be paid in produce by his tenants. After his collecting agents were mistreated, the owner sent his son to deal with the seriousness of the situation; but rather than respect the son, the tenants killed him and seized the vineyard. Both Dodd and Jeremias, therefore, felt that the entrance of the son was demanded by logical rather than theological motivation.

Dodd was uncertain whether Mark 12,9b is original, not because it is an unnatural conclusion or because it sounds like a *vaticinium ex eventu*, but because Jesus did not normally answer the questions his parables asked. Dodd had no doubt, however, that the stone quotations were later additions and that Mark 12,5 should also be excluded since it invites allegorical interpretation.

Despite his de-allegorizing, Dodd still felt that the climax of iniquity in the story suggested a similar climax in the situation to which it is to be applied; i.e., the parable suggests "the impending climax of the rebellion of Israel in a murderous assault upon the Successor of the prophets."[6] The veiled allusions may have been understood by the hearers, and by implication the parable predicts the death of Jesus and

---

[4] *The Parables of the Kingdom* (London: Nisbet & Co., 1936), pp. 124–132.
[5] *The Parables of Jesus* (London: SCM Press, 1963), 70–77.
[6] Dodd, p. 130.

the judgment on his slayers. Thus, while Dodd has swept away all allegory with one hand, he has brought it back with the other. Matthew Black noticed this inconsistency in Dodd's approach and justly criticized Dodd of trying to run with the allegorical hare and still hunt with the Jülicher hounds[7].

Jeremias' treatment is similar, but more detailed. In his view, the parable as it stands is pure allegory with every major factor from the "vineyard" (Israel) to the "other people" (the Gentiles, Matthew 21,43) accounted for, but a comparison of the various versions, especially the Gospel of Thomas, shows that the following allegorical features in Mark and Matthew are secondary:

1) The allusion to Isaiah 5, which is based on the LXX and which is omitted by Luke and Thomas.

2) The sending of the servants. There are no allegorical features in the simple account of Thomas and Luke. Mark 12,5b is a reference to the fate of the prophets, and Matthew has a reference to the earlier and later prophets in his two missions.

3) The christological coloring of the sending of the son. The actual story as in Thomas closed with the murder of the son. Matthew and Luke have the son killed outside the vineyard to correspond to Jesus' death outside the city. Mark has begun the allegorizing with $υἱὸν ἀγαπητόν$ and the citation of Psalm 118,22. All christological interpretations are absent from Thomas.

4) The final question of the Synoptists. It is missing from Thomas and the question refers to the LXX form of Isaiah 5 since the Hebrew text is not in the form of a question. If the question is secondary, obviously the answer is too[8].

The original parable vindicates the offer of the gospel to the poor, as do so many other parables in Jeremias' opinion. The form of the story thought to be original is preserved in Thomas with Luke being least allegorical of the Synoptics.

Like Dodd, Jeremias was also inconsistent in his attempts to do away with all allegory. With regard to the only son, Jeremias felt that we must distinguish between what Jesus meant and what the audience understood. For Jeremias there was no doubt that Jesus had himself in mind in the sending of the son, but the mass of hearers would not have equated the son with the Messiah[9]. However, that Jesus and some of his hearers knew the identity of the son involves an "allegorical" interpretation.

---

[7] "The Parables as Allegory," *BJRL*, XLII (1959–1960), 283.

[8] These four points are a summary of Jeremias' discussion in *The Parables of Jesus*, pp. 70–76.

[9] Ibid., 72f.

With regard to the original meaning of the parable, Jeremias took Mark 12,9 as the key to the meaning, but earlier in his attempt to remove allegory, he had omitted this verse from the original story[10]. Additional inconsistencies appear in Jeremias' treatment of Mark 12,10 || in other connections. Earlier he had given good reasons for accepting the authenticity of the Old Testament citation at the end of the parable[11], and in a later study he at least implied the authenticity of the quotation[12]. Even in his study of the parables, he indicated that Jesus in his esoteric self-revelation often used metaphors such as the rejected and later exalted stone[13].

Such inconsistencies in Jeremias' analysis have been noted before[14], and a few changes were made in the ninth German edition. That Jesus intended a reference to himself with the figure of the son is stated in more muted terms[15], and the inconsistency of seeing Mark 12,9 as secondary and yet the key to the meaning of the original parable is removed[16]. The parable is no longer seen as a vindication of the offer of the gospel to the poor, but instead as *"ein Drohwort"* which preaches judgment on the leaders of the people[17]. These corrections help, but there are still difficulties in Jeremias' treatment, as will be pointed out later[18].

A considerable number of other de-allegorizing approaches have been proposed since Jeremias' work. Despite disagreements over details, these approaches are basically alike in assumptions and procedures[19].

---

[10] *Ibid.*, 74 and 76.

[11] J. Jeremias, "λίθος, λίθινος," *TDNT*, IV, 274 n. 48.

[12] *The Eucharistic Words of Jesus* (London: SCM Press, 1966), p. 259. This edition contains the author's revisions to 1964.

[13] *The Parables of Jesus*, pp. 219f. He may have been thinking of the citation as an independent logion, but this is not expressed.

[14] See Jane E. and Raymond R. Newell, "The Parable of the Wicked Tenants," *NovT*, XIV (1972), 229–232, and John A. T. Robinson, "The Parable of the Wicked Husbandmen: A Test of Synpotic Relationships," *NTS*, XXI (1975), 449.

[15] *Die Gleichnisse Jesu*. 9th ed. (Göttingen: Vandenhoeck and Ruprecht, 1977) p. 70.

[16] *Ibid.*, 74.

[17] *Ibid.*

[18] See *infra*, especially pp. 26–29, 47–48, 52–55 and 61.

[19] One of the most elaborate de-allegorizing approaches is that of Michel Hubaut, *La parabole des vignerous homicides*. Cahiers de la *Revue Biblique* 16 (Paris: Gabalda, 1976). This study offers a detailed and speculative account of the tradition history of our parable from a rather brief, authentic word of Jesus (p. 131) through various stages of redaction to the present forms in the Synoptics.

One other such approach will be mentioned. B. M. F. van Iersel argued that the unevenness between the allegory and the allegorized reality (indicated by non-allegorical details in the story) points to an *Urform*, and on this basis he reconstructed the original story line-by-line by selecting the words and phrases from each of the Synoptics that he considered original[20]. He relied primarily upon the account of Mark, Semitisms, rare occurrences, simplicity, and the lack of allegory. The theme of inheritance (Mark 12,7) was retained as original since it is not allegorical, and it was seen as the key to understanding the parable. The mention of "inheritance" insures the presence of the son in the story, but he is only an incidental element. The message of the parable relates to the tenants. God has bestowed good on the leaders of Israel, but now must punish them and give that which is good to others. As Dodd and Jeremias, van Iersel was not consistent in his interpretation. Although he omitted all allegory, he interpreted the owner as God, the tenants as the leaders of Israel, and the son as an indirect and discreet self-designation by Jesus. Inconsistency between analysis and interpretation is fairly common in the de-allegorizing approach.

Werner Georg Kümmel

The leader of the opposition to the approach propagated by Dodd and Jeremias has been W. G. Kümmel[21]. Rather than the story of a thoroughly natural event, Kümmel thought the parable contains a series of improbabilities, especially in the repeated sending of servants and the sending of the son when the previous emissaries had been mistreated. He felt that the image side of the parable has been constructed on the fact side, i.e., that this story is undeniably an allegory. The attempts to reproduce an *Urform* are methodologically warranted only if they proceed from concrete observations of the text and not just from the desire to produce an account free from allegory.

Because of the Semitisms that occur in all parts of the text except Mark 12,5 and the occurrence of words that are not characteristic of

---

[20] *"Der Sohn" in den synoptischen Jesusworten* (Leiden: E. J. Brill, 1961), pp. 124–145.

[21] "Das Gleichnis von den bösen Weingärtnern (Mark 12,1–9)," *Aux sources de la tradition chrétienne. Mélanges offerts à M. Maurice Goguel* (Neuchatel: Delachaux & Niestle S. A., 1950), 120–131. Cf. *Promise and Fulfilment* (London: SCM Press, 1957), pp. 82–83.

Mark, Kümmel was fairly certain that the parable is a tradition that has been taken over by Mark. From his linguistic and stylistic studies, he concluded that no part of the text of Mark is divergent in style or speech, and therefore, that any hypothesis of secondary expansion is not sufficiently established.

Kümmel also objected to the way that Dodd and Jeremias explained away the improbabilities of the hatred of the tenants, the patience of the owner, and the sending of the son. The first two were explained as due to the fact that the owner was a foreigner, but he objected that ἀπεδήμησεν is not sufficient to substantiate this. There is no hint of political conditions as justification for the tenants' behavior. Thus the concept that the parable is based on economically and politically tense times is insufficiently supported. The improbability of the sending of the son cannot be explained away on stylistic and logical grounds either. Such a sending of a son by a father is not likely human behavior.

Furthermore, the designation υἱός ἀγαπητός echoes the baptism and transfiguration. On this basis, Kümmel declared that it is impossible to find a convincing way that is free from methodological objections to trace the parable back to a simpler form or to deny its essentially allegorical character.

While Kümmel followed Jülicher's view of the parables, he admitted that Jesus' parables contain series of metaphors and occasional unlikely features, and said that one should not reject this parable in its allegorical form on *a priori* grounds. He affirmed that Jesus attacked the Jews for their rejection of the prophets, anticipated his own destruction, and expected a space of time between his death and parousia. On the other hand, Kümmel found two overwhelming objections to the authenticity of this parable. The first is that the punishment of the tenants (Jews) and the transfer of the promise to others is depicted plainly as a direct result of the murder of the son. Jesus' other teachings do not indicate that his death should unleash this punishment; rather, this is an early Church idea. The second objection centers on the entrance of the son. The parable presupposes that the hearers recognize the son as the eschatological salvation bringer and that they equate the son with Jesus. The hearers could do this only if they knew the title "Son of God" as a messianic title, but there is no proof that "Son of God" was a current Jewish messianic title in pre-Christian or early tannaitic times. No Jew, when he heard of the sending and death of the son would have thought of the Messiah. If Jesus composed the parable, he made it hardly understandable by the introduction of the son. The title "Son of God" was an early Church designation of the resurrected Christ. Both of these objections indicate for Kümmel that the origin of the parable is in the early Church[22].

Novel Approaches

Because of the inconsistencies in previous approaches and the impasse reached in interpretation, several recent studies have offered what can only be called novel approaches to the parable. John Dominic Crossan has used a de-allegorizing approach similar to Jeremias' and has concluded that the non-allegorical account in Thomas is the original form of the story. Rather than referring to Jesus and his offer of the gospel to the poor, however, Crossan viewed the parable as a most disedifying and immoral story. As the Parable of the Unjust Steward, it stresses the crisis in which Jesus' hearers stand and gives an example of the prudent grasping of one's immoral choice[23]. Recently, however, on the basis of a structuralist approach Crossan has indicated that more and more he prefers to view the parable as a terribly foolish action by the owner similar to the Parable of the Rich Fool[24]. Even more recently Crossan has moved to an appreciation of allegory that would seemingly invalidate his quest for a form free from allegory[25].

---

[22] See also Charles E. Carlston, *The Parables of the Triple Tradition* (Philadelphia: Fortress Press, 1975), pp. 40–45; 76–78, and 178–190; and Dino Merli, "La parabola dei vignaioli infedeli," *Bibbia e Oriente*, XV (1973), 97–108, both of whom assign the parable to the early church, and the latter sees the parable as not composed before 70 A.D.

[23] "The Parable of the Wicked Husbandmen," *JBL*, XC (1971), 451–465; and *In Parables* (New York: Harper and Row, Publishers, 1973), pp. 86–96 and 111. See also the suggestion of Tim Schramm, *Der Markus-Stoff bei Lukas* (Cambridge: Cambridge University Press, 1971), pp. 168–169.

[24] "Structuralist Analysis and the Parables of Jesus," *Semeia*, I (1974), 208f. Other structuralist attempts to interpret the parable have been made (e. g., Crossan, "The Servant Parables of Jesus," *Semeia*, I (1974), 17–55; Robert W. Funk, "Structures in the Narrative Parables of Jesus," *Semeia*, II (1974), 56, 60–61, and 72; and Yvan Almeida, *L'Opérativité sémantique des récits-paraboles* (Louvain: Éditions Peeters, 1978), pp. 153–195, but they have not been very productive. (See also *infra*, p. 11, n. 30.) Structuralist exegesis has tended to be extremely subjective, and care should be taken to avoid making a structural grid a criterion for evaluating the value or authenticity of the form of a parable. See e. g., Anthony C. Thiselton, "Structuralism and Biblical Studies: Method or Ideology?" *ET*, LXXXIX (1978), 329–335.

[25] "Parable, Allegory, and Paradox," *Semiology and the Parables*, ed. Daniel Patte (Pittsburgh: The Pickwick Press, 1976), 247–281, especially 264–273.

In a different direction, Jane E. and Raymond R. Newell have suggested that Jesus was showing his audience of Zealot sympathizers that violence leads to self destruction[26]. In still another direction, but reviving a view put forward by A. Gray[27], Merrill Miller has proposed that the son in the parable is a reference to John the Baptist[28].

Pheme Perkins has followed many in stripping the parable of secondary features, particularly Mark 12,9b∥ which says the owner will destroy the tenants, and then has interpreted the parable as an image of what is implied in Jesus' policy of non-violence and love of one's enemy. The parable is a practical representation of how to "overcome evil with good," and shows that God will not use violence and vengeance to deal with situations of injustice. The conclusion the evangelists have drawn is seen as based on the destruction of Jerusalem[29]. Needless to say, this solution is not derived from the parable, and it appears that an agenda has been brought to the interpretive task[30].

These novel approaches, it seems fair to say, reflect the frustrations that some feel with more traditional approaches and with the difficulties inherent in the parable itself. The parable seems all too obviously to be later Christian theology if secondary features are noticed, but without the secondary features, no satisfactory and convincing explanation has appeared[31].

---

[26] "The Parable of the Wicked Tenants," *NovT*, XIV (1972), 226–237.

[27] "The Parable of the Wicked Husbandmen," *The Hibbert Journal*, XIX (1920–21), 42–52.

[28] *Scripture and Parable: A Study of the Biblical Features in the Parable of the Wicked Husbandmen and Their Place in the History of the Tradition*. Unpublished Ph. D. Dissertation, Columbia University, 1974.

[29] Pheme Perkins, *Hearing the Parables of Jesus* (New York: Paulist Press, 1981) pp. 181–194.

[30] Mention should be made of the suggestion of "intertextuality" by Paul Ricoeur in "The Bible and the Imagination," *The Bible as a Document of the University*, ed. Hans Dieter Betz (Chico, California: Scholars Press, 1981), 54–65. Ricoeur adopted the work of Yvan Almeida, (see *supra*, p. 10, n. 24), pp. 153–195, and 250–255, who argued that the parables of the Wicked Tenants and the Sower should be read and understood together. Both parables contain a vegetation and spatial isotopy. These (and other) isotopies contain the power of metaphorization and lead to understanding. The addition of the Old Testament quotation to the Parable of the Wicked Tenants was effected by the terms in Isaiah 5 that lead from plant to stone (winepress, tower, hedge, etc.). For Ricoeur, the metaphor encompassing the two parables is "If the word is to increase, the body must decrease" (p. 65). However, there is very little to justify connecting the two parables, and it is certainly unfair to force a single meaning from two such disparate accounts.

[31] Note the comment by Schramm, p. 167, n. 2.

Chapter 2

What Method Should be Used?

The previous chapter indicated the variety of approaches that have been posited for the Parable of the Wicked Tenants. Obviously other studies have been done besides the ones summarized above, but most are dependent on these or take similar approaches, and these are sufficient to show that methods and presuppositions for interpretation are crucial. Clearly not all of the methods and presuppositions used in the various approaches are legitimate.

Of all the questions that must be addressed, the most important is that concerning the *genre* of the story. This, of course, involves the discussion of parable and allegory. Since the publication of Jülicher's study on the parables, the term "allegory" has engendered negative reactions. For example, Jeremias recognized that both apocalyptic and rabbinic literature use allegory[1] and that rabbinic parables contain traditional metaphorical elements[2], but he found it necessary to remove all allegory from the Gospel parables. On what grounds does he deny to the Parable of the Wicked Tenants the common metaphorical associations of the owner of the vineyard, the vineyard, and the servants – associations which he otherwise permits[3]? For van Iersel the justification for seeking an *Urform* of the parable lies in the non-allegorical details[4], but this justification is valid only on the questionable assumptions that every detail of an allegory must have significance and that partial allegories or mixed forms do not occur.

The procedure that strips all allegorical features from the parable when determining its form, but then revives the allegorical significance

---

[1] *The Parables of Jesus* (London: SCM Press, 1963), pp. 219f.
[2] *Ibid.*, 89.
[3] *Ibid.*, 70; Cf. the comment of C. F. D. Moule, "Important and Influential Books: J. Jeremias' *The Parables of Jesus* and *The Eucharistic Words of Jesus*," ET, LXVI (1954–55), 48.
[4] *"Der Sohn" in den synoptischen Jesusworten* (Leiden: E. J. Brill, 1961), pp. 130f.

for interpretation cannot be permitted. However, it is difficult to interpret the parable without taking notice of the meaning of the allegorical (or metaphorical) features. This is easily seen when one reads the account of Thomas where the significance of the features may be ignored and where a meaningful interpretation is then extremely subjective, as is evident in the initial study of Crossan and in the study of J. and R. Newell[5]. But if one interprets the tenants of the parable as referring to the leaders of Israel or the owner as God, on what grounds does he or she deny the significance of the other major features[6]? If one attempts to distinguish what Jesus meant or had in mind from what the audience understood (as Jeremias), the result is still that Jesus intended the major features of the story to have metaphorical significance.

This, of course, lands us in the middle of the discussion of the nature of parable and allegory, and our analysis of this story cannot proceed until some decision with regard to the validity or invalidity of allegory and allegorical features is reached.

Can a Parable be an Allegory?

As is usually the case where there is continued controversy over an academic point, the absence of uniform definitions with this question has created havoc, and this is especially the case with the word "allegory." The answer to our question depends largely upon just what one means by "allegory."

Although the discussion of parable and allegory borders on being a "tired discussion," significant changes are being made. One must, of course, go back to Jülicher, and once again homage must be paid to him for freeing us from the imaginative hermeneutical approach of allegorizing the Gospel parables. Obviously, however, the question that concerns us is *allegory* itself and has no relation to *allegorizing*, the extreme practice of the post-apostolic Church whereby the elements in the parables could be interpreted as one saw fit (the practice against which Jülicher was reacting)[7].

---

[5] See *supra*, pp. 10–11.
[6] Matthew Black, "The Parables as Allegory," *BJRL*, XLII (1959–1960), 282. Cf. J. J. Vincent, " The Parables of Jesus as Self-Revelation," *SE*, I (1959), 85.
[7] See Dan Otto Via, Jr., *The Parables* (Philadelphia: Fortress Press, 1967), p. 14; and Hans-Josef Klauck, *Allegorie und Allegorese in synoptischen Gleichnistexten* (Münster: Aschendorff, 1978), pp. 354–355.

Jülicher combated this perversion by denying that Jesus used allegory or even allegorical traits. Where these are found, the evangelists are to blame. According to Jülicher, the parables are simple and straightforward comparisons that do not require interpretation. There can be no question of several points of comparison between the imagery and the idea, for parables illustrate only a single point of contact between the two. Allegory, in contrast to the authentic speech of the parable, is inauthentic speech in that it means other than the actual meaning of the words. The allegory is an artificial figure, and for this reason it is unlikely that Jesus used it. Rather than reveal, the allegory hides; it must be laboriously interpreted by the initiated so that every point of the imagery half has its correspondent in the thought being portrayed[8].

It is not necessary to trace the history of research on the parables since Jülicher[9], but the crucial issue has been the question of the possibility of allegory and allegorical traits. There are some who are willing to accept Jülicher's distinctions as proposed, but Norman Perrin's statement that subsequent research has validated all of Jülicher's conclusions except that of a truth of the widest possible application is misleading to say the least[10]. There are, in fact, very few studies of the parables since Jülicher that do not modify his views to some extent either in theory or in practice[11].

The most important of the early objections to Jülicher's distinctions came from Paul Fiebig. He pointed out that Jülicher should have relied more on rabbinic parables and the Hebrew thought world instead of Aristotle and the Greek thought world[12]. Fiebig amassed numerous

---

[8] *Die Gleichnisreden Jesu* (Freiburg i. B.: Akademische Verlagsbuchhandlung von J. C. B. Mohr, Vol. I, 1888; Vol. II, 1889), I, 65, 70–73, 77–78, 84–86, 109 and 121.

[9] See *supra*, p. 1, n. 1.

[10] *Rediscovering the Teaching of Jesus* (London: SCM Press, 1967), p. 257.

[11] To mention only a few: A. T. Cadoux, *The Parables of Jesus* (London: James Clarke & Co., n. d.), pp. 50f.; C. H. Dodd, *The Parables of the Kingdom* (London: Nisbet & Co., 1936), pp. 21 and his interpretation of our parable, pp. 130f.; Jeremias, pp. 18f. and his interpretation of Jesus' own mind in our parable, pp. 72f.; B. T. D. Smith, *The Parables of the Synoptic Gospels* (Cambridge: Cambridge University Press, 1937), p. 24; Eta Linnemann, *Parables of Jesus*, trans. John Sturdy (London: SPCK, 1966), p. 8, who made the same generalization as Perrin, but cf. pp. 28f. (the only certain allegory that she found is Matthew 22,1–14); and Sallie McFague Te Selle, *Speaking in Parables: A Study in Metaphor and Theology* (Philadelphia: Fortress Press, 1975), pp. 72f. This is to say nothing of those who directly oppose Jülicher.

[12] *Altjüdische Gleichnisse und die Gleichnisse Jesu* (Tübingen: Verlag von J. C. B. Mohr, Paul Siebeck, 1904).

rabbinic parables to show that they were essentially the same as the Gospel parables in form and that they evidenced allegory and mixtures of parable and allegory.

The charge has been made against Fiebig that what he has called rabbinic allegories and mixed forms of parable and allegory are not allegories or mixed forms at all. From the German side, Rudolf Bultmann said that Fiebig's allegorical features in the rabbinic similitudes are nothing of the kind. Rather, they are examples of customary metaphors or may simply be cases where the correspondence between the image and the reality has been expressed in the primitive form of an identification[13]. From the British side, B. T. D. Smith admitted that at least two rabbinic allegories exist, but he discounted these two as "the exceptions which prove the rule that the rabbis did not compose allegories."[14] He explained Fiebig's mixed forms as being due to argument by analogy where different elements of the object illustrated must be represented in the parable. If the choice of figures to represent these elements was influenced by metaphorical associations, the result is not an allegorical parable. The reason for this is that the Jew can speak of identity when he means no more than correspondence[15]. Smith pointed to an extreme example of this principle in a rabbinic parable of a farmer, his steward, and the produce. The interpretation which is attached shows that God is the farmer, Moses is the steward, Israel is the wheat, and the other nations are the straw and the thorns. On these correspondences Smith commented:

> We have here a true similitude, the point of which is that Israel is to God what wheat is to the farmer, the object of his special concern. The exposition is not an allegorical interpretation: it does but call attention to the aptness and Scriptural character of the details of the picture[16].

---

[13] *The History of the Synoptic Tradition*, trans. John Marsh (Oxford: Basil Blackwell, 1963), p. 198. He virtually admitted, however, that allegorical features do occur in rabbinic similitudes when he left an avenue of escape by saying, ". . . and we could always ask whether the somewhat allegorical features of rabbinic similitudes were not secondary too."

[14] Smith, pp. 24f. The two examples appear in Pirke Aboth II.19 and III.25.

[15] Smith, p. 26.

[16] *Ibid.*, 26–27. Shoḥer Tob Psalm 2,12; cf. Asher Feldman, *The Parables and Similes of the Rabbis* (Cambridge: Cambridge University Press, 1924), p. 67. The parable reads:

Why is Israel compared to wheat? To tell thee that it is with him as with a farmer who has in his house a steward; when he comes to reckon with him, he does not say "How many baskets of straw, or how many bundles of stubble dost thou bring into

Fiebig's side of the argument has been taken up by several studies that point out that the Hebrew equivalent of παραβολή is מָשָׁל, a term which in both the Old Testament and the rabbinic writings covers a broad range of ideas, one of which is allegory[17].

It should be clear from the little that has been said that what some scholars have called allegory is not allegory at all in the minds of others. Jülicher did draw his categories from the world of Greek rhetoric, primarily Aristotle, and it was necessary for Fiebig and many since to point to the wide range of ideas that could be conveyed by מָשָׁל. As Bultmann[18] and Linnemann[19] have insisted, however, a clarity of concept is needed. One's main concern should be that no violence is done to the material in classifying it. Jülicher's critics, on the other hand, maintain that he did great violence to the material by using too narrow a concept of parable.

The crux, of course, is how one defines allegory. To go back to Jülicher again, his formal definition is simple enough: "... derjenigen Redefigur, in welcher eine zusammenhängende Reihe von Begriffen (ein Satz oder Satzkomplex) dargestellt wird vermittelst einer zusammenhängenden Reihe von ähnlichen Begriffen aus einem anderen Gebiete."[20] This is very close to the common definition of allegory as an extended metaphor or a series of related metaphors, but in practice, Jülicher's definition is more complex than this. Besides this criterion of

---

the storehouse?" He gives him the thorns for fuel, and casts the straw to the wind. What is it that he does say? "Set your mind on how many *kor* of wheat thou bringest into the store, because that alone is the source of life to the world." The farmer is the Holy One, blessed is he, to whom the whole world belongs. . . . The steward is Moses. . . . What saith the Holy One, blessed be he, to him? "Regard not the heathen, for they are like straw," . . . And the nations are further likened unto thorns. But Israel is compared to wheat; and therefore the Lord spake unto Moses saying, "When thou takest the sum of the children of Israel."

Smith neglected that the other nations are likened to straw and thorns.

[17] Friedrich Hauck, "παραβολή," *TDNT*, V, 747f.; Black, "The Parables as Allegory," pp. 275f.; Raymond E. Brown, "Parable and Allegory Reconsidered," *NovT*, V (1962), 37f.; Maxime Hermaniuk, *La parabole évangélique* (Louvain: Bibliotheca Alfonsiana, 1947), pp. 62–189; J. Arthur Baird, *The Justice of God in the Teaching of Jesus* (London: SCM Press, 1963), pp. 26–28; Geraint Vaughan Jones, *The Art and Truth of the Parables* (London: SPCK, 1964), pp. 57–59 and 88–109; and Madeleine Boucher, *The Mysterious Parable* (Washington: The Catholic Biblical Association of America, 1977), pp. 11–25.

[18] Bultmann, p. 198.
[19] Linnemann, p. 131.
[20] Jülicher, I, 84.

form, Jülicher limited allegory in terms of its purpose and effect by saying that it is inauthentic speech in that it means other than what it says. Thus allegory actually hides its meaning and must be laboriously interpreted[21]. The obscure and artificial character of the allegory are prime reasons for Jülicher's rejection of it as a speech form of Jesus. One should note that Jülicher did not deny the use of allegory in the Semitic world. He admitted that the vineyard parable of Isaiah 5 is an allegory, but he asserted that the prophet immediately dropped the allegory to speak as plainly as possible[22]. He also admitted the several correspondences between image and reality in the parable given by Nathan (II Samuel 12,1–7), but he made nothing of them. For him, the parables of Jesus are artistically and rhetorically higher than these two Old Testament examples[23]. A discrepancy in Jülicher's approach is evident (Jesus' parables are too simple for the artificial allegory of rhetoricians, yet higher forms than Old Testament allegory), but our main concern is with his definition of allegory. He defined an allegory according to form, but in actual practice his definition is limited to those forms that cause obscurity.

It is this confusion in the definition of allegory that has created trouble in research on the parables. Bultmann distinguished parable from allegory by saying that the former involves a transference of judgment from one sphere to the other while allegory is concerned with disguising some situation in secret or fantastic forms so as to serve prophetic and other purposes[24]. A common definition is that allegory is a description in code which must be interpreted point by point by the initiate[25]. Obvi-

---

[21] Ibid., 65, 77f., and 121.   [22] Ibid., 65f.   [23] Ibid., 109.

[24] Bultmann, p. 198. On p. 199 he rejected Mark 12,1–12 as almost entirely allegorical and therefore a late community product. By his own definition of parable, however, this passage is not allegorical because it involves the transference of judgement from one sphere to another.

[25] Linnemann, pp. 6f. and Smith, p. 21. The latter claimed that it is the use of symbols rather than metaphors which is characteristic of an allegory. Exactly how he distinguished symbol and metaphor is not clear. Jones, pp. 108f., took the opposite approach by saying that the academic argument whether parables are allegories or not resulted from a failure to distinguish symbolism and allegory. W. G. Kümmel, "Das Gleichnis von den bösen Weingärtnern (Mark 12,1–9)," *Aux sources de la tradition chrétienne. Mélanges offerts à M. Maurice Goguel* (Neuchatel: Delachaux & Niestle S. A., 1950), p. 128, is an example of the lack of clarity in definition. He stated that Jesus did not use allegories, but that his parables contain series of metaphors.

ously, viewing allegory as necessarily a disguising of a situation so that only initiates can understand makes allegory a very unpopular and inferior *genre*.

Jülicher's analysis of parable and allegory was based upon a distinction between simile and metaphor, the simple forms he understood to provide the basis for parable and allegory respectively. He thought that the simile is a self-evident comparison that retains the original meaning of the word. The metaphor, however, is substituted for the idea being compared and cannot retain its original meaning; therefore, it is inauthentic speech. Rather than help the interpreter, the metaphor makes his task more difficult by its confidential character[26]. Just how far modern studies have moved from Jülicher is evident in such titles as *Speaking in Parables: A Study in Metaphor and Theology*[27] or *Die Gleichnisse Jesu als Metaphern*[28].

Hermaniuk, with the aid of the definitions of Quintilian, correctly pointed out that Jülicher's description of metaphor is extreme. The metaphor by its structure is less clear than the simile, but not all metaphors are obscure. A metaphor may be clear when the use of images and the disclosing of truths do not go beyond the average. A metaphor may be obscure when there is an absence of analogy between the image and the idea or when there is novelty in the image or thought[29]. There are many metaphors that are commonly used and whose meanings are quite clear. It is primarily with such metaphors that one is dealing in the rabbinic and Synoptic parables (God as king, Israel as vineyard, etc.).

Recent protests against Jülicher's position have been louder and more powerful. If J. Duncan M. Derrett could earlier speak of a trend in

---

[26] Jülicher, I, 55–59.
[27] By Sallie TeSelle, see *supra*, p. 14, n. 11.
[28] By Hans Weder, (Göttingen: Vandenhoeck & Ruprecht, 1978).
[29] Hermaniuk, pp. 42f. Cf. G. B. Caird, *The Language and Imagery of the Bible* (London: Duckworth, 1980), p. 162. Quintilian (*Instit. Orat.* VIII, VI.4) said that the metaphor is so natural that it is often used unconsciously or by the uneducated. In contrast, Jülicher claimed that the metaphor is for the educated and mature. Quintilian said virtually the same about the use of allegory as he did of metaphor (cf. VIII. VI.51). Amos N. Wilder, *Early Christian Rhetoric* (London: SCM Press, 1964), p. 80, spoke of the advantage of the metaphor in communication. On p. 92 he described the parables of Jesus as extended metaphor. He did not define his meaning of allegory. See p. 80, n. 2, "The parable of the sower, for example, is a developed image and a revealing metaphor, not an instructive simile or allegory."

Britain to recognize allegory in Jesus' parables[30], one can only speak now in terms of a widespread movement. The studies of M. Boucher[31], H.-J. Klauck[32], H. Weder[33], G. B. Caird[34], and David Flusser[35] all reject Jülicher's negative views of metaphor and allegory.

Through the influence of modern literary critics[36], allegory is being given a much greater appreciation. Allegory is no longer defined merely as a series of related metaphors, and the old attempts to distinguish between parable and allegory on the basis of the number of points of comparison are rejected. In fact, for Boucher and Klauck, comparing parable and allegory is like comparing apples and oranges. Allegory is viewed as a device of meaning and not in itself a literary form[37]. A story with two levels of meaning (literal and metaphorical) is an allegory. To put it another way, allegory is an extended metaphor in narratory form. The issue is not whether metaphors are used, but whether the meaning of the whole is metaphorical[38]. The main point in all of this is the recognition that allegory is a perfectly legitimate device and that allegory or allegorical features cannot be set aside just by saying that they are allegorical. Recently, J. D. Crossan has rejected his earlier distinctions between parable and allegory and has pointed to four valid functions of allegory determined by literary critics:

1. Allegory circumvents opposition.

---

[30] "Allegory and the Wicked Vinedresser," *JTSns*, XXV (1974), 426.
[31] *The Mysterious Parable.*
[32] *Allegorie und Allegorese.*
[33] *Die Gleichnisse Jesu als Metaphern.* See also John Drury, "The Sower, the Vineyard, and the Place of Allegory in the Interpretation of Mark's Parables," *JTSns*, XXIV, (1973), 367–379.
[34] Caird, pp. 160–171.
[35] *Die rabbinischen Gleichnisse und der Gleichniserzähler Jesus. 1. Teil: Das Wesen der Gleichnisse* (Bern: Peter Lang, 1981), especially pp. 121–130 and 137.
[36] Such as Angus Fletcher, *Allegory: The Theory of a Symbolic Mode* (Ithaca, N.Y.: Cornell University Press, 1964) and E. Honig, *Dark Conceit: The Making of Allegory* (New York: Oxford University Press, 1959).
[37] Boucher, p. 20; Klauck, p. 135. Cf. Flusser, p. 121, "Wenn Allegorie bedeutet, daß die Gleichnisse Jesu in ihren Sujets und in allen ihren Motiven eine bloße Einkleidung von etwas anderem sind, dann sind sie keine Allegorien. Wenn aber Allegorie bedeutet, daß ein erzähltes Ereignis nicht ein bloßes Geschehnis ist, sondern daß die Erzählung nicht autonom ist und auf eine "Moral der Geschichte" zielt, und daß sowohl das Sujet als auch einige seiner Motive eine genau bestimmbare Bedeutung auf einer anderen Ebene haben, dann sind sowohl die Gleichnisse Jesu als auch die rabbinischen Gleichnisse Allegorien."

2. Allegory creates separation between those who really understand and those who do not.
3. Allegory establishes continuation with a previous story and thereby achieves greater power through that which is known.
4. Allegory reveals structuration so that it is read on different levels[39].

The relevance of the first and third functions for the story of the Wicked Tenants is obvious.

While it is not the purpose of this study to resolve the problem of definitions, it seems that the new appreciation for allegory has destroyed what little "clarity of concept" we had with regard to such terms as allegory and parable. With Boucher's analysis, for example, we are left with only three categories for the New Testament stories (example stories, similitudes, and parables)[40]. Consequently, there are no special terms to distinguish between a story with points of comparison throughout (like the Parable of the Ewe Lamb in II Samuel 12,1f.) and a parable that has only one or few points of comparison (like the Parable of the Seed Growing Secretly in Mark 4,26–29)[41].

---

[38] See also E. J. Tinsley, "Parable and Allegory: Some Literary Criteria for the Interpretation of the Parables of Christ," *The Church Quarterly*, III (1970), 32–39; and cf. Flusser, p. 137.

[39] John Dominic Crossan, "Parable, Allegory, and Paradox," *Semiology and the Parables*, ed. Daniel Patte (Pittsburgh: The Pickwick Press, 1976), 264–271. Crossan understandably backed off from the second function as of less significance in a prophetic tradition. Its pertinence for a discussion of Mark 4,1–12 is clear though. Crossan viewed structuration as the most important function because he found there license for viewing interpretation as "play." This emphasis on polyvalent reading, however, does not do justice to the contexts of the Biblical stories and is, I think, a turn in the wrong direction. See *infra*, p. 29.

[40] Boucher, p. 38.

[41] However, one should note that some of the examplary stories (Luke 10,29–37 and 16,19–31) also have two levels of meaning. Even on the older definitions of allegory and parable, what was said of one could be said of the other: both are forms of comparison used not for their own sake, but for the subject at hand; both are secondary to and derive their forms from the idea being expressed; neither can be translated into self-understandable text and dispensed with more easily than the other. The distinction between parable and allegory has always been a relative one. See Via, pp. 7 and 14f.; Dodd, p. 21; Jones, p. 108; Edwyn Hoskyns and Noel Davey, *The Riddle of the New Testament* (London: Faber and Faber, 1931), p. 181; and Vincent, p. 81. According to the latter, "Some kind of allegory is scarcely avoidable in any kind of comparison." Robert W. Funk, "Structure in the Narrative Parables of Jesus," *Semeia*, II (1974), p. 68, even suggested that Jesus' frequent use of an authority figure to model God is a fundamental weakness in his parables and drives us in spite of ourselves in the direction of allegory!

Nor will it do to attempt to distinguish forms on the basis of obscurity or disguising, which was Jülicher's real basis for rejecting allegory and has been used against allegory by many others. If a parable is an extended metaphor, in the whole or in the parts as well, the degree of clarity will depend on the degree of analogy between image and idea and the amount of newness in the image[42]. A good number of the images used by Jesus would have been completely obvious to his hearers because of the repeated associations they had. Some images might have been less clear due to the novelty of the teaching about the Kingdom of God. It is hard to believe, however, that any Jew would have needed to decipher such terms as "king" and "vineyard" when used in traditional ways.

Because of the imprecision of definitions, I have little doubt that the parable – allegory debate will continue to haunt us for some time[43]. Many people will still use allegory to refer to a series of related metaphors in distinction from stories without such inner-relatedness. While clarity of concept is important, the most significant point is that one cannot discard whole stories or pieces of stories merely by saying that they are allegorical. While later hands may tend to add or underline metaphorical significance, the very nature of parables assumes metaphorical significance from the outset.

In this connection additional insight can be derived from the rabbinic parables. The message of the Synoptic parables differs from that of the rabbinic parables and the former are not exegetical as the latter tend to

---

[42] Hermaniuk, pp. 48f. It should be noted that the question of obscurity is not a new question. Quintilian reported that some people denied that his examples were allegories because for them allegory involves an element of obscurity while in his examples the meaning is obvious (*Instit. Orat.* VIII.VI. 58).

[43] Notice the attempt of Gerhard Sellin ("Allegorie und 'Gleichnis'," *Zeitschrift für Theologie und Kirche*, LXXI, 1978, 281–335) to validate Jülicher's rejection of allegory, but he did so by viewing parable as extended metaphor (contrary to Jülicher) and allegory as composed from symbol (as B. T. D. Smith earlier, see *supra*, p. 17, n. 25). He rightly empasized the importance of the contexts of the parables, but overemphasized the element of obscurity in allegory and that allegory is addressed to initiates. He admitted that there are no pure allegories and that allegories are in a second respect metaphorical (p. 302). His suggestions that allegory brings no new information and has no place in literature today (p. 311) are surprising. Such defacing of allegory does not do justice to the creative, cognitive process which is involved in human speech. See Graham Hough, "The Allegorical Circle," *The Critical Quarterly*, III (1961), 199–209, who traced much of the depreciation of allegory back to English Romanticists and who argued that allegory in its broadest sense is a pervasive element in all literature.

be, but it is virtually beyond debate that the Synoptic and rabbinic parables are alike in form[44].

David Flusser, as others before him, has argued that Jesus derived the form and many of the elements of his parables from early rabbinic material[45]. Despite the paucity of early rabbinic parables, he seems to be correct[46].

Without question, in both rabbinic and Synoptic parables, metaphorical elements are present[47]. Such a recognition requires that one be

---

[44] Fiebig, *Altjüdische Gleichnisse und die Gleichnisse Jesu, passim;* and his *Die Gleichnisreden Jesu im Lichte der rabbinischen Gleichnisse des neutestamentlichen Zeitalters* (Tübingen: Verlag von. J. C. B. Mohr, Paul Siebeck, 1912), *passim;* W. O. E. Oesterley, *The Gospel Parables in the Light of their Jewish Backgrounds* (London: SPCK, 1936), *passim;* Hauck, pp. 750f.; and Hermaniuk, pp. 153f. and 264; and Johannes B. Bauer, "Gleichnisse Jesu und Gleichnisse der Rabbinen," *Theologisch-praktische Quartalschrift,* CXIX (1971), 297–307. Jewish scholars rarely react to the term "allegory" as some NT scholars do. J. Z. Lauterbach, "Parable," *The Jewish Encyclopedia* (1905), IX, 512 defined משל/παραβολή as a "short religious allegory"; cf. Feldman, pp. vii and 20f.

While it is true that Jesus' parables are not told to illustrate the interpretation of an OT passage, the implied corollary that they bear no relation to the OT is not true. It appears that several of Jesus' parables may be actualizations of OT texts.

[45] Flusser, *passim,* especially pp. 141–175. See also I. Abrahams, *Studies in Pharisaism and the Gospels,* First Series (Cambridge: Cambridge University Press, 1917), p. 91; and Fiebig, *Die Gleichnisreden Jesu,* p. 268.

[46] *Contra* John Dominic Crossan, *Cliffs of Fall* (New York: The Seabury Press, 1980), pp. 48–49, who argued that the criterion of dissimilarity applies to form rather than content with regard to Jesus' teaching. Consequently, he viewed Jesus' teaching in parables as a new form of teaching. The foundation for this position is a brief statement from Jacob Neusner that rabbinic material prior to 70 A. D. contains no similitudes. (See his *The Rabbinic Traditions About the Pharisees Before 70,* Leiden: E. J. Brill, 1971, III, 85–86; or "Types and Forms in Ancient Jewish Literature: Some Comparisons," *History of Religions* XI, 1971, 376.) Neusner's statement, however cannot be used as support for Crossan's argument, but points instead to the paucity of material prior to 70 A.D. In his *First Century Judaism in Crisis* (Nashville: Abingdon Press, 1975), pp. 118–121, Neusner pointed to the similarity of a parable of Jesus and one of Yohanan ben Zakkai. Flusser would point not only to this parable of Yohanan (b Shab 153a), but also to Old Testament parables such as II Samuel 12,1–7, the parabolic speech of Antigonos of Sokho recorded in Pirke Aboth I.3, to the parabolic imagery of John the Baptist in Matthew 3,12||, and to late rabbinic examples which seem to preserve stories current in Jesus' day and adopted by him. In addition, Flusser would allow for the influence of Greek thought on the rabbinic parable form. It is worthy of note that there are no parables in the Apocrypha and Pseudepigrapha, apparently none at Qumran, none added from Diaspora Judaism, and none told in Aramaic. If a rabbi spoke Aramaic, he switched to Hebrew for the telling of the parable (See Flusser, pp. 17–20). Did Jesus do the same?

[47] Parables with such features are often called "mixed forms," See the arguments

willing to speak of more than one point of correspondence between image and idea[48]. That there may be several points of contact between image and idea can be easily seen in rabbinic examples:

1. To what may this be compared? To a human king who owned a beautiful orchard which contained splendid figs. Now, he appointed two watchmen therein, one lame and the other blind. (One day) the lame man said to the blind, "I see beautiful figs in the orchard. Come and take me upon thy shoulder, that we may procure and eat them." So the lame bestrode the blind, procured and ate them. Some time after, the owner came and inquired of them, "Where are those beautiful figs?" The lame man replied, "Have I then feet to walk with?" The blind man replied, "Have I then eyes to see with?" What did he do? He placed the lame upon the blind and judged them together. So will the Holy One, blessed be He, bring the soul, [re] place it in the body, and judge them together[49].

2. R. Simeon b. Halafta said: Unto what may this be likened? Unto one man living in Galilee and possessing a vineyard in Judea, and another living in Judea and owning a vineyard in Galilee. He who dwelt in Galilee used to go to Judea to hoe his garden and the one from Judea went to Galilee to hoe his. On coming together they said unto each other: "Instead of thee coming to my domain, take charge of my garden which is situated within thy region, and I shall in return guard thy property which is within my confines." Even so when David said, "Keep me as the apple of the eye," the Holy One, blessed be He, said unto him, "Keep My commandments and live." Thus said the Holy One, blessed be He, unto Israel, "Keep ye My precepts, the precept of reading the *Shema* morning and evening, and I shall guard you," even as it is written, "The Lord shall keep thee from all evil; He shall keep thy soul."[50]

3. Because Egypt enslaved Israel, she was punished and justice was exacted both in Egypt and at the sea. They were like robbers who had broken into the king's vineyard and destroyed the vines. When the king discovered that his vineyards had been destroyed, he was filled with wrath, and descending upon the robbers, without help from anything or anyone, he cut them down and uprooted them as they had done to his vineyard[51].

4. For whose sake did God reveal Himself in Egypt? For the sake of Moses. R. Nissim illustrated by a parable of a priest who had an orchard of figs, in which

---

or qualifications of the following: Fiebig, *Altjüdische Gleichnisse und die Gleichnisse Jesu*, p. 98; and *Die Gleichnisreden Jesu*, p. 231; Hermaniuk, pp. 169f.; Jones, pp. 76f. and 108f.; Hauck, pp. 750f.; Via, p. 13; Jeremias, pp. 18f and 88f.; Bauer, p. 298; and Martin Dibelius, *From Tradition to Gospel*, trans. Bertram Lee Woolf (London: Ivor Nicholson and Watson, 1934), pp. 255f.

[48] Jülicher's emphasis on only one point of comparison is not the necessary deterrent to allegorizing.

[49] b Sanh 91a and b. Jones, p. 66, classified this story as an allegory and commented on its similarity to Mark 12,1–11.

[50] Tanch קדושים (Buber, p. 38a, 57): see Feldman, p. 218.

[51] ExR XXX.17.

there was an unclean field. When he wished to eat some of the figs, he told one of his men to go and say to the tenant: "The owner of the orchard bids you bring him two figs." He went and told him; whereupon the tenant replied: "Who is this owner of the orchard? Go back to your work." Then the priest said: "I will go myself to the orchard." His men said: "Will you go to an unclean place?" He replied: "Even if there be a hundred forms of uncleanness I will go, so that my messenger may not be put to shame." So when Israel was in Egypt God said to Moses: "Come now therefore, and I will send thee unto Pharaoh" (Ex. 3,10), so he went and was asked: "Who is the Lord, that I should hearken unto His voice? . . . I know not the Lord (ib. v,2) get you unto your burdens (ib. 4)." Then God said: "I will Myself go to Egypt," as it is said: The burden of Egypt etc. (Isa. XIX,1). Whereupon His angels said: "Wilt thou go to an unclean place?" The reply was: "Yes, so that My messenger Moses may not be put to shame."[52]

These examples could be multiplied easily, but these should suffice to show that it is an error to limit the Synoptic parables to one point of contact. One could even say of each case that the parable was molded on the reality.

Consequently, while the historical context and argumentative nature of the parables show they were used for a specific purpose, it does not follow that this major point is the only truth evident in the narrative. The Parable of the Good Samaritan was told to illustrate the proper attitude to one's neighbor, regardless of who he or she may be, but it is also a scathing rebuke of the Jewish leaders. The parable of Nathan (II Samuel 12,1f.), acclaimed by all as a classic parable, is a condemnation of David, but there are certainly connections between the rich man and David, the poor man and Uriah, and the ewe-lamb and Bathsheba.

Whether one defines allegory as extended metaphor or a series of metaphors, the question "Can a parable be an allegory?" must be answered affirmatively. That individual features in Jesus' parables have significance for interpretation should occasion no surprise at all. This is not a license for fanciful exegesis since such significance must be rooted in the historical and literary context. One will still have to determine where features have been added or emphasized by a later hand, but allegory was a legitimate genre for Jesus to use.

The discussion of the nature of parable and allegory yields two conclusions for our purposes. First, one cannot reject the authenticity of

---

[52] ExR XV.19. For further examples, cf. S–B, I, 653f. and 865f.; Fiebig, *Altjüdische Gleichnisse und die Gleichnisse Jesu, passim;* and *Die Gleichnisreden Jesu, passim;* Hermaniuk, *passim;* and Feldman, *passim.*

the Parable of the Wicked Tenants merely by deciding it is allegory. While other issues remain to be discussed, the form of the story is in keeping with Old Testament and rabbinic parables. Whether one chooses to call this story a "parable," an "allegory," or both is not really important[53], but there is nothing in the story not in keeping with the essential nature of a parable[54]. The artificiality of rejecting this story on the basis of its form is underscored by the fact that there are two rabbinic versions of this parable:

1. This is to be compared to a king who had a field and he gave it to tenants. The tenants began stealing it. He (the king) took it from them and gave it to their sons. They turned out to be worse than their predecessors. He took it from their sons and gave it to their grandchildren. They, in turn, were worse than their antecedents. A son was born to him (the king). He said to them (the tenants), "Go forth from the midst of that which belongs to me. It is not my wish that you be in its midst. Give me my portion that I may make it known as my own."[55]

2. Like a king who had a small son; also he had a possession. The king wished to move to a foreign land. He spoke to a tenant; he should guard the possession and enjoy its produce until his son should wish it to be delivered to him. When the son of the king was grown, he claimed the possession. Immediately the tenant began to cry woe! Even so when the Israelites lived in Egypt, the

---

[53] Jones, pp. 96f., accepted the story as both parable and allegory; and A. M. Hunter, *Interpreting the Parables* (London: SCM Press, 1964), pp. 94 and 117, viewed it as an "allegorical parable."

[54] See also Xavier Léon-Dufour, "La parabole des vignerons homicides," *Sciences Ecclésiastiques*, XVII (1965), 366–371. Robert W. Funk, *Language, Hermeneutic, and Word of God* (New York: Harper & Row, 1966), p. 133, listed four essential clues to the nature of a parable: 1) the parable is a metaphor or simile which may ... be expanded into a story; 2) the metaphor or simile is drawn from nature or common life; 3) the metaphor arrests the hearer by its vividness or strangeness; and 4) the application is left imprecise in order to tease the hearer into making his own application. The Parable of the Wicked Tenants is in keeping with all four. The last characteristic I understand to mean that the hearer was forced to pass judgment himself. After the hearer had been forced toward a conclusion, the application may have been nailed down with a "Thou art the man."

[55] SDt. 32,9 § 312 (134b). In the interpretation God is the king, Abraham is the first group of tenants, Isaac is the second group. These first two were rejected because something "objectionable" i.e., Ishmael and Esau, arose from them. Jacob is the son because none of his descendents were objectionable. See the discussion of this parable in Eugene Mihaly, "A Rabbinic Defense of the Election of Israel," *HUCA*, XXXV (1964), 103–135, from which this translation comes. There is a shorter version of the parable which has only two groups of tenants. (See S–B, I, 874, and the discussion by Derrett, "Allegory and the Wicked Vinedressers," 427–431, but his reasons for preferring the long text are not clear. The third group of ousted tenants is not picked up in the interpretation.)

Canaanites lived in the land of Israel and guarded it and ate its fruit; but when they heard that the Israelites had come out of Egypt, they began to cry woe[56]!

The second conclusion from the discussion of parable and allegory is that the practice of wholesale de-allegorizing is not justified. The methods of Dodd, Jeremias, and especially van Iersel must be called into question. Later additions and redactional changes do have to be reckoned with, but any de-allegorizing will have to be supported by a comparison of the various Synoptic accounts of the parable[57]. Specifically with regard to our parable, Flusser commented on the well-intentioned de-allegorizing that has changed this parable into an "öde Ruine" and asserted correctly "Wenn man die Typologie vom Gleichnis von den bösen Winzern wegnimmt, dann verliert das Gleichnis sein Rückgrat."[58] On the other hand, there is also an unacceptable tendency to see specific allegorical or metaphorical significance when it is questionable that any exists[59]. The significance that an item has, will have to be adequately based in the story itself and neither imposed from the outside nor removed without adequate grounds, but that an item may carry some significance is to be expected.

Other Methodological Considerations

So far, our concern with method has been to correct misunderstanding with regard to allegory and allegorical features so that our parable may be approached without prejudice. Given the fact that the form is legitimate, there are still other methodological considerations that are necessary. Can one move back to an earlier form of the story and if so, how? Certainly no full treatment of the important subject of methods for Gospels studies is possible, but several comments are in order.

---

[56] Tanch B בשלח 7 (29ª), S–B, I, 874f.
[57] On Thomas see *infra*, pp. 52–54.
[58] Flusser, pp. 125–126, and 137.
[59] As M. D. Goulder in "Characteristics of the Parables in the Several Gospels, *JTSns*, XIX (1968), 60, when he saw in the stoning of one servant (Matthew 21,35) a reference to the stoning of Zechariah. Hugh Montefiore, "A Comparison of the Parables of the Gospel According to Thomas and of the Synoptic Gospels," *NTS*, VII (1960–61), 236, thought that since Thomas omits καιρός in Mark 12,2‖, the Synoptic writers possibly understood this word allegorically as the moment of salvation. Jeremias, *The Parables of Jesus*, p. 77, accused Matthew of thinking of the covenant at Sinai with ἐξέδετο (21,33), despite the fact that both Mark and Luke have the same word in the same context, evidently without any allegorical meaning.

Recent attention has focused on the criteria and the employment of the criteria by which scholars have tried to determine the "authentic" elements in Jesus' teaching[60]. In most cases, the concern has been for more careful use of the criteria than was often the case in the past. In particular, several people have correctly pointed out the short-comings of the use of the principles of dissimilarity and coherence and have argued for a positive rather than a negative use of various criteria[61].

Increasingly, scholars are recognizing that the "laws" according to which traditions were conveyed are not laws at all, but at most "tendencies" which may change in a given instance. For example, an unwarranted assumption that has been applied to our parable is that the simpler account is the earlier[62]. If nothing else, the work of E. P. Sanders has shown that one must proceed with extreme caution when trying to ascertain relative antiquity on the basis of length or amount of detail[63]. The longer is not necessarily the later since the tradition moved both ways, partly due to the author's style and partly to what he considered needed explanation or was nonessential. If one assumes the priority of Mark, he or she may well see a de-allegorizing tendency in the accounts of our parable in Luke and Thomas, as Martin Hengel did[64]. Rather than just saying that Luke and Thomas represent the original version since

---

[60] See the discussions on methods and criteria in M. Hooker, "Christology and Methodology," *NTS*, XVII (1970-1971), 480-487, (arguing against Perrin, *Rediscovering the Teaching of Jesus*, pp. 39f.); Richard N. Longenecker, "Literary Criteria in Life of Jesus Research: An Evaluation and Proposal," *Current Issues in Biblical and Patristic Interpretation*, ed. Gerald F. Hawthorne (Grand Rapids: William B. Eerdmans Publishing Co., 1975), 217-229; D. G. A. Calvert, "An Examination of the Criteria for Distinguishing the Authentic Words of Jesus," *NTS*, XVIII (1971-1972), 209-219; Neil J. McEleney, "Authenticating Criteria and Mark 7,1-23," *CBQ*, XXXIV (1972), 431-460; Heinz Schürmann, "Wie hat Jesus seinen Tod bestanden und verstanden?" *Orientierung an Jesus*, ed. Paul Hoffmann (Freiburg: Herder, 1973), 325-332; Karl Kertelge (ed.) *Rückfrage nach Jesus* (Freiburg: Herder, 1974); and Robert H. Stein, "The Criteria for Authenticity," *Gospel Perspectives*, Vol. I, ed. R. T. France and David Wenham (Sheffield: JSOT Press, 1980), 225-263.

[61] See especially the articles by Hooker and Calvert in the previous note.

[62] Montefiore, p. 237. This principle is used despite the fact that he recognized the tendency in Thomas to compress the parables. (Cf. p. 228.) Cf. Jeremias, *The Parables of Jesus*, p. 72; G. Quispel, "'The Gospel of Thomas' and the 'Gospel of the Hebrews'," *NTS*, XII (1965-1966), 379; and the discussions in E. P. Sanders, *The Tendencies of the Synoptic Tradition* (Cambridge: Cambridge University Press, 1969), pp. 46f and 88f.

[63] Sanders, pp. 82f. and 183f. and the whole of chapters two and three.

[64] "Das Gleichnis von den Weingärtnern Mc 12,1-12 im Lichte der Zenonpapyri und der rabbinischen Gleichnisse," *ZNW*, LIX (1968), 5-6.

they are simpler, it must be granted as equally possible that they may have abbreviated a longer original.

Sanders' caution that a Semitism does not necessarily indicate antiquity should also be heeded[65]. However, Sanders may have gone too far in playing down the importance of Semitisms. Since Aramaic was at least one of the languages used by Jesus and the Jewish Christians, one should expect the occurrence of Semitisms. The point is that caution should be used in assessing the importance of individual occurrences.

David Flusser's recent work on parables has raised other methodological concerns and in fact his book is in many ways a direct challenge to the classic treatment of parables by Jeremias. In addition to the rejection of wholesale de-allegorizing referred to above[66], Flusser has suggested that the Gospel of Thomas is much less significant for research on the words of Jesus than Jeremias and others have suggested[67]. He also argued that there is less theology, Christology, and eschatology in the parables than many think; instead, the parables of Jesus were originally moral paranesis and were readily adaptable to the new Christian community[68].

Of greater significance is Flusser's assertion that the contexts, introductions, and interpretations of the parables in the Synoptics are not only generally reliable, but necessary for a proper understanding. The interpretations are not later additions by the evangelists, but were attached to the parables by Jesus[69]. The implications of Flusser's arguments are far-reaching and will have to be examined in detail as we investigate the parable before us. Of methodological importance, however, is the fact that one cannot merely assume the kinds of principles on which much parable research has taken place.

In addition, one should approach the various accounts of this parable without a presupposition as to which is earliest. If one assumes that a certain account is the earliest and attempts to explain the others from it, adequate attention might not be given to the accounts that are considered adaptations. Even apart from the fact that the question of Synoptic relationships has been reopened[70], it has been too frequently over-

---

[65] Sanders, pp. 228f. and 249f.
[66] *Supra*, p. 26.
[67] Flusser, p. 128.
[68] *Ibid.*, pp. 120–123.
[69] *Ibid.*, pp. 61, 119–120, and 137.
[70] William R. Farmer, *The Synoptic Problem* (New York: The Macmillan Company, 1964); Sanders, *The Tendencies of the Synoptic Tradition*; Bernard Orchard,

looked that any one of the Gospels may preserve an older tradition in a given pericope. Such an awareness will at least allow all the traditions to be heard.

One other element requires mention here. Particularly in America, the term "polyvalence" has frequently been associated with parable research. The idea in the use of this term is that parables are not to be confined to *a* meaning, but by their very nature open up the reader to various meanings or levels of meaning[71]. It seems to me that this is an unfortunate turn of events that leads back to the very abuse of the parables against which Jülicher was reacting[72]. One can read parables into different contexts as, indeed, the re-use of rabbinic parables by Jesus and rabbis in various contexts shows. However, one must distinguish between *hearing* the parables in the context intended by Jesus and the re-use of parables by putting them into another context. In the former case, we interpret the parables; in the latter, we become the teller of the parable by retelling it in another context (which Crossan terms "play"). With regard to meaning, significance, and authorial intention, the discussions of E. D. Hirsch, Jr. and G. B. Caird provide a much saner approach to hermeneutical procedure[73].

What is required for an analysis of our parable is a careful comparison of the various accounts without assuming the priority of one account over the others. An attempt must be made on the basis of the differences in the texts to explain the movement of the tradition. The metaphorical or theological significance of special items will have to be evaluated in light of the cultural milieu of the story, the teaching of Jesus elsewhere, and the theology of the early church. Only then can we make some assessment of the origin and meaning of the story. The illusion that we can move behind the gospels to an *Urform* of the *ipsissima verba* of Jesus should be given up. The differences in the accounts, however, compel

---

Matthew, Luke, and Mark (Manchester: Koinonia Press, 1976); and Hans Herbert Stoldt, *Geschichte und Kritik der Markushypothese* (Göttingen: Vandenhoeck & Ruprecht, 1977) to point only to the most obvious.

[71] See particularly Crossan, *Cliffs of Fall*, pp. 51–104; and Mary Ann Tolbert, *Perspectives on the Parables: An Approach to Multiple Interpretations* (Philadelphia: Fortress Press, 1979), *passim*.

[72] Note that Crossan, *Cliffs of Fall*, pp. 96–97, referred to the four levels of meaning in medieval exegesis as he proposed reading parables within different systems.

[73] E. D. Hirsch, Jr., *Validity in Interpretation* (New Haven: Yale University Press, 1967), *passim*, and G. B. Caird, especially, pp. 37–61.

us to look for the "basic" form of the original story and to note the movement of the tradition and the tendencies of the evangelists as they shaped the story and placed it in their individual works.

Chapter 3

The Cultural Setting of the Parable

The objections to the Parable of the Wicked Tenants that are based on the fact that it is allegory operate in tandem with objections that the story is unnatural and psychologically improbable. The fact that the story seems unrealistic has reinforced the opinions that the parable is a secondary and "artless" creation from the church.

Some of such criticism raised against the parable results from sheer pedanticism and a woodenly literal reading of the text[1], but other points of criticism must be taken more seriously. To the twentieth century mind, the following may appear questionable:

1. A man would not plant a vineyard and then leave it.
2. A vineyard would not be given out immediately after construction since the first fruits come after five years.
3. The behavior of the tenants is improbable.
4. It is psychologically improbable that a man would repeatedly send slaves when they were repeatedly and progressively mistreated.
5. It is even more improbable that a man would send his only son.
6. There is no justification for the tenants' belief that they would inherit the vineyard.
7. It is questionable whether the owner could simply kill his tenants.
8. It is unlikely that the owner would give the vineyard to others; rather, he would look after it himself[2].

---

[1] Alfred Loisy, *L'Evangile selon Marc* (Paris: Emile Nourry, Editeur, 1912), p. 335, thought it bizarre that a man who planted his own vineyard would go on a long trip, but the owner probably would not have done more than supervise the initial endeavor. Ernst Lohmeyer, *Das Evangelium des Markus* (Göttingen: Vandenhoeck & Ruprecht, 1967), p. 244 and also "Das Gleichnis von den bösen Weingärtnern (Mark 12,1-12)," *ZST*, XVIII (1941), 243, objected to the owner asking his rent in grapes, but "fruit of the vineyard" cannot be restricted to fresh grapes. He also objected to the word πύργος, but see Alex. Pallis, *Notes on St. Mark and St. Matthew* (London: Oxford University Press, 1932), p. 41.

[2] For these objections see the following: W. G. Kümmel, "Das Gleichnis von den bösen Weingärtnern (Mark. 12,1-9)," *Aux sources de la tradition chretienne. Mélanges offerts à M. Goguel* (Neuchatel: Delachaux & Niestle S. A., 1950), 122f.; Lohmeyer,

Fortunately, a good deal of material has been preserved in the rabbinic writings and elsewhere that helps to elucidate the background with which we are dealing. In addition to regulations in the Mishnah and Talmud which govern the leasing and possession of property, there are numerous rabbinic parables that deal with the owner of a vineyard (or garden) and his tenants. Also, there are historical documents outside the rabbinic writings that report the leasing of land and the problems involved. A contract from the third century provides information about lease arrangements in the ancient world.

To Aurelius Serenus also called Sarapion son of Agathinus and Taposirias, of the illustrious and most illustrious city of Oxyrhynchus, from the Aurelii Ctistus son of Rufus and Dionysia and his son Ptolemacus . . . and Peloius . . . We voluntarily undertake to lease for one year more from Hathur 1 of the present 6th year all of the vinetending operations in the vineyard owned by you in the area of the village of Tanais and the adjoining reed-plantation whatever be the acreage of each, we, the party of Aurelius Ctistus, undertaking half and I, Peloius, the remaining half, which operations are, concerning the vineyard, plucking of reeds, collection and transport of them, proper pruning, making into bundles and binding, stripping and transport of leaves and throwing them outside the mudwalls, layering as many vine-shoots as are necessary, digging, scooping hollows round the vines and trenching, you, the landlord, being responsible for the arrangement of the reeds and we for assisting you in the work, we being responsible for the remaining operations after those mentioned, namely, breaking up the ground, picking off shoots, keeping the vines well tended, giving space to the growths, cutting back, needful thinnings of foliage; and concerning the reed-plantations, the bisection of each of the two, watering and continual weeding; and further we agree to assist you in the vineyard and the reed-plantation in superintending the asses which bring earth, in order that the earth may be thrown in the proper places, and we will perform the testing of the jars intended for the wine, and will put these, when they have been filled with wine, in the open-air shed, and plaster them, and move the wine, and strain it from one jar into another, and watch over them as long as they are stored in the open-air shed, the wage for all the aforesaid operations being 4500

Das Evangelium des Markus, pp. 244–247; B. T. D. Smith, *The Parables of the Synoptic Gospels* (Cambridge: Cambridge University Press, 1937), pp. 22 and 224; Loisy, pp. 336f.; Geraint Vaughan Jones, *The Art and Truth of the Parables* (London: SPCK, 1964), p. 93; Sherman E. Johnson, *A Commentary on the Gospel According to Mark* (London: Adam & Charles Black, 1960), p. 195; Josef Schmid, *The Gospel According to Mark,* trans. Kevin Condon (Staten Island: Alba House, 1968), pp. 215f.; Erich Klostermann, *Das Markusevangelium* (Tübingen: Verlag J. C. B. Mohr, Paul Siebeck, 195), p. 122; Walter Grundmann, *Das Evangelium nach Markus* (Berlin: Evangelische Verlagsanstalt, n. d.), pp. 239f.; and Ernst Haenchen, *Der Weg Jesu* (Berlin: Alfred Töpelmann, 1966), p. 399. See also the discussion by Vincent Taylor, *The Gospel According to St. Mark* (London: Macmillan & Co., 1952), pp. 472f.

silver drachmae, 10 artabae of wheat, and 4 jars of wine at the vat, which wages we are to receive in installments according to the progress of the operations. And we likewise undertake to lease for one year the produce of all the date-palms and fruit-trees which are in the old vineyard, for which we will pay as a special rent 1½ artabae of fresh dates, 1½ artabae of pressed dates, 1½ artabae of walnut-dates, ½ artaba of black olives, 500 selected peaches, 15 citrons, 500 summer figs before the inundation, 500 winter figs, 4 large white fat melons. Moreover we will in consideration of the above wages likewise plough the adjoining fruit-garden to the south of the vineyard, and will do the watering, weeding, and all other seasonal operations, only the arrangement of reeds in it and the strewing of earth being left to you, the landlord, the rent being secured against all risks. If our undertaking is guaranteed to us, we will perform all the seasonal operations of the vineyard and fruit-garden and reed-plantation at the proper times and to your satisfaction, your agents keeping a check on everything, and we will pay the special rent at the required time without delay, and at the end of the period we will deliver the objects of the lease under cultivation, well cared for by our operations, and free from rushes, weeds, and all coarse grass, you having the right of execution upon us, who are mutual securities for the payment of the rent, as is fitting. This undertaking is valid, and in answer to the formal question we have given our consent[3].

As this contract shows, the first and last objections listed above, which question the owner's leaving the vineyard to the oversight of others, are eliminated. A cursory examination of other sources substantiates that the possession of vineyards in distant places (as well as near home) was also a common feature in the life of Palestinian Jews[4]. It is unlikely that a man who was rich enough to own much land would cultivate it himself. The normal procedure was that he would live in a city and reserve his time for more important and pleasant duties by leasing the land to tenants. This practice is reflected over and over in both Palestinian and non-Palestinian material[5].

---

[3] P. Oxy. 1631. See the text and commentary in Bernard P. Grenfell and Arthur S. Hunt, eds. *The Oxyrhynchus Papyri* (London: Egyptian Exploration Society, 1920), XIV, 15–25. The translation above is from *The Loeb Classical Library's Select Papyri*, trans. A. S. Hunt and C. C. Edgar (London: William Heinemann, 1952), I, 54–59.

[4] Asher Feldman, *The Parables and Similes of the Rabbis* (Cambridge: Cambridge University Press, 1924), p. 128, and the whole chapter on viticulture. Cf. Tanch קדושים (Buber, p. 38a, 57); BB III.2; Song of Solomon 8,11f.; and II Chron. 26,10.

[5] Particularly Pesiq 99ª, and see the discussions of S–B, I, 869–875; Feldman, pp. 39f., 84f., and 127f.; and Martin Hengel, "Das Gleichnis von den Weingärtnern Mc 12,1–12 im Lichte der Zenonpapyri und der rabbinischen Gleichnisse," *ZNW*, LIX (1968), 12–21. Note particularly the papyrus published by Hengel which illustrates a situation similar to that of the parable. See Victor Tcherikover, *Hellenistic Civilization and the Jews*, trans. S. Appelbaum (Philadelphia: The Jewish Publication Society

The objection that a new vineyard would not be leased immediately is disposed of just as quickly. It is true that there would be no profit on a new vineyard before the fifth year, but it is not true that there would be no fruit (nor is the implication true that there would be no work to do). The fruit of the first three years, however much there might be, was forbidden as being the "fruit of uncircumcision." The fruit of the fourth year was set aside as holy, but could be redeemed, and the fruit of the fifth year could be enjoyed[6]. In addition to the work that the vines themselves would require, other plants would have been planted in the vineyard to fray the expenses of the early years[7].

The remaining objections are of a more serious nature. The objections of psychological improbability are the primary reasons why it has been charged that the whole parable has been formed on the reality being portrayed. To a certain degree, the importance placed on these improbabilities is unjustified. As Linnemann pointed out, the narrative supports the unnatural features by including motivations that justify them. A listener would not see the problems[8]. One must also consider the argument by David Flusser that the parables are more pseudo-realistic than realistic[9]. But would the events of this parable have seemed improbable to a first century Palestinian listener?

C. H. Dodd and J. Jeremias have both reminded us of the politically and economically tense conditions prevalent in Palestine. One cannot ignore the evidence mentioned by Jeremias which shows that large parts

---

of America, 1959), p. 336, for evidence of Jewish owners and Egyptian tenants in Egypt. See also Ramsay MacMullen, *Roman Social Relations 50 B. C. to A. D. 284* (New Haven: Yale University Press, 1974), pp. 5–6.

[6] See Lev. 19,23f.; Herbert Danby (ed.), *The Mishnah* (Oxford: Clarendon Press, 1933), p. 795; LvR XXV.8; b BK 68b; J. Duncan M. Derrett, "Fresh Light on the Parable of the Wicked Vinedressers," *Revue Internationale des Droits de L'Antiquitè*, 3me série, X (1963), 15f. (also in *Law in the New Testament*, London: Darton, Longman, and Todd, 1970, pp. 286–312).

[7] Derrett, p. 22; S–B, I, 872. See LvR XXIII.3 and the complex legislations in Kil. IV.1–V.8. Cf. Luke 13,6.

[8] Eta Linnemann, *Parables of Jesus*, trans. John Sturdy (London: SPCK, 1966), pp. 28f. Amos N. Wilder, *Early Christian Rhetoric* (London: SCM Press, 1964), p. 85, pointed to the hyperbole in Jesus' parables, and J. Alexander Findlay, *Jesus and His Parables* (London: The Epworth Press, 1950), pp. 8f.; stated that surprise is one of the main characteristics of the parables. See also Robert W. Funk, "The Parables; A Fragmentary Agenda," *Jesus and Man's Hope II* (Pittsburgh: Pittsburgh Theological Seminary, 1981), p. 289.

[9] David Flusser, *Die rabbinischen Gleichnisse und der Gleichniserzähler Jesus. 1. Teil. Das Wesen der Gleichnisse* (Bern: Peter Lang, 1981), p. 125.

of Palestine were controlled by foreign landlords[10]. The Zenon papyri show that as far back as 250 B. C. Baitianata in Galilee was a wine-growing area owned by Apollonius, one of the top officials under Ptolemy II (Philadelphos)[11]. A papyrus, which has been published by Hengel, gives the number of vines there and indicates that housing had been built for the tenants[12]. A large part of the better land in Palestine may have been owned by foreign landlords.

The same Zenon papyri show the reality of rebellion by the tenants. For example, Zenon sent an underagent, Straton, to collect a debt from Jeddus, presumably an elder of a Jewish village. Aid was requested from the local Ptolemaic forces, but the man who was to accompany Straton excused himself by an alleged sickness and sent a youth and a letter with Straton. The letter was ignored, and Straton and the youth were assaulted and driven out of the village[13]. As Hengel pointed out, the terminology used for the violent action is similar to that in Luke[14].

It is possible that the events of the Parable of the Wicked Tenants result from the fact that the owner is a foreign landlord, but there is nothing in the parable itself that demands this. Ἀπεδήμησεν does not necessarily mean "he went to a foreign country;" it may denote only absence[15]. Haenchen noted that the evangelist would not have depicted the good owner in such a way as to bring a foreigner to mind[16].

---

[10] Joachim Jeremias, *The Parables of Jesus* (London: SCM Press, 1963), pp. 74–75, and especially n. 97. See C. H. Dodd, *The Parables of the Kingdom* (London: Nisbet and Co., 1936), pp. 125–126.

[11] *Ibid.* See Pubblicazoni della Societa Italiana, *Papiri Greci e Latini*, 6,1920, no. 594.

[12] Hengel, pp. 12f. The number of vines was 80,000, and Hengel estimated that twenty-five workers would have been needed to care for them.

[13] C. C. Edgar (ed.), *Catalogue général des antiquités égyptiennes du Musée du Caire: Zenon Papyri* (Le Caire: Imprimerie de L'Institute Français D'Archaeologie Orientale, 1925), I, 38, no. 59018. The incident is preserved in the letter from Alexandros, the officer who was to accompany Straton, to his overseer, Oryas:

When they returned, they told me that he had in no way regarded my letter; rather, he had taken them forcibly and had ejected them from the village. (αὐτοῖς δὲ [χεῖρας] προσενεγκεῖν καὶ ἐγβαλ [ει]ν ἐκ τῆς κώμης.) I write to you. Farewell.

Cf. Hengel, pp. 14f. and 26f., who mentioned an incident involving a petition drawn up by tenants, and p. 27, an incident involving runaway slaves.

[14] Hengel, pp. 26f.

[15] B-A-G, p. 90; LSJ, p. 196; M-M, p. 61, Kümmel, p. 122, n. 10.

[16] Haenchen, p. 398, n. 8. Thus, the suggestion of Jane E. and Raymond R. Newell, "The Parable of the Wicked Tenants, *NovT*, XIV (1972), 234–237, that the parable is a warning against Zealot violence has no basis in the text. The suggestion also is completely out of keeping with the rabbinic use of the metaphors involved.

However, it is not really important whether the man was a foreigner or not. The least required is that he was not near enough to the vineyard for convenient direct supervision[17]. Even if both the owner and the tenants were Jews, the behavior of the tenants is understandable.

The conflict between landowner and tenant was more of an economic class struggle than rebellion against a foreign landlord. If the landowner were a foreigner, it would only have intensified the conflict. The problems caused by unreliable, greedy, and rebellious tenants hired by hard and merciless landowners are mentioned repeatedly in the rabbinic writings. Four parables have already been mentioned that illustrate some of these problems and there are others as well[18]. Similar to these tenant parables is a significant parable about an attempt to collect taxes from a province that was behind in payment:

> This may be compared to the case of a province which owed tax arrears to the king who sent a collector of the (king's) treasury to collect (the debt). What did the people of the province do? They rose and mulcted him and hanged him. People said: Woe to us, should the king become aware of these things. That which the king's emissary sought to do to us, we did to him[19].

More important than the parables are the complex legal pronouncements of the Mishnah and Talmud that try to deal with the friction between landowner and tenant[20]. From this evidence one can only conclude that the behavior of the tenants in the Gospel parable would have seemed all too common to first century listeners.

The owner's reluctance to use force is understandable in a first century milieu. Hengel has correctly reminded us of the legal system in first century Palestine[21]. The owner would have been at a distinct disadvantage if he had sought legal assistance. The local authorities

---

[17] See Derrett, p. 16.

[18] See *supra*, pp. 23–24; b Sanh 91a–b; ExR XV.19; SDt 32,9 § 312; and Tanch B בשלח (29a). In addition the following are of interest: DtR VII.4 – a garden was leased to two tenants; one did nothing, and the other planted trees, but cut them down; LvR XXIII.3 – an orchard was let out, but the tenants let it go to weeds; LvR V. 8 – this reflects the problems of a tenant borrowing from an owner. Cf. EcclR V.10.2. b Berakh 5b shows the attempts of an owner and a tenant to cheat each other out of the vine twigs. Cf. Hengel, pp. 24f., for further information on this class conflict.

[19] LvR XI.7.

[20] See the complexity of the regulations in BM V.8; VIII.6–X.5; BB X.4; VII.8; b BM 103b–110b, 112b. Cf. Maimonides XIII.I.8 (pp. 27–31 of YJS): and Hengel, pp. 28f.

[21] Hengel, pp. 26f.

would more likely favor the tenants than the owner who lived some distance away. As the New Testament reveals, the administration of justice often sought the way of least resistance (Mark 15,6–15; Luke 18,1–8; and Acts 24,26f.), and for the local authorities the maintenance of peace would have been more important than legal aid for an outsider. If force were used, the tenants would probably abandon the vineyard and cause even more trouble. The wisest course of action for the owner was to repeat his request in hope that the tenants would respond[22]. While this may account for the second or even the third sending of servants, it will not support the long series of sendings reported in Mark 12,5. Whether this long series should be attributed to hyperbole or improbability, which some have felt are characteristic of Jesus' parables, will have to be determined later.

The sending of the son and especially the justifying of this action by saying that the tenants would respect him seem to be particularly naive to the modern reader. Derrett has brought forth rabbinic evidence which shows that this would not have been the case with the first century listener[23]. When someone had been wronged in early Palestine, his only recourse was to make a formal protest before witnesses warning that legal action would be taken. Neither this protest nor the adjuring of witnesses could be made by servants[24]. Nor was it possible for one to deal through an agent; if he desired to do so, it was necessary to transfer his right (or part of it) to the representative[25]. For this reason it was necessary to send the son. (With typical parable conciseness, we are not told why the father could not come.) The father would probably have transferred a small portion of ownership to the son to make him a legal claimant[26]. Alternatively, but less likely is Ernst Bammel's view that complete ownership was transferred to the son as a gift from his

---

[22] *Ibid.*, 27. Note particularly the instance in the Zenon papyri (PCZ 50915) in which Zenon wrote five letters rather than use force to regain what was legally his. Cf. the discussion of the inadequacies of justice and the abuse of the defenseless in MacMullen, pp. 6–13.

[23] Derrett, p. 31; and cf. Hengel, p. 30.

[24] Sheb. IV.12 (cf. RH I.8); b BB 38a–39a is significant. "What constitutes protest? . . . If, however, he says: 'So and so is a robber who has seized my land wrongfully and tomorrow I am going to sue him,' this is a protest."

[25] b BK 70a.

[26] Derrett, p. 31; and Hengel, p. 30. Although there is nothing determinative in the text, Derrett may be correct in saying that it is unlikely that the son would have made the trip unaccompanied.

father[27]. At any rate, the expectation of the father that the son would be respected becomes understandable. His coming would indicate to the tenants that definite legal action was being taken to protest their seizure of the vineyard. There still may be questions that one would like to ask of the parable at this point, but the sending of the son is not artificial or incomprehensible.

The other feature which seems particularly naive to the modern reader is that the tenants assert that they would gain the inheritance if they killed the son. It is not necessary to resort to the regulations governing the claiming of proselyte and ownerless land[28]. It was a general rabbinic law that a person without title deeds could sustain a claim to rightful ownership if he could prove three years undisputed possession[29]. The extensive discussions relating to usucaption (or seizure) of land reveal how common it was for tenants to attempt to become owners. The Mishnah states explicitly that tenants cannot secure title by usucaption[30], but the necessity of the statement and the Gemaras betray the reality of the attempts[31]. There is an additional factor that may have influenced the thinking of the tenants. In rabbinic law, if one abandoned hope of recovering lost or stolen property, he renounced his claim to ownership[32]. To this point the father had been unable to come to the vineyard, and the tenants must have felt that there was some chance the owner would give up. If the father did come and could not produce evidence, the stronger of the two parties could take possession[33].

There is always the problem of date when dealing with the rabbinic

---

[27] "Das Gleichnis von den bösen Winzern (Mk. 12,1–9) und das jüdische Erbrecht," *Revue Internationale des Droits de L'Antiquité*, 3me serie, VI (1959), 13.

[28] BB III.3; b BB 53a–55a; b Gitt 39a; and b Gerim 61a.

[29] BB III.1–6; b BB 28a and 35b. See Bammel, p. 14; Derrett, p. 28; and Hengel, p. 28.

[30] BB III.2–3. Cf. Maimonides XIII.IV.13 (pp. 241f. YJS).

[31] b BB 28a–36b; b BM 110a; p Bik I, 64^b, 55 (S–B, I, 872). Cf. Maimonides XIII.IV.11–16 (pp. 230–258 YJS).

[32] b BM 21a–22a; b BK 66a–70a and 114a. Cf. Derrett, p. 32.

[33] b BB 34b. Derrett, pp. 11–42, postulated that the tenants' rejection of the servants was a claim that the owner owed them for their output in the initial lean years. Only at the coming of the son were they tempted to steal the vineyard. His reconstruction is too elaborate and without basis. The first three years were not valid for usucaption (b BB 36a) and κενός does not mean "stripped of their possessions" as he suggested. (Cf. LXX Gen. 31,42; Deut. 15,13; and Job 22,9.) In the Gospel accounts the tenants are guilty from the beginning.

material, but the point being made here does not depend on specific texts or details. Rather, these texts, as others before them, are witness to the kind of relations that existed between landowners and tenants, and that is sufficient for our purposes. The most important point derived from the rabbinic writings is not so much how the tenants might gain possession, but that the laws were ambiguous and that this type of land seizure went on. The tenants, no doubt, were not experts in rabbinic law, and there is question whether their possession would ever be legal possession[34]. They were not concerned, however, with legal possession; they were interested in actual possession. At any rate, the tenants' statement, καὶ ἡμῶν ἔσται ἡ κληρονομία, may mean no more than "possession will be ours," for κληρονομία is not limited to the concept of inheritance. The Old Testament usage of נחלה and the LXX translation of this term by κληρονομία show repeatedly that the idea of inheritance is secondary to that of possession[35]. Of particular interest is III Kings 20 (21),15f. which uses κληρονομεῖν for Ahab's taking possession of Naboth's vineyard[36].

The remaining feature of the parable that has been questioned is whether the owner could just kill the tenants. Some of Jesus' other parables and some of the rabbinic parables involve killing or physical punishment as well[37]. For example, b BK 27b states that a man is entitled to take the law into his own hands to protect his interests and that he may "break another's teeth" and tell him "I am taking possession of what is mine." From the Greek papyri, one lease agreement states that if any of the conditions are infringed upon, the tenants will be liable to

---

[34] In b BB 47a it is stated that in some cases the grandson of a robber cannot secure title by usucaption (whereas usually he can), and it is explained that the kind of person meant is like those of a certain family who do not shrink from committing murder to extort money (and thus people are afraid to protect their property). Cf. Maimonides XIII.IV.13 (pp. 244–245 YJS).

[35] Werner Foerster and J. Herrmann, "κληρονόμος, συγκληρονόμος, κληρονομέω, κατακληρονομέω, κληρονομία," *TDNT*, III, 770, 774–775, and 778. Charles E. Carlston, *The Parables of the Triple Tradition* (Philadelphia; Fortress Press, 1975), pp. 183f., failed to realize this, and therefore, insisted on the improbability of the story.

[36] See also vs. 3 and 6, and cf. Neh. 9,24–25; and Judges 3,13.

[37] In Jesus' parables note Matthew 18,34; Luke 12,46; and 19,27. In the rabbinic writings see ExR XXX.17; LvR XI.7; XIII.5; and b Sanh 91a–b. See also Hans-Josef Klauck, "Das Gleichnis vom Mord im Weinberg (Mk 12,1–12; Mt. 21,33–46; Lk 20,9–19)," *Bibel und Leben*, XI (1970), 134; and Rudolph Pesch, *Das Markusevangelium* (Freiburg: Herder, 1977), II, 219.

arrest and imprisonment[38]. It is not necessary to justify legally the owner's punishment of the tenants. Under the circumstances, probably no objection would or could be made if he did kill the tenants. Our concern is that this feature of the parable is in keeping with rabbinic parables and the inadequate administration of justice at that time.

Thus the claim that the Parable of the Wicked Tenants is an artificial story whose features are not in keeping with everyday life cannot be substantiated as long as one does not limit "everyday life" to our twentieth century experiences. The rabbinic parables and regulations show that the events of the story were quite common and understandable in the early Palestinian culture. There is nothing objectionable about the basic features of the story[39].

---

[38] B. G. U. 1121 (See *Select Papyri*, I, 125f., no. 41). This papyrus is important also for the statement that if the contract is broken the owner can evict them (ἐγ[βα]λλειν) and lease the land to others (ἑτέροις). Cf. Matthew 21,41 ∥. See also P. Columbia 270 (*Memoirs of the American Academy in Rome*, vol. VI, American Academy in Rome, 1927, pp. 147–167; available in *Select Papyri* I, pp. 118f., no. 39). Note the extreme punishment of debtors recorded by Philo. *De spec. leg.* III, 159–162, and Josephus' account of a Galilean rebellion against the nobility in which supporters of Herod were drowned (*Antiq.* XIV.450) and of Herod's attempts to deal with rebellion (*Antiq.* XIV.415f. and 432f.).

[39] Cf. Hengel, p. 34; and Hans Dombois, "Juristische Bemerkungen zum Gleichnis von den bösen Weingärtern (Mk. 12,1–12)," *Neue Zeitschrift für Systematische Theologie und Religionsphilosophie*, VIII (1966), 361–373. The latter did not make use of the rabbinic evidence.

Chapter 4

An Analysis of the Parable and its Development

To some extent, it is true that the differences in the various accounts have been over-emphasized since the context, the basic form, and the meaning of the parable are the same for each of the three Synoptic evangelists[1]. At the same time, however, there are several differences that are significant for determining one's approach to the parable. These differences should suggest an explanation of the movement of the tradition and should give some insight into the individual accounts.

An attempt such as B. van Iersel's to reconstruct an *Urform* from the various accounts is neither possible nor justified. Each of the Synoptic accounts reveals different Semitisms and stylistic features of its writer. It is obvious that we are dealing with three distinct Greek reconstructions of a Semitic parable (but the accounts are not necessarily independent of each other). The account in Thomas is part of a long tradition as well. The shaping of the evangelists will allow one to trace at least part of the development of the story and can legitimately establish the essential features of the parable.

---

[1] Geraint Vaughan Jones, *The Art and Truth of the Parables* (London: SPCK, 1964), p. 91. Matthew included two other parables that Mark and Luke omitted or placed elsewhere, but the setting and sequence are the same otherwise.

Comparison of the Various Accounts

Matth 21 ³³⁻⁴⁶	Mark 12 ¹⁻¹²	Luk 20 ⁹⁻¹⁹
³³ "Ἄλλην παραβολὴν ἀκούσατε. ἄνθρωπος ἦν οἰκοδεσπότης ὅστις ἐφύτευσεν ἀμπελῶνα, καὶ φραγμὸν αὐτῷ περιέθηκεν καὶ ὤρυξεν ἐν αὐτῷ ληνὸν καὶ ᾠκοδόμησεν πύργον, καὶ ἐξέδοτο αὐτὸν γεωργοῖς, καὶ ἀπεδήμησεν. ³⁴ ὅτε δὲ ἤγγισεν ὁ καιρὸς τῶν καρπῶν, ἀπέστειλεν τοὺς δούλους αὐτοῦ πρὸς τοὺς γεωργοὺς λαβεῖν τοὺς καρποὺς αὐτοῦ. ³⁵ καὶ λαβόντες οἱ γεωργοὶ τοὺς δούλους αὐτοῦ ὃν μὲν ἔδειραν, ὃν δὲ ἀπέκτειναν, ὃν δὲ ἐλιθοβόλησαν. ³⁶ πάλιν ἀπέστειλεν ἄλλους δούλους πλείονας τῶν πρώτων, καὶ ἐποίησαν αὐτοῖς ὡσαύτως.	¹ Καὶ ἤρξατο αὐτοῖς ἐν παραβολαῖς λαλεῖν. ἀμπελῶνα ἄνθρωπος ἐφύτευσεν, καὶ περιέθηκεν φραγμὸν καὶ ὤρυξεν ὑπολήνιον καὶ ᾠκοδόμησεν πύργον, καὶ ἐξέδοτο αὐτὸν γεωργοῖς, καὶ ἀπεδήμησεν. ² καὶ ἀπέστειλεν πρὸς τοὺς γεωργοὺς τῷ καιρῷ δοῦλον, ἵνα παρὰ τῶν γεωργῶν λάβῃ ἀπὸ τῶν καρπῶν τοῦ ἀμπελῶνος· ³ καὶ λαβόντες αὐτὸν ἔδειραν καὶ ἀπέστειλαν κενόν. ⁴ καὶ πάλιν ἀπέστειλεν πρὸς αὐτοὺς ἄλλον δοῦλον· κἀκεῖνον ἐκεφαλαίωσαν καὶ ἠτίμασαν. ⁵ καὶ ἄλλον ἀπέστειλεν· κἀκεῖνον ἀπέκτειναν, καὶ πολλοὺς ἄλλους, οὓς μὲν δέροντες, οὓς δὲ ἀποκτέννυντες.	⁹ Ἤρξατο δὲ πρὸς τὸν λαὸν λέγειν τὴν παραβολὴν ταύτην. ἄνθρωπος ἐφύτευσεν ἀμπελῶνα, καὶ ἐξέδοτο αὐτὸν γεωργοῖς, καὶ ἀπεδήμησεν χρόνους ἱκανούς. ¹⁰ καὶ καιρῷ ἀπέστειλεν πρὸς τοὺς γεωργοὺς δοῦλον, ἵνα ἀπὸ τοῦ καρποῦ τοῦ ἀμπελῶνος δώσουσιν αὐτῷ· οἱ δὲ γεωργοὶ δείραντες αὐτὸν ἐξαπέστειλαν κενόν. ¹¹ καὶ προσέθετο ἕτερον πέμψαι δοῦλον· οἱ δὲ κἀκεῖνον δείραντες καὶ ἀτιμάσαντες ἐξαπέστειλαν κενόν. ¹² καὶ προσέθετο τρίτον πέμψαι· οἱ δὲ καὶ τοῦτον τραυματίσαντες ἐξέβαλον. ¹³ εἶπεν δὲ ὁ κύριος τοῦ ἀμπελῶνος· τί ποιήσω;

37 ὕστερον δὲ ἀπέστειλεν πρὸς αὐτοὺς τὸν υἱὸν αὐτοῦ λέγων· ἐντραπήσονται τὸν υἱόν μου. 38 οἱ δὲ γεωργοὶ ἰδόντες τὸν υἱὸν εἶπον ἐν ἑαυτοῖς· οὗτός ἐστιν ὁ κληρονόμος· δεῦτε ἀποκτείνωμεν αὐτὸν καὶ σχῶμεν τὴν κληρονομίαν αὐτοῦ· 39 καὶ λαβόντες αὐτὸν ἐξέβαλον ἔξω τοῦ ἀμπελῶνος καὶ ἀπέκτειναν. 40 ὅταν οὖν ἔλθῃ ὁ κύριος τοῦ ἀμπελῶνος, τί ποιήσει τοῖς γεωργοῖς ἐκείνοις; 41 λέγουσιν αὐτῷ· κακοὺς κακῶς ἀπολέσει αὐτούς, καὶ τὸν ἀμπελῶνα ἐκδώσεται ἄλλοις γεωργοῖς, οἵτινες ἀποδώσουσιν αὐτῷ τοὺς καρποὺς ἐν τοῖς καιροῖς αὐτῶν. 42 λέγει αὐτοῖς ὁ Ἰησοῦς· οὐδέποτε ἀνέγνωτε ἐν ταῖς γραφαῖς· λίθον ὃν ἀπεδοκίμασαν οἱ οἰκοδομοῦντες, οὗτος ἐγενήθη εἰς κεφαλὴν γωνίας· παρὰ κυρίου ἐγένετο αὕτη, καὶ	6 ἔτι ἕνα εἶχεν, υἱὸν ἀγαπητόν· ἀπέστειλεν αὐτὸν ἔσχατον πρὸς αὐτοὺς λέγων ὅτι ἐντραπήσονται τὸν υἱόν μου. 7 ἐκεῖνοι δὲ οἱ γεωργοὶ πρὸς ἑαυτοὺς εἶπαν ὅτι οὗτός ἐστιν ὁ κληρονόμος· δεῦτε ἀποκτείνωμεν αὐτόν, καὶ ἡμῶν ἔσται ἡ κληρονομία. 8 καὶ λαβόντες ἀπέκτειναν αὐτόν, καὶ ἐξέβαλαν αὐτὸν ἔξω τοῦ ἀμπελῶνος. 9 τί οὖν ποιήσει ὁ κύριος τοῦ ἀμπελῶνος; ἐλεύσεται καὶ ἀπολέσει τοὺς γεωργούς, καὶ δώσει τὸν ἀμπελῶνα ἄλλοις. 10 οὐδὲ τὴν γραφὴν ταύτην ἀνέγνωτε· λίθον ὃν ἀπεδοκίμασαν οἱ οἰκοδομοῦντες, οὗτος ἐγενήθη εἰς κεφαλὴν γωνίας· 11 παρὰ κυρίου ἐγένετο αὕτη, καὶ	πέμψω τὸν υἱόν μου τὸν ἀγαπητόν· ἴσως τοῦτον ἐντραπήσονται. 14 ἰδόντες δὲ αὐτὸν οἱ γεωργοὶ διελογίζοντο πρὸς ἀλλήλους λέγοντες· οὗτός ἐστιν ὁ κληρονόμος· ἀποκτείνωμεν αὐτόν, ἵνα ἡμῶν γένηται ἡ κληρονομία. 15 καὶ ἐκβαλόντες αὐτὸν ἔξω τοῦ ἀμπελῶνος ἀπέκτειναν. τί οὖν ποιήσει αὐτοῖς ὁ κύριος τοῦ ἀμπελῶνος; 16 ἐλεύσεται καὶ ἀπολέσει τοὺς γεωργοὺς τούτους, καὶ δώσει τὸν ἀμπελῶνα ἄλλοις. ἀκούσαντες δὲ εἶπαν· μὴ γένοιτο. 17 ὁ δὲ ἐμβλέψας αὐτοῖς εἶπεν· τί οὖν ἐστιν τὸ γεγραμμένον τοῦτο· λίθον ὃν ἀπεδοκίμασαν οἱ οἰκοδομοῦντες, οὗτος ἐγενήθη εἰς κεφαλὴν γωνίας;

ἔστιν θαυμαστὴ ἐν ὀφθαλμοῖς ἡμῶν;	ἔστιν θαυμαστὴ ἐν ὀφθαλμοῖς ἡμῶν;	
43 διὰ τοῦτο λέγω ὑμῖν ὅτι ἀρθήσεται ἀφ' ὑμῶν ἡ βασιλεία τοῦ θεοῦ καὶ δοθήσεται ἔθνει ποιοῦντι τοὺς καρποὺς αὐτῆς.		
44 καὶ ὁ πεσὼν ἐπὶ τὸν λίθον τοῦτον συνθλασθήσεται· ἐφ' ὃν δ' ἂν πέσῃ λικμήσει αὐτόν		18 πᾶς ὁ πεσὼν ἐπ' ἐκεῖνον τὸν λίθον συνθλασθήσεται· ἐφ' ὃν δ' ἂν πέσῃ λικμήσει αὐτόν.
45 καὶ ἀκούσαντες οἱ ἀρχιερεῖς καὶ οἱ Φαρισαῖοι τὰς παραβολὰς αὐτοῦ ἔγνωσαν ὅτι περὶ αὐτῶν λέγει·		
46 καὶ ζητοῦντες αὐτὸν κρατῆσαι ἐφοβήθησαν τοὺς ὄχλους, ἐπεὶ εἰς προφήτην αὐτὸν εἶχον.	12 καὶ ἐζήτουν αὐτὸν κρατῆσαι, καὶ ἐφοβήθησαν τὸν ὄχλον, ἔγνωσαν γὰρ ὅτι πρὸς αὐτοὺς τὴν παραβολὴν εἶπεν. καὶ ἀφέντες αὐτὸν ἀπῆλθον.	19 καὶ ἐζήτησαν οἱ γραμματεῖς καὶ οἱ ἀρχιερεῖς ἐπιβαλεῖν ἐπ' αὐτὸν τὰς χεῖρας ἐν αὐτῇ τῇ ὥρᾳ, καὶ ἐφοβήθησαν τὸν λαόν, ἔγνωσαν γὰρ ὅτι πρὸς αὐτοὺς εἶπεν τὴν παραβολὴν ταύτην.

The Gospel of Thomas Account

⁶⁵ He said: A good (χρηστός) man had a vineyard. He gave it to tenants that they might cultivate it and he might receive its fruit (καρπός) from them. He sent his servant so that the tenants might give him the fruit (καρπός) of the vineyard. They seized his servant (and) beat him, a little more and they would have killed him. The servant came (and) told it to his master. His master said, Perhaps he did not know them. He sent another servant; the tenants beat him as well. Then (τότε) the owner sent his son. He said, Perhaps they will respect my son. Since (ἐπεί) those tenants knew that he was the heir (κληρονόμος) of the vineyard, they seized him (and) killed him. He who has ears, let him hear.

⁶⁶ Jesus said: Show me the stone which the builders rejected. It is the cornerstone.

⁶⁷ Jesus said: He who knows the All but fails (to know) himself has missed everything.

The Context

All three Synoptic Gospels place this parable in the context of the dispute with the Jewish leaders toward the end of Jesus' ministry and in connection with the question of his authority. The objection has been raised that the parable is too caustic to come in its present position since in the preceding and following events, Jesus showed the greatest reserve in answering the questions of his opponents[2]. The proximity of the parable to the question of authority should not be overly stressed since Matthew records an additional parable between them[3], but the parable serves well as a veiled answer to that question and surely the Gospel writers intended this[4]. One should realize that with their questions, the Jewish leaders were attempting to trap Jesus into making a public statement that would serve to condemn him. His answers were not

---

[2] Alfred Loisy, *L'Evangile selon Marc* (Paris: Emile Nourry, Editeur, 1912), p. 343; Erich Klostermann, *Das Markusevangelium* (Tübingen: Verlag J. C. B. Mohr, Paul Siebeck, 1950), p. 120; and Arthur Gray, "The Parable of the Wicked Husbandmen," *The Hibbert Journal*, XIX (1920-21), p. 45.

[3] See M.-J. Lagrange, *Evangile selon Saint Matthieu* (Paris: J. Gabalda et Cie, Editeurs, 1941), p. 413.

[4] Ernst Lohmeyer, *Das Evangelium des Markus* (Göttingen: Vandenhoeck & Ruprecht, 1967), p. 244: and Walter Grundmann, *Das Evangelium nach Markus* (Berlin: Evangelische Verlagsanstalt, n. d.), p. 238.

reserved out of great respect for his opponents, but so that they would have nothing with which to bring a charge against him. That he would then use a parable in a caustic way against the Jewish leaders is in keeping with his general attitude toward them. Nothing has been brought forward to prevent one from agreeing with Hengel and a variety of others that this parable has been preserved in its original context[5]. At least one would have to grant that the parable is suitable for the last events in the life of Jesus, whether used by him or by the Church.

One additional feature of the context should be mentioned. All three Synoptists assume the presence of the common people[6] and agree that the parable was directed against the Jewish leaders. Luke reports that the parable was addressed to the people, and this is in keeping with his general tendency to emphasize the common people[7]. Matthew and Mark have the parable addressed to the Jewish leaders.

The Setting (Matthew 21,33; Mark 12,1; Luke 20,9; Thomas Logion 65)

According to Matthew, the owner of the vineyard was an οἰκοδεσπότης, which probably reflects the common rabbinic בעל הבית [8]. Thomas adds that he was a "good" man. Montefiore thought that this descrip-

---

[5] Martin Hengel, "Das Gleichnis von den Weingärtern Mc 12,1–12 im Lichte der Zenonpapyri und der rabbinischen Gleichnisse," *ZNW*, LIX (1968), 38; see also J. A. T. Robinson, "The Parable of the Wicked Husbandmen: A Test of Synoptic Relationships," *NTS*, XXI (1974–1975), 444; and David Flusser, *Die rabbinischen Gleichnisse und der Gleichniserzähler Jesus. 1. Teil: Das Wesen der Gleichnisse* (Bern: Peter Lang, 1981), p. 74. T. W. Manson said somewhat sarcastically that the criticism that rejects the context of this parable will be capable of getting rid of anything in the Gospels. (*The Teaching of Jesus*, Cambridge: Cambridge University Press, 1935, p. 104.)

[6] Matthew 21,23,26,46; Mark 11,32; 12,12,37; Luke 20,1,6,9,19.

[7] H. Strathmann, "λαός," *TDNT*, IV,50; Jerome Kodell, "Luke's Use of *Laos*, 'People,' Especially in the Jerusalem Narrative (Lk 19,28–24,53)," *CBQ*, XXXI (1969), 327–343; and see Hans Conzelmann, *The Theology of St. Luke*, trans. Geoffrey Buswell (London: Faber and Faber, 1960), p. 164, n. 1.

[8] Karl Heinrich Rengstorf, "οἰκοδεσπότης, οἰκοδεσποτέω," *TDNT*, II, 49; and Hengel, p. 17. B. van Iersel (*"Der Sohn" in den synoptischen Jesusworten*, Leiden: E. J. Brill, 1961, pp. 131f.) noted the occurrences of the word in the Synoptics (7/1/4) and that it occurs only twice outside figurative language (Mark 14,14 and Luke 22,11) and concluded that Matthew has added the word in this parable as a typical parable expression. Just because the word is omitted by the other two accounts does not make it a Matthean addition. It may well have had a counterpart in a Semitic version. The word is used more frequently in Matthew because of the author's interest in

tion was original[9], but this is unlikely. It is not the kind of feature that would have been omitted, but it is the kind that would have been added to insure that it is understood that the owner did nothing to cause the tenants' rebellion.

The most important feature of the setting is the vineyard itself. Matthew and Mark describe the planting and construction of the vineyard with words borrowed from the LXX account of Isaiah 5,2. There are slight divergencies between Matthew and Mark and neither is in exact agreement with the LXX. It has often been said that this allusion is secondary in that the LXX is used and that it is omitted by Luke and Thomas[10]. That some LXX wording was used is no proof at all since this may reflect only an assimilation to the LXX in either the oral or written period[11], nor is it strictly true to say that Luke omits the allusion. From the features of the Isaiah account, Matthew and Mark report the planting of the vineyard (as opposed to the vine, ἄμπελος, in LXX Isaiah 5,2, but ἀμπελὼν is mentioned in 5,1b) and three acts performed to improve the vineyard. Luke reports the planting of the vineyard, but omits the improvements as superfluous details. The omission of the details in Luke could be said to be an argument for their secondary insertion only if ἐφύτευσεν ἀμπελῶνα in Luke 20,9 is neither dependent on the identical words in Matthew and Mark, nor goes back to ἐφύτευσα ἄμπελον of Isaiah 5. Such a position is difficult to defend[12]. It is even less likely that the other two accounts added the Isaiah 5 elements as a result of the Lukan phrasing. The claim that Luke omitted the allusion to Isaiah 5 is therefore unfounded. It is much more likely that

---

similitudes. Five of the seven occurrences of the word in Matthew are in material peculiar to this book and six of the occurrences are in parables. It would be more accurate to say that it is a typically parabolic word.

[9] Hugh Montefiore, "A Comparison of the Parables of the Gospel According to Thomas and of the Synoptic Gospels," *NTS*, VII (1960–1961), p. 226.

[10] See particularly Joachim Jeremias, *The Parables of Jesus* (London: SCM Press, 1963), pp. 70f.; and Tim Schramm, *Der Markus-Stoff bei Lukas* (Cambridge: Cambridge University Press, 1971), pp. 156f.

[11] Cf. Krister Stendahl, *The School of St. Matthew* (Lund: C. W. K. Gleerup, 1954), p. 162; Robert Horton Gundry, *The Use of the Old Testament in St. Matthew's Gospel* (Leiden: E. J. Brill, 1967), pp. 179–180; cf. pp. 150 and 161, and Hengel, p. 19. Jeremias, p. 71 n. 80, thought that the LXX incorrectly translates Isaiah 5,2 (ויעזקהו), but עזק can include the idea of surrounding. Cf. BDB, 740; Jastrow, 1062; and the Aramaic עזקא ("clasp" or "ring").

[12] Despite the fact that Schramm, p. 157, attempted to do so.

the tradition Luke used did have the allusion to Isaiah 5 and that he omitted the irrelevant details. Such an omission is in keeping with his proclivity for neatness and efficiency. Another indication that Luke is not completely free from LXX influence is the soliloquy of the owner in 20,13. Τί ποιήσω may be characteristic of Luke[13], but it is also paralleled in the question of the vineyard owner in Isaiah 5,4.

Further, while it is possible that the allusions to Isaiah 5 were added later, one would have to ask what motivation there was to cause the addition. Not a great deal is established by the allusion, and in fact the allusion makes the understanding of the vineyard image more difficult, as we will see. The vineyard image was traditional enough for the hearers to know that the issue is about the relation to God. If the vineyard is to be interpreted as the Kingdom of God or something similar, why put in an allusion where the vineyard is interpreted as Israel? We will have to deal with the issue later, but the point here is that there does not seem to be adequate motivation to cause a later insertion of the allusion. The arguments for a secondary insertion of the allusion to Isaiah 5, therefore, seem rather weak[14].

The Thomas account states only that a good man had a vineyard. It is usually agreed that Thomas has no allusion to Isaiah 5, but G. Quispel thought that this statement in Thomas presupposes the Hebrew text of Isaiah 5,1 (היה ל) rather than the LXX[15]. However, this is rather slim evidence on which to base an allusion. Without prior knowledge that the parable alluded to Isaiah 5, the Thomas account would not cause one to look there. The significance one places on this omission depends upon his or her estimation of the Thomas account, and this question will be dealt with later.

The account of the leasing of the land to tenants (אריסין) and the departure of the owner is virtually the same in all the Synoptics[16]. The

---

[13] As suggested by M.-J. Lagrange, *Evangile selon Saint Luc* (Paris: J. Gabalda et Cie, Editeurs, 1941), p. 508. Cf. 12,17 and 16,3–4.

[14] At best, the insertion might picture the care of God in the planting of the vineyard, but that plays no part in the story.

[15] G. Quispel, *Makarius, das Thomasevangelium und das Lied von der Perle* (Leiden: E. J. Brill, 1967), p. 77. Cf. his "Das Thomasevangelium und das alte Testament," *Neotestamentica et Patristica* (Leiden: E. J. Brill, 1962), 245.

[16] On tenants in the ancient world, see S–B, I, 871–875; and J. Duncan M. Derrett, "Fresh Light on the Parable of the Wicked Vinedressers," *Revue Internationale des Droits de L'Antiquité*, 3ᵐᵉ série, X (1963), 16.

only difference is the Lukan explanatory addition, χρόνους ἱκανούς[17]. Thomas explains why the vineyard was given out (that the tenants might cultivate it and the owner might receive its fruits from them) and only assumes the owner's departure[18].

The Attempts to Collect the Produce (Matthew 21,34–37; Mark 12,2–6; Luke 20,10–13)

None of the accounts agrees with the others on the details of the sending of the servants and the son. Matthew emphasizes that the fruits are the owner's by the use of αὐτοῦ and reports that the owner first sent three servants (presumably) and that one was beaten, one was killed, and one was stoned. Then the owner sent a larger number of servants, and they were treated the same way. Finally, he sent his son. According to Mark, the owner sent one servant (who was beaten and sent away empty-handed), a second (who was beaten on the head and dishonored), a third (who was killed), and many others (some of whom were beaten and some of whom were killed). Then there was yet one remaining, an only son (υἱὸν ἀγαπητόν)[19] who was sent last (ἔσχατον). In the Lukan account, the owner sent one servant (who was beaten and sent away empty-handed), a second (who was beaten, dishonored, and sent away empty-handed), and a third (who was wounded and cast out). After some deliberation the owner sent his only son (τὸν υἱὸν μου τὸν ἀγαπητὸν). According to Thomas, the owner sent one servant (who was seized, beaten almost to death, and who reported to his master) and because the tenants may not have known him[20], a second was sent (who was beaten as well). Then the owner sent his son, and the tenants seized and killed him.

The climax for each writer is the killing of the son, but each reveals a different progression. With Matthew, there is an intensification of the importance of the envoys (three, more than at first, the son) although he does include a progression in the mistreatment of the first group of servants (beating, killing, stoning)[21]. In Mark, there is an intensification

---

[17] Lagrange, *Evangile selon Saint Luc*, p. 508. Cf. Luke 8,27; 23,8; and Acts 8,11.
[18] Montefiore, p. 236, attempted to see in the Gospels' emphasis on the owner's departure an allegorical reference to the invisible God, but this is surely going too far. The feature in the story does not correspond to Old Testament reality and should not be pressed.
[19] Ἀγαπητός should be understood as "only." See C. H. Turner, "Ο ΥΙΟΣ ΜΟΥ ΑΓΑΠΗΤΟΣ," *JTS*, XXVII (1926), 113–129.
[20] Literally, "Perhaps he did not know them."
[21] Stoning would have been the punishment par excellence. The same order

of the treatment the servants receive, but it is of little significance because several servants are killed. His emphasis on the son is expressed in the description of the son. Luke records a progression in the mistreatment by reserving death for the son and also emphasizes the son by describing him as the "only son" (as Mark). The progression in Thomas is in the revealing of the rebellion of the tenants to the owner.

We have already looked at the logic of the sending of the son. It should be added here that the attempts to omit the sending of the son are without foundation[22]. Only after the tenants see the son do they desire to possess the vineyard[23]. Apart from the sending of the son there is no real climax and no bridge from the patience of the owner to his anger[24].

One should observe several other features in this section. Each of the writers justifies the sending of the son by saying that the tenants will respect him, but Luke and Thomas qualify the statement with "perhaps" (ἴσως). Matthew and Thomas have the possessive pronoun with the first envoy whereas Mark and Luke do not. The Markan paratactic style is evident as are several stylistic features of Luke[25]. Προσέθετο πέμψαι in Luke may be a Semitism, but more likely it is a Lukan biblicism[26]. Luke and Thomas also agree in the wording for the reason the first servant was sent (Luke 20,10 – ἵνα ... δώσουσιν αὐτῷ).

(killing ... stoning) occurs in Matthew 23,37 ‖ Luke 13,34. Cf. W. Michaelis, "λιθάζω, καταλιθάζω, λιθοβολέω," *TDNT*, IV, 267; Lagrange, *Evangile selon Saint Matthieu*, p. 414. Cf. the similar order in Matthew 23,34 and Luke 11,49–51.

[22] *Contra* Hans-Josef Klauck, "Das Gleichnis vom Mord im Weinberg (Mk 12,1–12; Mt 21,33–46; Lk 20,9–19)," *Bibel und Leben*, XI (1970), 123 and 134 (although a different tone is expressed in his *Allegorie und Allegorese in synoptischen Gleichnistexten*, Münster: Aschendorff, 1978, pp. 302-304); and B. T. D. Smith, *The Parables of the Synoptic Gospels* (Cambridge: Cambridge University Press, 1937), p. 224.

[23] Tullio Aurelio, *Disclosures in den Gleichnissen Jesu* (Frankfurt: Peter Lang, 1977), p. 195.

[24] Ernst Haenchen, *Der Weg Jesu* (Berlin: Alfred Töpelmann, 1966), p. 398 n. 8 and 399; and Klaus Berger, *Exegese des Neuen Testaments* (Heidelberg: Quelle & Meyer, 1977), p. 62. B. van Iersel, p. 143, argued that the concept of inheritance would not have carried significance for the early church and that its inclusion assumes the entrance of the son. Robinson, p. 447, stated that the contrast between servant and son is a common feature of the parables of Jesus. See Luke 15,19 and John 8,35.

[25] Jeremias, p. 72, n. 84.

[26] Προστιθέναι 2/1/7 and Acts 6 times. Πέμπειν 4/1/10 and Acts 32 times. Cf. Acts 12,3. See John Martin Creed, *The Gospel According to St. Luke* (London: Macmillan and Co., 1930), p. 245.

The Rejection of the Son (Matthew 21,38–39; Mark 12,7–8, Luke 20,14–15a)

Each of the Synoptics shows a recognition of the son by the tenants and the premeditation of the tenants to kill the son. Matthew and Mark have δεῦτε ἀποκτείνωμεν whereas Luke has only ἀποκτείνωμεν. The former is a possible allusion to Genesis 37,20[27], but the similarity is probably only due to the analogous situation rather than the intention of the writer.

The other important difference in this section is that Matthew and Luke report that the son was thrown out and then killed whereas Mark reports that the son was killed and then thrown out.

In this section, Thomas abandons the standpoint of the owner and finishes the story from the standpoint of the narrator. The account explains that since the tenants knew the son was the heir, they seized and killed him.

The Ending (Matthew 21,40–44; Mark 12,9–11; Luke 20,15b–18)

According to Thomas, the parable is over. It remains only to add "he who has ears, let him hear." The Synoptic writers have additional material to report. In each Jesus asks the listeners what the owner will do. According to Mark and Luke, he answered his own question by saying that the tenants would be destroyed and the vineyard given to others. Luke adds that the listeners responded with μὴ γένοιτο. According to Matthew, the listeners give the answer with the qualification that the new tenants will pay the fruits to the owner. With slight variations, all three report that Jesus then asked his hearers if they had never read Psalm 118,22 (Matthew and Mark include v. 23). Thomas records the quotation of Psalm 118,22 as the next logion (66), introduced by "Jesus said." (The same introduction is used for logion 67, which is almost certainly an interpretation of the Old Testament quotation.) Matthew records Jesus' explanation of the parable, and, according to most manuscripts, adds a further saying about the stone which is paralleled in Luke. All three Synoptics agree that the Jewish leaders understood that the parable was directed against them and wanted to seize Jesus, but could not for fear of the crowds.

---

[27] Hengel, p. 18; Henry Barclay Swete, *The Gospel According to Mark* (London: Macmillan and Co., 1898), p. 254; and Merrill Miller, *Scripture and Parable: A Study of the Biblical Features in the Parable of the Wicked Husbandmen and Their Place in the History of the Tradition.* Unpublished Ph. D. Dissertation, Columbia University, 1974.

The Development of the Tradition

As mentioned previously, some scholars have held the view that the version of Thomas is probably the closest to the original. On this view Luke represents the least corrupt of the Synoptics while Matthew is farthest removed since his account is the most "allegorical." That Thomas does not have the allusion to Isaiah 5, the christological hints, or the final question, and that he has only the simple threefold sending (which is common to folk stories) are the main reasons for this view. C. H. Dodd, with J. Jeremias following him, had suggested such a reconstruction even before Thomas was found[28].

In recent years the arguments for an independent and early tradition in Thomas have met serious resistance. Andreas Lindemann has argued that all the parables in Thomas are secondary to those of the canonical Gospels[29]. Specifically with regard to our parable, Wolfgang Schrage has argued from an analysis of the Coptic versions that Thomas is dependent on the canonical tradition[30]. Schrage's conclusions overall may not be conclusive[31], but he did show several points in this parable where Thomas appears to be dependent on the Synoptics. Of particular importance are the counterparts in Thomas to δώσουσιν αὐτῷ in Luke 20,10 and ἴσως in 20,13[32]. The latter is a *hapax legomenon* in the New Testament and is an amplification to prevent the misunderstanding that God made an error. This does not necessarily prove that Thomas is dependent on Luke, but at least it shows that Thomas is dependent on the same tradition as Luke. (The Coptic counterpart to ἴσως occurs

---

[28] C. H. Dodd, *The Parables of the Kingdom* (London: Nisbet & Co., 1936), pp. 126–130; and Joachim Jeremias, *Die Gleichnisse Jesu* (2d Auflage; Zürich: Zwingli Verlag, 1952), pp. 54f. Others who have argued that Thomas presents a pre-Synoptic stage of the parable include R. McL. Wilson, *Studies in the Gospel of Thomas* (London: A. R. Mowbray & Co., 1960), pp. 101f.; Montefiore, pp. 247f.; John Dominic Crossan, "The Parable of the Wicked Husbandmen," *JBL*, XC (1971), 456f.; Robinson, p. 451; Schramm, p. 165; and Jane E. and Raymond R. Newell, "The Parable of the Wicked Tenants, *NovT,* XIV (1972), pp. 226f.

[29] "Zur Gleichnisinterpretation im Thomas-Evangelium," *ZNW*, LXXI (1980), 214–243.

[30] *Das Verhältnis des Thomas-Evangeliums zur synoptischen Tradition und zu den koptischen Evangelienübersetzungen* (Berlin: Verlag Alfred Töpelmann, 1964).

[31] See R. McL. Wilson, *Gnosis and the New Testament* (Oxford: Basil Blackwell, 1968), pp. 96–97; and his review of Schrage's book in *VC*, XX (1966), 118–123.

[32] Schrage, p. 140. See also William R. Schoedel, "Parables in the Gospel of Thomas: Oral Tradition or Gnostic Exegesis?" *CTM*, XLII (1972), 557–560.

earlier in the Thomas account in the statement of the owner, "Perhaps he did not know them.")

There is another point, however, which throws a cloud of suspicion on the Thomas account[33]. Syr^s omits Mark 12,4 so that only two servants precede the "many others" and the sending of the son. Likewise, syr^c, which is not extant for Mark, omits the sending of the third servant in Luke 20,12. According to F. C. Burkitt, "the rest of v. 12 is lost in c through homoeoteleuton,"[34] but this is questionable. Syr^s does record the sending of the third servant in Luke, but it is evident that the text has been tampered with. It follows neither the Lukan style as the preceding verse nor the Lukan sequence[35]. Clearly the Old Syriac texts of Mark and Luke represent a harmonizing tendency to bring their accounts into line with the two-fold sending in Matthew. It seems evident that Thomas, which probably has a Syrian provenance[36], is

---

[33] See my "The Parable of the Wicked Husbandmen: Is the Gospel of Thomas Version the Original?" *NTS*, XXI (1974), 142–144.

[34] *Evangelion Da-Mepharreshe* (Cambridge: Cambridge University Press, 1904), I, 383. The text of syr^s for Mark 12,2–6 is as follows:

And he sent in the time of the fruits unto the husbandmen his slave that they might send him of the fruits of his vineyard. And they took hold of him and beat him and sent him away empty. And again he sent unto them another slave, and him also they killed, and many others – some of them they beat and some of them they killed. One beloved son had he: he sent *him* unto them, and said: Perhaps they will have reverence for my son.

(Note "perhaps" which does not appear in the text of Mark.) The text of syr^c for Luke 20,10–13 is as follows:

And at one of the times he sent his slave unto the husbandmen that they should give him of the fruits of the vineyard. And they beat him and sent him away empty. And he went on and sent another slave of his, and this one also they wounded and put him forth. Saith the master of the vineyard: What shall I do? I will send my beloved son; perchance they will have reverence for him.

[35] Syr^s at Luke 20,11 has w'wsp following the Lukan style and records the events that parallel the *third* servant in Luke. In 20,12, the Lukan biblicism is not present, and the treatment of the servant is not that reported in the Greek. Other features of the syr^s account show tampering. Note the reintroduction of the Isaiah 5 element (v. 9) and the changes in vs. 16 and 19. If 20,12 has been re-inserted into the text of S, the omission in C is not due to homoeoteleuton. It should be remembered that Mark 12,4 is omitted in syr^s.

[36] E. Hennecke, *New Testament Apocrypha*, ed. W. Schneemelcher, trans. R. McL. Wilson (London: Lutterworth Press, 1963), pp. 286f.; H. E. W. Turner and Hugh Montefiore, *Thomas and the Evangelists* (London: SCM Press, 1962), pp. 44f.; and Wilson, *Studies in the Gospel of Thomas*, pp. 10f. Barbara Ehlers, "Kann das Thomasevangelium aus Edessa stammen? Ein Beitrag zur Frühgeschichte des Christentums in Edessa," *NovT*, XII (1970), 283–317, argued against a Syrian provenance

dependent on this tradition. The Old Syriac itself may well be dependent on the Diatessaron. While one cannot rule out the possibility of the dependence of Thomas on the Diatessaron, at least we may say that Thomas appears to be dependent upon a Syriac harmonizing tradition[37]. The two-fold sending of servants in Thomas then stems from a post-Synoptic rather than a pre-Synoptic stage of the parable. This has to cast doubt on the other claims that have been made for Thomas and suggests that some features of the Thomas account appear to have been determined by Gnostic concerns. The lateness of the account makes it hard to doubt that the omission of the allusion to Isaiah 5 is due to a negative attitude to the Old Testament[38]. The omission of the final question and answer are probably due to a tendency to de-eschatologize[39]. In line with the late character of the account, the excuse for the tenants' behavior should be seen as a later addition to make the story more palpable. If this is the case, obviously we should confine our analysis to the Synoptic accounts[40].

---

for Thomas, but see the response by A. F. J. Klijn, "Christianity in Edessa and the Gospel of Thomas," *NovT*, XIV (1972), 70–77.

[37] That the Old Syriac was dependent on Tatian, see Burkitt, II, 234. On harmonistic tendencies and the relation of Thomas and Tatian, see Quispel, *Markarius, das Thomasevangelium und das Lied von der Perle*, p. 7 et passim; and his "L'Evangile selon Thomas et le Diatessaron," *VC*, XIII (1959), 87–117; A. F. J. Klijn, *A Survey of the Researches into the Western Text of the Gospels and Acts: Part II, 1949–69* (Leiden: E. J. Brill, 1969), pp. 8f., who mentioned the tendency of Thomas and the Diatessaron to harmonize Matthew and Luke and the possibility of a curious text of the Gospels in Syria; Hennecke, p. 293; Turner and Montefiore, pp. 25f.; Wilson, *Studies in the Gospel of Thomas*, pp. 126f.; Robert M. Grant with David Noel Freedman, *The Secret Sayings of Jesus* (London: Collins, 1960), p. 151; and George Howard, "Harmonistic Readings in the Old Syriac Gospels," *HTR*, LXXIII (1980), 473–491.

[38] Schoedel, p. 559; see Montefiore, p. 228; and Bertil Gärtner, *The Theology of the Gospel of Thomas*, trans. Eric J. Sharpe (London: Collins, 1961), p. 150; cf. Thomas logion 52.

[39] Ernst Bammel, "Das Gleichnis von den bösen Winzern (Mk. 12,1–9) und das jüdische Erbrecht," *Revue Internationale des Droits de L'Antiquité*, 3me série, VI (1959), 17; Haenchen, p. 404; and Schoedel, pp. 559f. The last also argued that the differences in Thomas were due to Gnostic concerns.

[40] Others arguing that Thomas is secondary include B. Dehandschutter, "La parabole des vignerons homicides (Mc. XII, 1–12) et l'évangile selon Thomas," *Bibliotheca Ephemeridum Theologicarum Lovaniensium*, XXXIV (1974), 203–219; Klauck, "Das Gleichnis vom Mord im Weinberg," 136; *Allegorie und Allegorese in synoptischen Gleichnistexten*, pp. 292f.; Hans Weder, *Die Gleichnisse Jesu als Metaphern* (Göttingen: Vandenhoeck & Ruprecht, 1978), p. 152; Miller, p. 369; Michel Hubaut, *La parabole des vignerons homicides*, Cahiers de la *Revue Biblique* 16 (Paris: Gabalda,

On grounds similar to the arguments for the priority of Thomas, several have argued that Luke represents the earliest account. Most recently, David Flusser has chosen to presuppose R. L. Lindsey's theory of Lukan priority which is based on the fact that Luke is more easily translated into Hebrew[41]. Flusser would argue that our parable supports this theory since the allusion to Isaiah 5 in Matthew and Mark derives from the LXX, and since Matthew's description of the owner as an οἰκοδεσπότης is so Greek that it cannot be translated literally into Hebrew[42]. Quite apart from questions about the methodology of this different approach to the Synoptic problem, there is little in the accounts before us that supports an argument that Luke's version is the earliest. In fact, there are several factors that speak against this. We have already pointed out that the use of the LXX may be the result of accommodation later in the tradition[43]. It is true that Luke presents a neat progression and climax, but the author's reconstruction reveals his stylistic and symmetrical preferences[44]. Evidence of the author's style does not necessarily cast suspicion on the validity of his report, but a comparison with the other two accounts shows several points where Luke has smoothed the story (v. 9 – the omission of irrelevant details; v. 10 – δώσουσιν αὐτῷ; the progression and preservation of the climax; v. 13 – the deliberation of the owner and the addition of ἴσως; v. 17 – the omission of Psalm 118,23). Rather than being the earliest, Luke's account has been neatly edited and is a later version.

In line with the popular assumption of the priority of Mark, several scholars have suggested that Mark's account is the earliest and have

---

1976), p. 134; Xavier Léon-Dufour, "La parabole des vignerons homicides," *Sciences Ecclésiastiques*, XVII (1965), 368f. Heinz Schürmann ("Das Thomasevangelium und das lukanische Sondergut," *BZ*, VII, 1963, 236–260) had earlier expressed the suspicion that Thomas was dependent on a source that had already harmonized the Synoptics.

[41] Flusser, pp. 195–198. See Robert Lisle Lindsey. *A Hebrew Translation of the Gospel of Mark* (Jerusalem: Dugith Publishers, 1973).

[42] Flusser, pp. 197–198. Flusser still, however, argued that Jesus intended to allude to Isaiah 5 with the words recorded in Luke.

[43] See *supra*, p. 47.

[44] Jeremias, *The Parables of Jesus*, p. 72 n. 84, recognized this but still preferred the Lukan account to that in either Matthew or Mark. W. G. Kümmel, "Das Gleichnis von den bösen Weingärtnern (Mark. 12,1–9)," *Aux sources de la tradition chretienne. Mélanges offerts à M. Goguel* (Neuchatel: Delachaux & Niestle S. A., 1950), p. 126, called his hand on this.

pointed to the fact that his account is the least systematic[45]. W. Farmer has countered that the account of the sending in Mark represents an attempt to conflate the Lukan three-fold sending with the Matthean parallel series, a suggestion that bears consideration[46].

Recently J. A. T. Robinson has argued for the priority of Mark on other grounds. His conclusion is based on the fact that Mark has the highest proportion of words common with one of the other Gospels at those points which he has determined are the most primitive state of the tradition[47]. Certain anomalies force him to argue for a hypothetical *Grundschrift*, an *Ur-Markus*, however. Already his whole procedure has been called into question[48], and it must be admitted that his argument does not convince. It is particularly hazardous to attempt to judge relationships on the basis of a hypothetical *Urform*.

If one wants to ascertain which is the earliest account, he or she should seek the one that most easily explains the shape of the other two. Despite the charges that have been leveled at the Matthean account, there is evidence that it represents the earliest version of this parable[49]. There are several indications that this parable was in "Q" (or better, the double tradition). Of major significance are the agreements of Matthew and Luke against Mark in the addition of the second stone saying, the expulsion of the son before death, and that the listeners responded to Jesus' question. Many have been quick to accuse Matthew of allegorizing the parable, but there is no real reason to detect more allegory in Matthew than in Mark or Luke. It seem strange that J. Jeremias would argue ἐξέδετο in Matthew 21,33 is proof of the author's allegorizing the giving of the covenant at Sinai when Mark and Luke both have the same word, apparently without allegorical significance[50]. It is also strange that

---

[45] Kümmel, p. 126; M.-J. Lagrange, *Evangile selon Saint Marc* (6th ed.; Paris: J. Gabalda et Cie, Editeurs, 1942), p. 308. Adolf Jülicher thought that the irregularity of v. 5b confirmed its accuracy. (See *Die Gleichnisreden Jesu*, Freiburg i. B.: Akademische Verlagsbuchhandlung von J. C. B. Mohr, Vol. I, 1888; Vol. II, 1889, II, 389.)

[46] William R. Farmer, *The Synoptic Problem* (New York: The Macmillan Company, 1964), p. 249.

[47] Robinson, pp. 443–461.

[48] See Bernard Orchard, "J. A. T. Robinson and the Synoptic Problem," *NTS*, XXII (1976), 346–352.

[49] See also the arguments of Léon-Dufour, pp. 392–393; and Heinrich Kahlefeld, *Gleichnisse und Lehrstücke im Evangelium* (Frankfurt: Josef Knecht, 1964), pp. 89–90.

[50] Jeremias, *The Parables of Jesus*, p. 77.

the two-fold sending of servants in Thomas has been judged non-allegorical while the two-fold sending in Matthew represents the earlier and later prophets[51]. It is true that Matthew records that the owner sent more than one servant each time, but this is probably in keeping with reality. The owner would not send only one servant to bring back a large quantity of produce, even if it were all wine. More important, Matthew would not have limited the number in the first group of servants to three if he were trying to depict accurately a group of the prophets. Regardless of the significance of the servants, none of the accounts presents an accurate picture of God's sending the prophets. The sequence in Matthew and Luke at least is determined primarily by the requirements of the story, rather than by an attempt to underline the meaning of the servants.

The Matthean account is also more understandable as a story. The owner sent three servants to collect his produce, and they were met with violent rebellion. He sent a larger number of servants to repeat his demands, but they were treated the same way. Then he sent his son to take legal action. While the Lukan account is feasible, the Markan account is improbable. It is true that improbability and hyperbole are features of Jesus' parables, but these do not seem to be the reasons for the Markan progression. Rather, it appears that Mark was trying to underline the meaning of the envoys.

If the Matthean account of the envoys is earliest, the development of the other two representations can be explained. The Matthean account reports two groups and the son. The use of triads to assist the conveyance of traditional material is well-known, but the story in Matthew presents a second triad in the treatment of the servants. This may have rendered the Matthean presentation too bulky for convenient reproduction. If so, the sending of three individual servants in Mark and Luke represents a simplification of Matthew in that they used only his first group. (Therefore Matthew is not a "tidying-up" of Mark as is some-

---

[51] Jeremias, *The Parables of Jesus*, p. 72; and Lagrange, *Evangile selon Saint Marc*, p. 308, understood the former and latter prophets according to the division of the canon; Ernst Lohmeyer and Werner Schmauch, *Das Evangelium des Matthäus* (Göttingen: Vandenhoeck & Ruprecht, 1967), p. 313, understood the Matthean three-fold sending of the servants and son to represent the periods of the history of the people as presented in the genealogy of Jesus in Matthew 1. Charles E. Carlston, *The Parables of the Triple Tradition* (Philadelphia: Fortress Press, 1975), pp. 40f.; likewise unjustly allegorized the Matthean account. I would argue that all such explanations are reading into the parable.

times suggested.) The addition of Mark 12,5b was necessitated in that three servants did not do justice to the plurality presented in Matthew. Luke, with his preference for symmetry, confined the number to three and reserved killing for the son. It may be that the Markan account is a conflation of Matthew and Luke as Farmer suggested[52], but it is just as possible that Luke omitted Mark 12,5b. The assumption of Markan priority leaves unexplained the complexity of Mark 12,5b, which is obviously cumbersome and an uncommon mode of progression. The Matthean triad is more customary and will account for the forms in Mark and Luke[53].

There are other reasons for believing that Matthew presents the earliest form of the parable, and one of the most important is his treatment of the son. Both Mark and Luke refer to the son as υἱὸς ἀγαπητός ("only son") while Matthew uses simply υἱός. It is questionable that ἀγαπητός was strictly a christological title since it is used quite frequently throughout Acts and the Epistles as a designation for individual Christians. However, υἱὸς ἀγαπητός is used by all three Synoptists of Jesus in the accounts of the baptism and transfiguration. Except for this parable and the baptism and transfiguration accounts, the only time ἀγαπητός occurs in the Synoptics is in the application of Isaiah 42,1 to Jesus (Matthew 12,18). If the tradition Matthew used for this parable had had ἀγαπητός he certainly would not have omitted it. The absence of ἀγαπητός in Matthew cannot be regarded as insignificant, and the attempts to explain it as an omission by Matthew are rather lame[54]. The

---

[52] Farmer, p. 249. Redundancy (or duality) is a Markan characteristic. See F. Neirynck, "Duplicate Expressions in the Gospel of Mark," *ETL*, XLVIII (1972), 150–210.

[53] The sending of servants in Matthew 22,3–4 uses words similar to 21,34–36, and it could be said that this is Matthew's style. However, again this is a situation where more than one servant would be sent (it would take one servant too long to call all the guests), and again the Lukan parallel (14,17f.) shows the style of Luke. If either of the Matthean parables has influenced the other, the Parable of the Marriage Feast has been the recipient of the influence. See Richard J. Dillon, "Towards a Tradition-History of the Parables of the True Israel (Matthew 21,33–22,14)." *Bib*, XLVII (1966), 6–7. Many rabbinic parables contain common features (as servants and their actions), and some are made on the same pattern as others. The similarities of the two parables may be due to rabbinic practice.

[54] *Contra* Th. de Kruijf, *Der Sohn des lebendigen Gottes* (Romae: e Pontifico Instituto Biblico, 1962), p. 140. Lohmeyer and Schmauch, pp. 312f., noticed the lack of emphasis on the son and on p. 315 pointed to features that suggest the Matthean version is earlier than Mark. The points they mention against Matthew will be taken

superiority of the Matthean text at this point forced Robinson to argue for a hypothetical *Ur-Markus* behind the Synoptics[55]. Both Mark and Luke have emphasized the son in other ways as well. Mark took pains to point out that this is the only son and that he was sent last (ἔσχατον). Luke emphasized the son by reserving death for him and by using the climactic three plus one formula. While Mark and Luke made certain of the identity of the son, no attempt to emphasize him was made by Matthew. Certainly neither Matthew nor any of the early Church wanted to play down christology. The only logical conclusion is that the Matthean tradition preceded those of Mark and Luke.

Whereas a few years ago such a conclusion would have been viewed as extreme, several recent studies have either taken this position or have made some attempt to account for the earlier material in Matthew. M. Hubaut granted the arguments for a "Q" tradition, but because of several features in Matthew, argued for a pre-Matthean version[56]. M. Miller granted that the two-fold sending in Matthew is original while ἀγαπητός is not[57]. Likewise, Bernard Orchard preferred the sending of the servants in Matthew[58], and X. Léon-Dufour argued that the Matthean form preserves a more ancient tradition[59].

---

up below. Wolfgang Trilling, *Das wahre Israel* (3d ed.; München: Kösel-Verlag, 1964), pp. 56-57, offered feeble explanation for the omission of ἀγαπητός and although he thought Mark was earlier, viewed the account in Matthew as the most self-contained. See his *Christusverkündigung in den synoptischen Evangelien* (München: Kösel-Verlag, 1969), p. 168. Charles Carlston, p. 42, attempted to explain the omission of ἀγαπητός as an attempt to soften the tragic error of the father even though he viewed Matthew as heightening the polemic. Hans-Josef Klauck, *Allegorie und Allegorese in synoptischen Gleichnistexten*, p. 291, suggested that Matthew omitted the term because his emphasis is less Christological and more ecclesiological and paranetic, even though in his "Das Gleichnis vom Mord im Weinberg," 124, he admitted that there is no satisfying answer for the omission. It should be added that Hubaut, p. 128, viewed ἀγαπητός as emerging either from LXX Isaiah 5,1 or from Isaac typology.

[55] Robinson, pp. 447 and 455-456.
[56] Hubaut, pp. 12, 28f., 95f., 101f., and 128f. Schramm, pp. 159-160, also argued that Matthew had a parallel tradition, but he viewed Luke and Thomas as having earlier forms.
[57] Miller, p. 373.
[58] Orchard, p. 349.
[59] Léon-Dufour, pp. 379 and 392f. Josef Blank, "Die Sendung des Sohnes," *Neues Testament und Kirche*, ed. Joachim Gnilka (Freiburg: Herder, 1974), p. 24, argued that Mark 12,1-12 is secondary to the "sayings source." See also Rafael Silva, "La parábola de los renteros homicidas," *Compostellanum*, XV (1970), 352, who viewed Matthew as closer to the message of Jesus.

The one point that speaks most clearly against an earlier account in Matthew is that Matthew and Luke report that the son was thrown out of the vineyard and then killed, whereas Mark records that he was killed and then thrown out. It is usually accepted that Matthew and Luke have tried to bring the story into line with the events of Jesus' death outside the city[60]. While this seems evident on the first analysis and is possible, it is not as convincing after further investigation. Neither Matthew nor Luke explicitly mentions that Jesus' crucifixion was outside the city. This view necessitates as well that the vineyard be interpreted as the city of Jerusalem[61]. It may be that Mark was trying to heighten the offense of the murder for the sake of his Gentile readers by showing the desecration of the corpse[62]. David Daube pointed out that leaving the body unburied as Mark implies would be a flagrant case of *niwwul* (disgrace)[63]. Another factor that should be considered is that the tenants would not have wanted to jeopardize their profits by rendering the vineyard unclean by killing someone within its boundaries[64]. It is for this reason that Derrett postulated an impossible reconstruction. On his view, the son would have received the death blow in the tower away from the vines with the hope that the body could be carried to the wall before death[65]. If the tenants had been concerned about laws of uncleanliness, they would have thrown the son out before killing him. One should remember that it was a normal procedure to expel a person before

---

[60] Dodd, p. 130; Jeremias, *The Parables of Jesus*, p. 73; E. Earle Ellis, *The Gospel of Luke* (London: Nelson, 1966), p. 232; Lagrange, *Evangile selon Saint Luc*, p. 510; van Iersel, p. 139; Hengel, p. 36; Montefiore, p. 237; and Julius Schniewind, *Das Evangelium nach Markus* (Göttingen: Vandenhoeck & Ruprecht, 1952), pp. 153ff.

[61] Alfred Plummer, *Gospel According to S. Luke* (Edinburgh: T. and T. Clark, 1898), p. 461; and Sigfred Pedersen, "Zum Problem der vaticinia ex eventu (eine Analyse von Mt. 21,33–46 par; 22,1–10 par)," ST, XIX (1965), p. 171. Cf. Swete, p. 254, and I. Howard Marshall, *The Gospel of Luke* (Grand Rapids: William B. Eerdmans Publishing Company, 1978), p. 731.

[62] Léon-Dufour, p. 379; and Rudolf Pesch, *Das Markusevangelium* (Freiburg: Herder, 1977), II, 220. The attempts to point to passages such as Matthew 27,32 or Luke 4,29 to show that Matthew and Luke know of the crucifixion outside the city do not prove the point, *contra* Hubaut, p. 52, and Klauck, *Allegorie und Allegorese in synoptischen Gleichnistexten*, p. 290. The acceptance by both these scholars of the reading of D at Matthew 21,39 has little to commend it. The reading in D and its allies is more likely a harmonization to Mark.

[63] *The New Testament and Rabbinic Judaism* (London: Athlone Press, 1956), p. 302.

[64] A. T. Cadoux, *The Parables of Jesus* (London: James Clarke & Co., n. d.), p. 40, Cf. Marshall, p. 731.

[65] Derrett, pp. 35f.

killing him[66]. Thus once again there is good reason to believe that the Matthean account is the earliest.

I am not arguing for the priority of Matthew as a whole, nor is it to be denied that Matthew may have underlined certain features such as the giving of the fruit or the treatment of the servants. But without question, the Matthean version has every indication of being more self-contained and of preserving the earliest form.

With regard to the question and answer concerning what the owner will do, Jeremias has asserted that both are secondary since the question refers back to the LXX form of Isaiah 5,5 while the Hebrew text of Isaiah 5,5 does not have a question[67]. Jeremias has made a mistake, however, for there is not a question in the LXX at Isaiah 5,5[68]. The allusion is to Isaiah 5,4 where both the Hebrew and the LXX have a question. There are no grounds for excluding the question and some form of the answer even though the answer differs in the three Synoptics. Again preference should be given to the Matthean account[69]. The parable is much more effective if the hearers pronounce their own judgment in keeping with classic parable form (cf. Nathan's parable to David in II Samuel 12,1f.). H.-J. Klauck pointed out in connection with his analysis of Mark 12,1–12 that a parable ending with a rhetorical question answered by the person who asked it is a singular phenomenon[70]. Also, one should notice that the answer given in Matthew contains a formal legal pronouncement and a Psalm allusion. Various theories have been produced to account for κακοὺς κακῶς, but the evidence presented by Lohmeyer and Schmauch shows conclusively that the first part of the answer was a common Greek legal expression which was also current in Palestine[71]. The second part of the answer, that the vineyard would be given to others, has been unnecessarily allegorized by modern interpreters, but more likely reflects the wording of rental agreements[72]. The final part of the answer is probably an

---

[66] I Kings 21,13; Luke 4,29; Acts 7,58; but there are exceptions. Cf. John 8,59 and Acts 14,19.
[67] Jeremias, *The Parables of Jesus*, p. 74. Cf. Hubaut, p. 140.
[68] Robinson, p. 449, also noticed the mistake.
[69] Lohmeyer and Schmauch, p. 315; cf. Dodd, p. 127, who thought that Matthew has *restored* the more usual conclusion.
[70] Klauck, *Allegorie und Allegorese in synoptischen Gleichnistexten*, p. 288. However, Klauck used this point to argue that the parable originally ended with v. 8.
[71] Lohmeyer and Schmauch, pp. 313f. Cf. Josephus, *Antiq.* VII. 11.8 and XI.5.4.
[72] See P. Columbia VI. 270 col. 1 and B. G. U. 1121 (partially restored) where it is

allusion to Psalm 1,3. Lohmeyer and Schmauch thought that the legal pronouncement and the Psalm allusion fit the situation well since those who answered were representatives of the highest Jewish tribunal and would have spoken both the language of law and that of religion[73].

The inclusion of the final question and the stone quotation from Psalm 118,22 as valid parts of the parable has been maintained by relatively few scholars until recently, even though the quotation follows the parable in Thomas. The opinion of the majority has been that these are additions of the early Church to supply the missing reference to the resurrection. The presence of a quotation is not (or should not be) a cause for suspicion since P. Fiebig pointed out that it is common for rabbinic parables to end with a scripture citation[74]. Concerning the wording of the quotation, all three evangelists correspond in an exact reproduction of the LXX (which is in virtual agreement with the Hebrew), but this is of no significance since most formal quotations have been assimilated to the LXX[75]. The reasoning behind the rejection of the quotation is that Psalm 118,22 was a favorite verse of the early Church and sounds like a reference to the resurrection, especially since there appears to be no logical connection to the parable itself[76]. The Synoptists hint in other passages that Jesus used this verse of himself

---

stated expressly that if the tenants do not fulfill the conditions of the contract, the owner shall be at liberty to rent the land to others (ἑτέροις). These texts are available in *Select Papyri* I (Loeb Series) pp. 119–129.

[73] Lohmeyer and Schmauch, pp. 313f.

[74] Paul Fiebig, *Die Gleichnisreden Jesu im Lichte der rabbinischen Gleichnisse des neutestamentlichen Zeitalters* (Tübingen: Verlag von J. C. B. Mohr, Paul Siebeck, 1912), pp. 78, 86, and 239. Cf. Joachim Jeremias, "λίθος, λίθινος," *TDNT*, IV, 274 n. 49.

[75] See *supra*, p. 47, n. 11. Gundry, p. 20, mentioned that the LXX presupposed a pointing of נִפְלָאת as a niphal participle rather than the MT niphal perfect. The omission in Luke of Psalm 118,23 is again due to his proclivity to omit irrelevant parts, rather than to theological motivation as Traugott Holtz argued in his *Untersuchungen über die alttestamentlichen Zitate bei Lukas* (Berlin: Akademie-Verlag, 1968), p. 161.

[76] Jülicher, II, 405; Loisy, p. 341; Dodd, p. 128; Smith, p. 224; Jeremias, *The Parables of Jesus*, pp. 73f.; Lohmeyer, *Das Evangelium des Markus*, p. 246; van Iersel, pp. 125f.; Hengel, p. 1; Alfred Suhl, *Die Funktion der alttestamentlichen Zitate und Anspielungen im Markusevangelium* (Gütersloh: Gütersloher Verlagshaus Gerd Mohn, 1965), pp. 141f.; Klauck, *Allegorie und Allegorese in synoptischen Gleichnistexten*, pp. 288f.; Weder, pp. 149f. Others have suggested that the quotation may have been an independent parable or quoted in another connection. See Alexander Balmain Bruce, *The Parabolic Teaching of Christ* (London: Hodder and Stoughton, 1882), p. 458; and Morna Hooker, *Jesus and the Servant* (London: SPCK, 1959), p. 98.

(Mark 8,31; Luke 9,22; and 17,25)[77], although some have attributed this to the work of the early Palestinian Church[78].

Since Jülicher at least, it has been strongly maintained that the addition of the quotation was not only illogical, but also disruptive. It has always been recognized that the rejected stone represented the rejected son in the parable, but the reasoning behind this equation has not been explained. It is in the Hebrew/Aramaic form of this identification that the reason for the use of the quotation should be sought. The addition of Psalm 118,22 is based on the Semitic wordplay between אבן and בן[79]. Paranomasia is, of course, frequent in both testaments and should occasion no surprise[80], and this wordplay is so common that one can justly call it a traditional wordplay. (Since the marshalling of evidence for the wordplay would be somewhat disruptive at this point, occurrences of the wordplay in a variety of sources and a discussion of the issues involved is provided as an appendix. See *infra*, pp. 113–118.) No Jew would have missed the connection between the parable and quotation, regardless of whether Hebrew or Aramiac was used. It is especially interesting that one of the accounts of this parable in the Palestinian Syriac Lectionary records 'bn' in two manuscripts. As A. F. J. Klijn has pointed out[81], in the Syriac New Testament אבן has been replaced by *kyp*' almost completely. אבן ('bn) occurs in only one other place[82]. It appears that, 'bn' was retained in the lectionary for the wordplay[83]

---

[77] See Jeremias, "λίθος, λίθινος," p. 274 n. 48; and C. E. B. Cranfield, *The Gospel According to Saint Mark* (Cambridge: Cambridge University Press, 1959), p. 368.

[78] E. g., H. E. Tödt, *The Son of Man in the Synoptic Tradition* (London: SCM Press, 1965), pp. 166f.; Reginald H. Fuller, *The Foundations of New Testament Christology* (New York: Charles Scribner's Sons, 1965), pp. 118 and 137; and Ferdinand Hahn, *The Titles of Jesus in Christology* (London: Lutterworth Press, 1969), pp. 40f.

[79] Philip Carrington, *According to Mark* (Cambridge: Cambridge University Press, 1960), pp. 249–250 and 256, recognized the wordplay. Cf. also John Lightfoot, *Horae Hebraicae et Talmudicae*, ed. Robert Gandell (Oxford: Oxford University Press, 1859), ii, 435; and A. Finkel, "The Pesher of Dreams and Scriptures," *RQ*, IV (1963), 367. The wordplay was first suggested to me in private conversation by Matthew Black. Now see his "The Christological Use of the Old Testament in the New Testament," *NTS*, XVIII (1971–1972), 12.

[80] See particularly Matthew Black, *An Aramaic Approach to the Gospels and Acts* (3d ed.; Oxford: Clarendon Press, 1967, pp. 144f., 141f., 160f., 228f., and 276.

[81] "Die Wörter 'Stein' und 'Felsen' in der syrischen Übersetzung des Neuen Testaments," *ZNW*, L (1959), 99–105. See *infra*, pp. 117–118.

[82] I Peter 2,8.

[83] Agnes Smith Lewis and Margaret Dunlop Gibson (eds.), *The Palestinian Syriac*

When the wordplay is recognized, the addition of the quotation is entirely understandable and in keeping with rabbinic practice. However, it is surprising that some have acknowledged the presence of the wordplay, because of the influence of Matthew Black, and still argue that the quotation is a later secondary addition[84]. There is no basis for attempting to explain the quotation as a later addition, and it is highly improbable that a proof text would have been added along these lines at a later date. I am aware of no other place in the New Testament where a quotation is used on this basis. Indeed, it seems too indirect for the Church. The quotation, therefore, should not be separated from the rest of the parable[85]. As we will see, this connection is reinforced by the significance of the term "builders" and is determinative for understand-

---

Lectionary of the Gospels (London: Kegan Paul, Trench, Trubner & Co., 1899), pp. 152–154. Codex B and C have '*bn*'; Codex A has *dkyp*'. The passage occurs in another lectionary where *dkyp*' occurs in all manuscripts.

[84] E. g., Pesch, p. 222; and Hubaut, p. 62. Note Hubaut's comment on the strangeness of the quotation. It is strange only if one does not see the role the quotation plays in connection with the parable.

[85] See Stendahl, pp. 69 and 212; Vincent Taylor, *The Gospel According to St. Mark* (London: Macmillan & Co., 1952), p. 477; Swete, pp. 255f.; Cranfield, pp. 368f.; Gundry, p. 69; E. Earle Ellis, "Midrash, Targum and New Testament Quotations," *Neotestamentica et Semitica*, ed. E. Earle Ellis and Max Wilcox (Edinburgh: T. & T. Clark, 1969), p. 67; R. N. Longenecker, *The Christology of Early Jewish Christianity* (London: SCM Press, 1970), pp. 51–52, cf. his "Some Distinctive Early Christological Motifs," *NTS*, XIV (1967–1968), 536–538; John Bowman, *The Gospel of Mark* (Leiden: E. J. Brill, 1965), p. 223; Miller, pp. 140f.; Michael Giesler, *Christ the Rejected Stone* (Pamplona: Ediciones Universidad de Navarra, 1974), pp. 127f.; and Berger, p. 61. Obviously, the reasons why people have kept the quotation and parable together vary.

Lohmeyer, *Das Evangelium des Markus,* p. 247, linked the stone saying to the servant concept and concluded that if the servant concept is traceable to the preaching of Jesus, the use of the stone quotation can scarcely be denied to him. The servant and stone images were also linked by Bertil Gärtner, "טליא als Messiasbezeichnung," *SEA*, XVIII–XIX (1953–1954), pp. 101f. and Pius Sciascia, *Lapis Reprobatus* (Rome: Pontificium Athenaeum Antonianum, 1959), pp. 52f. Seraphinus M. Gozzo. *Disquisitio critico-exegetica in parabolam N. Testamenti de perfidis vinitoribus* (Romae: Pontificium Athenaeum Anatonianum, 1949), p. 97, argued that the stone quotation and the parable were two allegories which belonged together and formed one speech, but the basis of his statement was not sufficiently presented. Dino Merli, "La parabola dei vignaioli infedeli (Mc. 12,1–12)," *Bibbia e Oriente,* XV (1973), 97–108, argued that the quotation belonged to the parable (which he viewed as a meditation on Isaiah 5,1–7) and was added because the allegory did not do justice to the place Jesus occupied in the "building." He attributed the allegory to the Church. Carlston, p. 181, attempted to say that the quotation shows Mark's redactional activity, but the verses he offered as proof (2,21, 27; and 11,23) have no relevance to the discussion.

ing the parable[86]. Whoever composed the parable also concluded it with the quotation from Psalm 118.

There are still two verses in the Matthean account, one of which is paralleled in Luke, which cause considerable difficulty and must be taken into consideration. The prevalent opinion concerning Matthew 21,43 is that it is a Matthean redaction to highlight the historical event of the transfer of the kingdom from the Jews to the Church[87].

Matthew 21,44, however, is often ignored as an interpolation from Luke 20,18, which is itself considered a Lukan redaction as a further comment on the stone or as a floating tradition that was joined because of the key word "stone."[88]

The suggestion that Matthew 21,43 is an explanation of the parable by Matthew, which has merit, has been most forcefully presented by W. Trilling. His main arguments were that the style is Matthean, that δοθήσεται – ἀρθήσεται has been influenced by Matthew 13,22 || and 25,29 || (particularly since ἐκδιδόναι was used in v. 41), and that bearing fruit is a familiar theme in Matthew. While he recognized that βασιλεία τοῦ Θεοῦ is not typical in Matthew, he explained this by pointing to Matthew's flexibility in his use of kingdom phrases[89]. The decision is not nearly as clear cut as Trilling made it however. The only thing particularly Matthean in style is the introductory formula. The relation to the other passages with the δοθήσεται – ἀρθήσεται formula is open to question, especially since in those texts, the one who has receives more, whereas in this text the ones who have lose. While it is true that one would have

---

[86] See *infra*, pp. 96 and 101.
[87] Trilling, *Das wahre Israel*, pp. 58–62; Lohmeyer and Schmauch, pp. 314–315; Jeremias, *The Parables of Jesus*, p. 77; Georg Strecker, *Der Weg der Gerechtigkeit* (Göttingen: Vandenhoeck & Ruprecht, 1962), pp. 111 and 169; H. D. A. Major, T. W. Manson, and C. J. Wright, *The Mission and Message of Jesus* (London: Ivor Nicholson and Watson, 1937), p. 516; Kenzo Tagawa, "People and Community in the Gospel of Matthew," *NTS*, XVI (1969–1970), 161; Barnabas Lindars, *New Testament Apologetic* (London: SCM Press, 1961), p. 174; and Günther Bornkamm, Gerhard Barth, and Heinz Joachim Held, *Tradition and Interpretation in Matthew* (London: SCM Press, 1963), pp. 20 and 43.
[88] Jülicher, II, 401; Dodd, p. 128; Lindars, pp. 174 and 183f.; Trilling *Das wahre Israel*, p. 57 n. 15; Major, Manson and Wright, pp. 516 and 614; Ellis, *The Gospel of Luke*, p. 232; Walter Grundmann, *Das Evangelium nach Lukas* (Berlin: Evangelische Verlagsanstalt, [1964], p. 372; and Martin Rese, *Alttestamentliche Motive in der Christologie des Lukas* ([Gütersloh]: Gütersloher Verlagshaus Gerd Mohn, 1969), p. 171.
[89] Trilling, *Das wahre Israel*, pp. 58f.

expected ἐκδιδόναι to be carried over from v. 41, one would also expect ἀποδιδόναι instead of ποιειν. That the wording of v. 43 is different from v. 41 is difficult to explain on any theory of the origin of v. 43. Bearing fruit is a familiar theme in Matthew, but appears to be a familiar theme of the sayings tradition as well and is common throughout the New Testament[90]. It is true too that Matthew shows some flexibility in the terminology for the kingdom, but one cannot accept with Trilling that βασιλεία τοῦ Θεοῦ is not striking in Matthew. Particularly on the evidence of βασιλεία τοῦ Θεοῦ, it has been denied that Matthew is responsible for this verse[91].

The question over the inclusion of v. 44 is relevant to the analysis of v. 43. The reasons that v. 44 is often considered to be an interpolation from Luke are that the verse is omitted by certain manuscripts and that it seems out of place in its present context since logically it should precede v. 43[92]. This view, however, is not justified. If v. 44 were an interpolation from Luke, one would have expected the scribe to follow the sequence in Luke. That the sequence seems illogical may be the reason for the omission[93]. As far as the external evidence goes, by far the majority of the witnesses are in favor of retaining the verse. While the Old Latin and the Church Fathers are divided on the question, only syr^s of the Syriac manuscripts and only D and 33 of the Greek manuscripts omit v. 44. One reason for the quick acceptance of the omission of v. 44 in spite of the preponderant external evidence in its favor is that the passage qualifies as a possible "Western non-interpolation" and for the authority accorded this category in the past. Westcott and Hort were not oblivious to the fact that D is not a very pure text, but felt that in the "non-interpolations" it preserved the genuine text[94].

---

[90] Καρπός is used 19 times in Matthew and 12 in Luke. Seven of the occurrences in Matthew are in 7,16–20.

[91] Dillon, p. 17; Léon-Dufour, p. 394 n. 34; and Rudolf Schnackenburg, *God's Rule and Kingdom*, trans. John Murray (London: Nelson, 1963), p. 241. Βασιλεία τοῦ Θεοῦ occurs elsewhere in Matthew only at 6,33 (as a variant); 12,28; 19,24 (with variants); and 21,31. On the connection of 21,31 and 21,43, see *infra*, pp. 93 and 96.

[92] Trilling, *Das wahre Israel*, p. 57 n. 15; and Major, Manson, and Wright, p. 516. Cf. Strecker, p. 111; and Julius Schniewind, *Das Evangelium nach Matthäus* (Göttingen: Vandenhoeck, 1954), p. 219, who retained the verse, but commented on the order.

[93] G. F. Brandon, *The Fall of Jerusalem and the Christian Church* (London: SPCK, 1951), p. 244; and Gundry, pp. 84f.

[94] Brooke Foss Westcott and Fenton John Anthony Hort (eds.), *Introduction and*

Textual criticism has made significant advances since Westcott and Hort proposed their theory, and the increased number of manuscripts and the papyri have been the main reasons for these advances. In reporting on the significance of the papyri for textual criticism, Aland commented,

> One of the most important results of this change has been, for instance, that Westcott–Hort's so-called "western non-interpolations" have been, so to speak, stripped of their original nimbus and that, although interesting, they are no longer regarded, or should no longer be regarded, as authoritative[95].

The basis for this statement is set out in a textual analysis of the Western non-interpolations in Luke and John (eighteen passages in all)[96]. In most of the passages the situation is the same. The omission is supported by D, some of the Old Latin versions, usually part of the Syriac tradition, a few of the Church Fathers, and twice by the original hand of Sinaiticus. Significantly, in every passage but John 3,31–32 where the textual tradition is divided, P[75] goes with the long text. Aland considered each passage on both internal and external grounds and concluded in every case except two (one being John 3,31–32) that the evidence is decisively against the originality of the shorter Western reading. Jeremias had previously considered the internal evidence of the Western non-interpolations in Luke and had reached the same conclusion[97]. The case against the non-interpolations appears to be decisive[98].

The problem of Matthew 21,44 is an exact parallel except that no papyri are extant which cover this section of Matthew. That the Western non-interpolations have no claim to originality in Luke and John does not prove that the omission of Matthew 21,44 has no such claim, but it certainly prejudices the case against it. On external grounds

---

Appendix, Vol. II: *The New Testament in the Original Greek* (London: Macmillan and Co., 1896), pp. 120f., 149, and 175f. Cf. Burkitt, II, 228f. and 232. For a full discussion of the subject, see my "Western Non-Interpolations," *JBL*, XCI (1972), 369–379.

[95] Kurt Aland, "The Significance of the Papyri for Progress in New Testament Research," *The Bible in Modern Scholarship*, ed. J. Philip Hyatt (Nashville: Abingdon Press, 1965), p. 334.

[96] Kurt Aland, "Neue neutestamentliche Papyri II," *NTS*, XII (1965–1966), 193–210. The same material may be found in his *Studien zur Überlieferung des Neuen Testaments und seines Textes* (Berlin: Walter de Gruyter & Co., 1967), pp. 155–172.

[97] Joachim Jeremias, *The Eucharistic Words of Jesus* (London: SCM Press, 1964), pp. 145–159.

[98] See my "Western Non-Interpolations," pp. 369–379.

there appears to be little doubt that v. 44 was part of the original text. On internal grounds there appears to be just as little that substantiates the interpolation theory. The illogical sequence has already been mentioned as the probable reason for the omission of the verse. One should also note that Matthew 21,44 and Luke 20,18 do not correspond exactly. If Matthew 21,44 were an interpolation, surely the scribe would have followed the wording of Luke more closely.

There is a further consideration which is important for this discussion. It is commonly recognized that the first half of the saying in Matthew 21,44/Luke 20,18 is an allusion to the stone in Daniel 2,44–45 ($λικμήσει$ appears in Theodotion's text of Daniel but does not occur in the New Testament outside this saying)[99]. The allusion to Isaiah 8,14–15 is sometimes ignored but should not be. The thought is present in Isaiah 8,14, but the real allusion is to 8,15 ("Many among them shall stumble and fall and be broken . . .;" cf. the LXX, ". . . $πολλοὶ καὶ πεσοῦνται καὶ συντριβήσονται$").

While the allusions in v. 44 have been recognized, only R. Swaeles has suggested an allusion in Matthew 21,43 to Daniel 2,44[100]. The allusion is not verbal, but the thought is close. The $δοθήσεται$-$ἀρθήσεται$ formula, as noted above, is similar to Matthew 13,11–12, where one could also argue for an allusion in v. 11 to the thought of Daniel 2 and 7[101]. In addition, the statement of v. 43 that the kingdom of God will be given to a nation is reminiscent of Daniel 2,44. With the reference to the stone provided by Matthew 21,44, the allusion to Daniel 2,44–45 is strengthened. The author of Matthew 21,43–44 may have had in mind the fifth kingdom of Daniel 2 and, if so, turned this imagery against the Jewish leaders[102]. If this suggestion is right, it removes all doubt that v. 44 belongs in the text[103].

---

[99] See G. Bornkamm, "$λικμάω$," *TDNT*, IV, 281; and Miller, p. 179.

[100] R. Swaeles, "L'Arrière-fond scripturaire de Matt. XXI.43 et son lien avec Matt. XXI.44," *NTS*, VI (1959–1960), 310–313.

[101] *Ibid.*, 311, following L. Cerfaux, "La connaissance des secrets du Royaume d'après Matt. XIII et parallèles," *NTS*, II (1955–1956), 244. See Dan. 7,12–14 where dominion is taken from the beasts and given to the Son of Man. Hubaut, pp. 83–84, viewed Dan. 7,27 as part of the background of the judgment saying.

[102] Swaeles, p. 312. Cf. Dan. 7,13f., 27. Dillon's dismissal (p. 37 n. 5) of Swaeles' suggestion on the grounds that it requires the acceptance of the priority of Matthew is unfounded. As we have shown, there is every reason to believe that this is part of the double tradition. All that is required is that Matthew possibly preserved an earlier element.

[103] See my "Western Non-Interpolations," p. 377. For the view that v. 44 should

Swaeles pointed out that one problem with this view is that it is difficult to explain why ἔθνος is used in Matthew 21,43 instead of λαός which is used in Theodotion's text of Daniel 2,44[104]. The LXX text of Daniel 2,44 has ἔθνος but does not have λικμᾶν. Swaeles did not want to explain ἔθνος and λαός as going back to the Aramaic עַם (despite the fact that this is the word used in Daniel), since he thought that λικμᾶν directed one to the Greek Bible; therefore, he suggested that Matthew used ἔθνος in a sense of opposition to Theodotion's λαός, the people of the first alliance. This is possible, but it is not necessary to go this far. One should remember that the text of Theodotion which we know is based on a version in the second half of the second century A.D. of an Ur-Theodotion text which dates from the earlier part of the first century B.C.[105]. Whether ἔθνος or λαός was used in Ur-Theodotion is, of course, unknown. There probably is a dependence on Ur-Theodotion, but not necessarily since λικμᾶν is not that rare a word. At any rate, the presence of ἔθνος rather than λαός in Matthew 21,43 does not detract from the allusion to Daniel 2,44–45.

Some form of the saying about the destructive stone probably existed in rabbinic teaching prior to the New Testament usage. A rabbinic statement which is traceable to 200 A.D. is similar and is also connected to Daniel 2,45[106]. The stone in this statement is Israel, and the ones being

---

be in the text, besides Brandon, Gundry, and Swaeles, see Jeremias, *The Parables of Jesus*, pp. 77 n. 7 and 108 n. 78; Strecker, p. 111; Stendahl, p. 68; Léon-Dufour, p. 393 n. 33; and Miller, p. 201. The verse is placed in the apparatus in Tischendorf's eighth edition, in single brackets in the editions of W–H, Vogels (1955), and Nestle-Aland (twenty-sixth), in double brackets in the UBS (all three editions), and in the text without reserve in the editions of Merk and Bover.

[104] Swaeles, p. 312. Ἔθνος and λαός can be used interchangeably. See Georg Bertram and Karl Ludwig Schmidt, "ἔθνος, ἐθνικός," *TDNT*, II, 369.

[105] Sidney Jellicoe, *The Septuagint and Modern Study* (Oxford: Clarendon Press, 1968), pp. 83 and 87–94. H. Oort, "Lucas 20,18b," *Theologisch Tijdschrift*, XLIII (1909), 138–140, tried to date this saying, if not the whole of Luke, in the second century because he did not allow for Ur-Theodotion.

[106] EsR VII.10. The text reads:
R. Simeon b. Jose b. Lakunia said: In this world Israel are likened to rocks, as it says, *For from the top of the rocks I see him* (Num. 23,9); *Look unto the rock whence ye were hewn* (Is. 51,5). They were compared to stones, as it says, *From thence the shepherd of the stone of Israel* (Gen 49,24); *The stone which the builders rejected* (Ps 118,22). But the other nations are likened to potsherds, as it says, *And he shall break it as a potter's vessel is broken* (Is. 30,14). If a stone falls on the pot, woe to the pot! If a pot falls on a stone, woe to the pot! In either case, woe to the pot! So whoever ventures to attack them receives his deserts on their account. And so it says in the dream of

destroyed are the other nations. It is likely, therefore, that vs. 43–44 of Matthew not only use the Jewish understanding of Daniel 2 against the leaders, but also use one of their own proverbs as a medium for doing so.

The importance of the allusion of both vs. 43 and 44 in the Matthean ending to Daniel 2,44–45 is that it would explain the sequence. The order of the Matthean account would have been taken over from Daniel 2 and would appear illogical only if one does not see the allusion to the Old Testament passage. Nor would there be any longer a need to explain the addition of Luke 20,18 as due to the key word λίθος. If this parable was in the double tradition, then Luke has used only the stone saying and has omitted Matthew 21,43 as repetitious in that it really adds nothing to the conclusion of the parable given in Luke 20,16. If Mark knew of the saying, he omitted both parts as anticlimactic and cumbersome[107].

It is, of course, possible that Matthew has preserved the earliest account of the parable up through v. 42 and has added vs. 43–44 as his own comment. The introductory formula is Matthean, but it is unlikely that the rest of the saying is. Βασιλεία τοῦ Θεοῦ is non-Matthean and cannot be explained away. Secondly, Matthew certainly knew to whom the kingdom was given at the time of writing. If this were a Matthean redaction, surely he would have used the almost technical plural instead of the singular ἔθνος for the Church. It seems more likely to me that some form of vs. 43–44 were connected to the parable in the tradition that Matthew knew. The changes of ἐκδιδόναι to διδόναι and ἀποδιδόναι to ποιεῖν are difficult to explain on any theory. The former may have been due to the influence of the language in Daniel or both changes may be stylistic. Consideration will have to be given to these verses again in the next chapter.

To summarize, there is every indication that Matthew preserves the earliest account of this parable at least up through the quotation of Psalm 118,22. Obviously, to say this does not require the acceptance of Matthean priority overall, nor does it exclude the possibility of Matthean redactional elements, but the basic story is as preserved in Matthew,

---

Nebuchadnezzar, *Thou sawest a stone was cut out of the mountain without hands, and that it broke in pieces the iron, the brass, and the clay* (Dan. 2,45). (S–B, I, 877)

[107] That both Matthew 21,42 and 43 were convenient stopping places may be seen from the Palestinian Syriac Lectionary. See Lewis and Gibson, No. LXXVIII (which stops with v. 42) and No. CXLI (which stops with v. 43).

i.e., the construction of the vineyard with the allusion to Isaiah 5; the leasing; the two sendings of servants; no explicit christological emphasis on the son; the son cast out and killed; the judgment pronouncement by the hearers themselves; and the stone quotation. Whatever one thinks of the two verses that follow, the quotation in v. 44 should be considered part of the Matthean text. Verses 43–44 are probably a double tradition ("Q") saying which may contain an allusion to Daniel 2,44–45 and were either always connected to the parable or were taken over and added in the tradition used by Matthew as a fitting interpretation. If Mark knew of this saying, he omitted it completely. He has also shaped the sending of the servants to reflect the long line of the prophets and has underscored the christological significance of the son. Luke apparently knew of the final saying in Matthew 21,43–44 and omitted the first half as superfluous. He also shaped the story stylistically and underscored the christological significance of the son. Of course, literary dependence of Mark on Luke or vice versa is not excluded.

Chapter 5

The Origin and Meaning of the Parable

Since the origin and meaning of the parable are closely connected, they will be considered together. The major contours of the story will be dealt with individually to attempt to determine origin and significance. Obviously, some features of the parable will bear the same significance regardless of origin. It should be stressed that certain of the results of our study so far are more important for this stage of the investigation than others. The argument that the Matthean account preserves the earliest tradition, although important, will not materially affect one's conclusions about origin and meaning, whereas the decision rejecting the originality of Thomas will make certain options difficult to defend. The results of the investigation of parable as allegory, of the Palestinian thought world underlying the story, and the relevance of the stone quotation are all quite determinative.

Before dealing with the features of the parable, comment should be made with regard to the role of the parable in each of the gospel accounts. While few would question that the evangelists see the parable as a veiled answer to the question of authority, several people have suggested that broader connections should be seen in the various versions. Some have tied this parable in Mark's account to chapter 4, either because of common "isotopies"[1] or because of similar wording[2]. However, there is very little in theme or wording to connect the two chapters. Unlike the parables in Mark 4, this parable is understood without a private explanation. Mark's "parable theory" is not univocal[3], as this parable and 3,23–30 show.

---

[1] Yvan Almeida, *L'Opérativité sémantique des récits-paraboles* (Louvain: Editions Peeters, 1978), pp. 153–195, followed by Paul Ricoeur, "The Bible and the Imagination," *The Bible as a Document of the University*, ed. Hans Dieter Betz (Chico, California: Scholars Press, 1981), 54–65. See *supra*, pp. 10–11, notes 24 and 30.
[2] C. R. Kazmierski, *Jesus, the Son of God* (Echter Verlag, 1979), p. 135.
[3] Jan Lambrecht, *Once More Astonished* (New York: Crossroad, 1981), p. 132.

There is an additional suggestion of the connection of this parable with Mark's anti-temple bias[4]. Mark is certainly concerned to show the rejection of the religious authorities and the destruction of the temple and the preference of obedience to sacrifice. However, his concern seems to be more the rejection of the religious leaders than a rejection of the temple. In 11,17 and 12,41–44, the temple is seen as having a legitimate use in Jesus' time. At any rate, there is nothing in our parable that relates directly to statements about the temple[5].

Matthew's placement of the parable is significant because of the two parables that bracket it. The Parable of the Two Sons is in many ways parallel to the message of the Parable of the Wicked Tenants, and the Parable of the Marriage Feast has a similar structure as that of the Wicked Tenants. All three parables deal with the theme of judgment against those who reject God's message. As we will see, there are also parallels with the Lament over Jerusalem (Matthew 23,37–39 ‖ Luke 13,34–35) which are hardly accidental. Luke does not seem to have connections between the parable and the rest of his gospel that are not already present in Matthew or Mark.

The Owner and his Vineyard

In the discussion above on the form of this parable, we concluded that there is no basis for denying the metaphorical significance of the basic features of the story and that this parable is in keeping with rabbinic parables[6]. The Old Testament and rabbinic usage of a vineyard and its owner to depict Israel and her God is well-known[7], and the allusion to Isaiah 5 would suggest that something similar is involved here. Some have supported a denial of any metaphorical significance for the vineyard in this parable by saying that in other parables (like that of the Two Sons, Matthew 21,28–32, the Laborers in the Vineyard, Matthew

---

[4] John R. Donahue, *Are You the Christ?* (Missoula: Society of Biblical Literature, 1973), pp. 122–127.

[5] Donald Juel, *Messiah and Temple* (Missoula: Scholars Press, 1977), p. 136. Juel did go on to suggest connections with the temple, but the admission that there is no obvious connection is significant. On the possible connections, see *infra*, pp. 74 and 89–90 and 91 n. 81.

[6] See *supra*, pp. 13–26.

[7] Asher Feldman, *The Parables and Similes of the Rabbis* (Cambridge: Cambridge University Press, 1924), pp. 129f.; and Joachim Jeremias, *The Parables of Jesus* (London: SCM Press, 1963), p. 88.

20,1–16, or the Barren Fig Tree, Luke 13,6–9) the vineyard does not have metaphorical significance[8]. If one assumes that metaphorical significance could only mean that the vineyard stands for Israel, then such a position might be justified. However, the vineyard image cannot be limited to a representation of Israel. In the three vineyard parables referred to, the vineyard seems to stand for the "business" or concerns of God[9]. In our parable as well, to interpret the vineyard as Israel only creates problems. How can Israel be taken away and given to others? This problem and the illogical sequence in the preparation of the vineyard caused E. Lohmeyer to suggest that the vineyard stood for the temple and cultus[10]. There are points in favor of this suggestion, but they seem to stem from the fact that the cultus is to some degree the personification of the people, or possibly to ideas traditionally connected to Isaiah 5[11]. If any artificiality in the sequence of preparation exists, it should not be pressed since the words were taken over from the LXX. Lohmeyer evidently abandoned this interpretation in his Meyer commentaries[12].

---

[8] Hans-Josef Klauck, *Allegorie und Allegorese in synoptischen Gleichnistexten* (Münster: Aschendorff, 1978), p. 208; and Sören Ruager, *Das Reich Gottes und die Person Jesu* (Frankfurt: Verlag Peter Lang, 1979), p. 138.

[9] David Flusser (*Die rabbinischen Gleichnisse und der Gleichniserzähler Jesus. 1. Teil: Das Wesen der Gleichnisse,* Bern: Peter Lang, 1981, p. 170) recognized that images can be used for more than one purpose and that the vineyard in Matthew 20,1–16 and 21,28–32 signifies "die menschliche Leistung vor und für Gott." Still he viewed the vineyard in our parable as a symbol for Israel.

[10] Ernst Lohmeyer, "Das Gleichnis von den bösen Weingärtnern (Mark 12,1–12), *ZST,* XVIII (1941), 247f. Cf. Austin Farrer, *A Study in St. Mark* (Westminster: Dacre Press, 1951), p. 161; Lloyd Gaston, *No Stone on Another* (Leiden: E. J. Brill, 1970), p. 237; Robert Horton Gundry, *The Use of the Old Testament in St. Matthew's Gospel* (Leiden: E. J. Brill, 1967), p. 44; and Philip Carrington, *According to Mark* (Cambridge: Cambridge University Press, 1960), p. 251, who thought that the tower refers to the temple. See also the discussion by Donahue, pp. 122–123. While there is evidence to support this equation, it does not seem to have been intended by the author. J. Duncan M. Derrett, „Fresh Light on the Parable of the Wicked Vinedressers," *Revue Internationale des Droits de L'Antiquité,* 3me série, X (1963), 37f., interpreted the vineyard as the world, the messengers as warnings from God, and the others as possibly another creation and referred the story to the expulsion of Adam and Eve from the Garden of Eden!

[11] Juel, pp. 136–137, pointed to the Targum on Isaiah 5 as suggestive and speculated that Isaiah 5 had traditionally been applied to the temple and Jerusalem. IVQ Is^b II.11f. would support this idea. See *infra*, p. 91 n. 81.

[12] Ernst Lohmeyer, *Das Evangelium des Markus* (Göttingen: Vandenhoeck & Ruprecht, 1967), pp. 244f.; and Ernst Lohmeyer and Werner Schmauch, *Das Evangelium des Matthäus* (Göttingen: Vandenhoeck & Ruprecht, 1967), pp. 321f.

Often unnoticed in the discussions of the vineyard is the frequency with which people interpret the vineyard of Israel and then surreptitiously allow the image to slide so that later it is Jerusalem out of which Jesus is cast and then at the end of the parable it is the privileges of election that are taken away from Israel. The conclusion of the parable does provide additional insight into the vineyard image, but such shifts as these are unacceptable[13]. While on first glance it appears that the vineyard in Isaiah 5 is the nation of Israel, a closer look at the Old Testament usage of the vineyard imagery necessitates a modification of this conclusion. The terms "vine" and "vineyard" at times appear to refer to the nation as an entity (Jer. 2,21; Hosea 10,1). The basic image, however, is to the *people* as the possession of God, and often this is limited to the remnant (Psalm 80,9–20[14]; II Kings 19,30; Isaiah 3,14; 27,2f.; 37,31; Jer. 6,9; Hosea 14,6–9). The metaphorical vineyard in the Old Testament does not designate the nation so much as the elect of God and all the privileges that go with this election[15]. That this is the meaning in Isaiah 5

---

[13] Nor are the shifts caused by redactional efforts as Robert H. Gundry suggests for Matthew 21,43 in his *Matthew: A Commentary on his Literary and Theological Art* (Grand Rapids: William B. Eerdmans Publishing Company, 1982), p. 430, or as Francis Wright Beare suggests for Matthew 21,39 in his *The Gospel According to Matthew* (New York: Harper and Row, Publishers, 1981), pp. 429–430. The vineyard does not stand for Israel as a nation in any of the Synoptics. Gundry's procedure is often methodologically suspect because he reads in redactional and theological significance where none exists. For example, he argued that Matthew's "his fruits" in 21,34 implies all the fruits belong to the owner. His conclusion is that Matthew's theological symbolism of God demanding the totality of people's lives has swallowed up the economic realism that the owner got only part of the crop. This is reading into Matthew's account.

[14] Psalm 80,9–20 is very interesting and may be more relevant for our parable than is apparent on the surface. In v. 16, the people are referred to as a shoot (כנה) which God's right hand planted and then as the son (בן) which he strengthened. In v. 18 they are the man (איש) of his right hand and the son of man (בן-אדם) which he strengthened. The LXX uses υἱὸν ἀνθρώπου in v. 16 for בן. The targum interprets בן of v. 16 as the King Messiah (מלכא משיחא) If this passage bears no direct relation to the parable, at least it gives important evidence for the understanding of christological titles. Cf. also Isaiah 5,7 – ". . . and the man (איש) of Judah is his pleasant plant." Was Psalm 80 written as a sequel to Isaiah 5?

[15] Josef Schmid, *The Gospel According to Mark*, trans. Kevin Condon (Staten Island: Alba House, 1968), p. 217; Julius Schniewind, *Das Evangelium nach Markus* (Göttingen: Vandenhoeck & Ruprecht, 1952), p. 154; Pierre Bonnard, *L'Evangile selon Saint Matthieu* (Neuchatel: Editions Delachaux & Niestle, 1963), p. 315; Josef Blinzler, *Der Prozeß Jesu* (Regensburg: Verlag Friedrich Prestet, 1955), p. 200; and M.-J. Lagrange, *Evangile selon Saint Marc* (6th ed.; Paris: J. Gabalda et Cie, Editeurs, 1942), p. 311.

is clear in the lavish care of the owner and the explanation in v. 7b that the man of Judah is God's pleasant plant[16].

Focus is often placed on the fact that the parable in Isaiah 5 is of an unfruitful vineyard while the New Testament parable is of tenants who withhold the fruit from the owner. One should notice that parallels to the thought of the New Testament parable appear in Isaiah 3,14–15 ("Yahweh will enter into judgment with the elders of his people and with their leaders. You have eaten the vineyard; the spoil of the poor is in your houses. Is it nothing to you that you crush my people . . .?") and Jer. 12,10 ("Many shepherds have destroyed my vineyard . . .")[17].

The distinction between the vineyard as the nation and the more basic image of the vineyard as the chosen possession of God is important for interpreting the New Testament parable, but there is still a problem in understanding how the people of God can be given to others. Logically it is necessary to understand the vineyard as the privileges entrusted to the people, i.e., the law, the promises, and the working of God in past and present, or as the vineyard is interpreted in Matthew 21,43, the kingdom of God[18]. That which is taken and given to others is the special relationship to God which results from being his elect, or in short, election itself. This delimitation of the vineyard concept is not evident until the judgment pronouncement at the end of the parable. For this reason it is necessary to add that the allusion to Isaiah 5,2 should not be pressed. Its purpose is important, but it is only introductory. The allusion to Isaiah 5,2 conveys to the hearer that the parable is about the relation of God to his chosen people[19].

---

[16] On Isaiah 5 see Willy Schottroff, "Das Weinberglied Jesajas (Jes 5,1–7): ein Beitrag zur Geschichte der Parabel," *ZAW*, LXXXII (1970), 68–91; and Gale Yee, "A Form Critical Study of Isaiah 5,1–7 as a Song and a Juridical Parable," *CBQ*, XLIII (1981), 30–40. However, I would understand "house of Israel" and "man of Judah" as synonymous parallelism, rather than seeing the first as a reference to the northern ten tribes. See also Gerald T. Sheppard, "More on Isaiah 5,1–7 as a Juridical Parable," *CBQ*, XLIV (1982), 45–47.

[17] Sheppard, pp. 45–47 argued that originally Isaiah 3,14–15 belonged with 5,1–7. See also *infra*, p. 77 n. 20.

[18] Lohmeyer, *Das Evangelium des Markus*, p. 248; W. O. E. Oesterley, *The Gospel Parables in the Light of their Jewish Backgrounds* (London: SPCK, 1936), p. 120; and Georg Strecker, *Der Weg der Gerechtigkeit* (Göttingen: Vandenhoeck & Ruprecht, 1962), p. 170 n. 168. Armin Kretzer, *Die Herrschaft der Himmel und die Söhne des Reiches* (Stuttgart: Katholisches Bibelwerk, 1971), p. 167, took the kingdom in Matthew 21,43 as Yahweh's guidance and leading in Israel's history.

[19] Lohmeyer, *Das Evangelium des Markus*, p. 244; Erich Klostermann, *Das Mar-*

With regard to the origin of the parable, the vineyard image is so traditional that is does not provide a basis for determination.

The Tenants and the Servants

Most scholars have agreed that the tenants represent the Jewish leaders, since each Gospel writer indicates that these persons knew that the parable was directed against them. To suggest the tenants are a reference to all of Israel is an error[20]. That the religious leaders were intended seems obvious when one reads the parable with the knowledge of Jesus' conflict with the Jewish authorities and with the explanation of the Gospel writers, but *while* the story was being told, it would not have been clear who was reflected by the tenants. We too frequently read the parables (and the rest of Jesus' teaching) from the perspective of the Church. Accordingly, the parables are often deprived of their uniqueness and lose their force. As all would agree, we must hear the parables as Jesus' listeners would have heard them. From their standpoint, the meaning of the parable would not have been at all clear *at this point in the story*. The religious authorities can pass judgment (as in Matthew) without realizing that they have condemned themselves. We have taught ourselves to recapture the shock of hearing that it is the publican who is declared righteous in the Parable of the Pharisee and the Publican or that it is a Samaritan who appears in the story and performs mercy in the Parable of the Good Samaritan. A similar lesson needs to be learned with this parable. Especially if this story was a stock rabbinic parable, the hearers would have assumed that the tenants referred to outsiders, possibly to the Canaanites (as in Tanch B בשלח)[21] or to the Romans who

---

kusevangelium (Tübingen: Verlag J. C. B. Mohr, Paul Siebeck, 1950), p. 121; Walter Grundmann, *Das Evangelium nach Markus* (Berlin: Evangelische Verlagsanstalt, n. d.), pp. 239 and 241; Bonnard, p. 317; and Rudolf Pesch, *Das Markusevangelium* (Freiburg: Herder, 1977), II, 214. See ExR XXX.17, *supra*, p. 23.

[20] A few have thought that the tenants represent all of Israel since the prophets were sent to the whole nation and not just to the heirarchy. See e. g., M.-J. Lagrange, *Evangile selon Saint Luc* (Paris: J. Gabalda et Cie, Editeurs, 1941), p. 508; and C. G. Montefiore, *The Synoptic Gospels* (London: Macmillan and Co., n. d.), I, 275. However, the prophets often did direct their message against the leaders of the people. E. g., Isaiah 3,14; 28,14; Jer. 5,31; 12,10; 14,13f.; Ezek. 11,2; 13,2f.; 22,23f.; 34,2f.; Micah 3,9–12. See also *infra*, pp. 90–92. Pesch, pp. 215 and 220, saw a reference to Israel's hard-heartedness with the tenants and to her election with the vineyard.

[21] *Supra*, pp. 25–26.

were the present day tenants of Israel or generally to foreign powers that God permitted to "occupy Israel." The parable could be understood as saying that the rejection by the foreign powers of the requests of the people and the killing of her leaders (such as Judas Maccabaeus) would result in punishment for them. At this point one only knows that someone illegitimate is violating the concerns of God. In this way the parable draws in the hearers and requires a judgment to be made. Only at the end of the parable does one know to whom the tenants refer[22].

While there is virtual agreement about the significance of the tenants from our hind-sight point of view, it has often been asserted that the servants have no real significance and are only the necessary machinery of the story[23]. If the owner and his vineyard would have brought to mind the relation of God and Israel, however, as they probably would have done even if the allusion to Isaiah 5 were omitted, it is probable that the servants would have caused Jewish listeners to think of the prophets or at least of some special representatives of God[24]. In the Old Testament, the prophets are regularly referred to as servants of God[25], and regardless of which account one reads, a servant (or servants) sent by the vineyard owner to his vineyard would point to this identification[26]. The account in Matthew with its parallel to the lament over

---

[22] *Infra*, pp. 90–92 and 95–96.

[23] C. H. Dodd, *The Parables of the Kingdom* (London: Nisbet & Co., 1936), p. 219; Jeremias, p. 71; Vincent Taylor, *The Gospel According to St. Mark* (London: Macmillan & Co., 1952), p. 474; and B. M. F. van Iersel, *"Der Sohn" in den synoptischen Jesusworten* (Leiden: E. J. Brill, 1961), pp. 144f.

[24] Alfons Weiser, *Die Knechtsgleichnisse der synoptischen Evangelien* (München: Kösel-Verlag, 1971), pp. 49–57.

[25] I Kings 14,18; 15,29; II Kings 9,7, 36; 10,10; 14,24; 17,13, 23; 21,10; 24,2; Ezra 9,11; Isaiah 20,3; 44,26; 50,10; Jer. 7,25; 25,4; 26,5; 29,19; 35,15; 44,4; Ezek. 38,17; Dan. 9,6 and 10; Amos 3,7; and Zech. 1,6. The title was not reserved for the prophets however.

[26] Lohmeyer, *Das Evangelium nach Markus*, p. 245; Lagrange, *Evangile selon Saint Marc*, p. 307; Henry Barclay Swete, *The Gospel According to Mark* (London: Macmillan and Co., 1898), p. 251; Matthew Black, "The Parables as Allegory," *BJRL*, XLII (1959–1960), 282; E. Earle Ellis, *The Gospel of Luke* (London: Nelson, 1966), p. 233; Grundmann, p. 239; Schniewind, p. 153; C. E. B. Cranfield, *The Gospel According to St. Mark* (Cambridge: Cambridge University Press, 1959), p. 367; W. G. Kümmel, "Das Gleichnis von den bösen Weingärtnern (Mark. 12,1–9)," *Aux sources de la tradition chrétienne. Mélanges offerts à M. Goguel* (Neuchatel: Delachaux & Niestle S. A., 1950), 124 and 127; Wolfgang Trilling, *Das wahre Israel* (3d ed. München: Kösel-Verlag, 1964), p. 64; Pesch, p. 216; and Hans Weder, *Die Gleichnisse Jesu als Metaphern* (Göttingen: Vandenhoeck & Ruprecht, 1978), p. 150.

Jerusalem ("killing and stoning") and that in Mark with its long string of emissaries allude to the prophets more overtly than that in Luke, but the reference probably would have been recognized in the latter as well. At the same time, it should be repeated that none of the accounts of the servants is formed on prophetic history, nor is one justified in attempting to see individual prophets represented in any of the accounts[27]. The version in Mark may reflect the patience of God, but this feature is not present in Matthew or Luke.

The parable depicts the servants as having been persecuted and killed, whereas the Old Testament is reticent about the fate of the prophets. The only reported murders of prophets in the Old Testament involve two relatively insignificant men, Zechariah, the son of Jehoiada (II Chron. 24,20f.) and Uriah (Jer. 26,20), but the killing of the prophets is a frequent New Testament theme[28]. Since this view of the prophets' fate was that of the early Church, it is sometimes suggested that this feature is an argument for the origin of the parable (or at least this part of it) in the early Church. This reasoning, however, does not take into account that the view that the Jews killed their own prophets was widespread in pre-Christian Judaism. According to apocryphal accounts of the prophets' lives, at least five of the more important prophets were killed[29], and Jubilees I, 12–13 sounds very much like our parable at this point. From every indication in the Gospels, this view was that of Jesus as well (Matthew 5,12; 23,29–37 ||), and there is, in fact, the probability that I Thessalonians 2,15–16 and the tradition from Matthew rely on a common source[30]. It should be added that in the Old Testament there are

---

[27] Weiser, pp. 55f. He did suggest that with λιθοβολεῖν in v. 35 Matthew may have thought of the stoning of Zechariah in II Chron. 24,41, but this is unlikely. Certainly Matthew's readers could not be expected to pick up such a nuance. Enoch 89 does depict individuals in the history of Israel with metaphorical language. See Lagrange, *Evangile selon Saint Marc*, p. 307.

[28] Matthew 23,31f. ||; Acts 7,52; Hebrews 11,36–38; I Thess. 2,15.

[29] Amos, Micah, Isaiah, Jeremiah, and Ezekiel; according to later accounts Joel and Habakkuk were added to the list. See *Vitae Prophetarum* and Pesiq R 26; cf. Hans Joachim Schoeps, "Die jüdischen Prophetenmorde," *Aus frühchristlicher Zeit* (Tübingen: Verlag J. C. B. Mohr, Paul Siebeck, 1950), pp. 126–143. See also the treatment of the violent fate of the prophets in Odil Hannes Steck, *Israel und das gewaltsame Geschick der Propheten* (Neukirchen-Vluyn: Neukirchener Verlag des Erziehungsvereins, 1967), although I disagree with his analysis of the Parable of the Wicked Tenants.

[30] Cf. I. Thess. 2,14–16 and Matthew 23,31b–32. See R. Schippers, "The Pre-

frequent hints that the whole story about the persecution of the prophets has not been told[31].

So far in the parable then, we have been dealing with traditional metaphors and subject material used to describe the relation of God and his people. Although the intention of the parable has not been revealed at this point, it is clear that someone illegitimate has rejected the messengers God has sent. Theoretically these features could have arisen from Jesus, from the early Church, or from a non-Christian Jew.

The Son

With the entrance of the son into the parable, we are apparently no longer dealing with a stock metaphor. The son of the vineyard owner does appear in rabbinic parables, but is not a frequent designation. In the two rabbinic versions of our parable referred to earlier, the son is Jacob in one and Israel as a nation in the other[32]. If our parable has its origin in the early Church, the understanding of the son as the crucified Lord is obvious, even in the Matthean account where the meaning is not made explicit. If the parable is an authentic parable of Jesus, several questions are raised. First of all, especially if the entrance of the son in the story was motivated by legal considerations, is it possible that the son is just "part of the machinery" of the parable? Secondly, to whom is reference made with the mention of the son? Finally, if the son in the parable is to convey some significance, what would the listeners or readers have understood by the term? Obviously the questions are inter-related and an answer to one question will have implications for the other questions.

There are those like B. van Iersel who have argued that the son is an incidental feature whose absence would cause no important changes[33]. Nearly all interpreters who have said that the son is merely a necessary

---

Synoptic Tradition in I Thessalonians II 13–16," *Placita Pleiadia* (Leiden: E. J. Brill, 1966), pp. 230–233.

[31] I Kings 18,13; 19,10, 14; 22,27; II Chron. 16,10; 36,15–16; Neh. 9,26; Jer. 2,30; 37,15. Lohmeyer, *Das Evangelium des Markus*, p. 245, objected that the prophets were the bearers of God's message, and in the vineyard imagery the guardians of the vineyard. However, the prophets often denounced those who were supposed to be the guardians of the vineyard (*supra*, p. 77, n. 20). That the servants were sent to collect the fruit is required by the story and should not be pressed.

[32] *Supra*, pp. 25–26.

[33] van Iersel, p. 144.

part of the story have had to go on and make christological pronouncements about the self-consciousness of Jesus in their interpretations[34], but one could theoretically view the parable as a warning of judgment and attach no significance to the son. However, this interpretation is almost impossible if one holds that Jesus was aware of his filial relationship to the Father and is not very probable on any grounds. While it is true that the presence of a son or sons in other parables of Jesus usually carries no specific metaphorical significance[35], the situation with this parable is different in that the son is the point on which the parable turns, and it is only natural that some emphasis is placed on this part of the story. None of the rabbinic parables ignores the significance of the climax of its plot. Even if the identity of the son was not immediately perceived, special importance would have to be accorded to his coming.

The question to whom reference is made with the son would require little consideration were it not for an attempt to see in the killing of the son a reference to the death of John the Baptist. Arthur Gray had made this suggestion because he viewed any self reference by Jesus as too direct in response to the question of authority (Mark 11,27–33) and because the verb tenses in the quotation of Psalm 118,22–23 are past[36]. Merrill Miller likewise viewed the parable as constructed on the death of John the Baptist[37]. The only item in favor of this view is the connection

---

[34] *Ibid.;* Dodd, pp. 130–131; Jeremias, p. 72; and Wolfgang Trilling, *Christusverkündigung in den synoptischen Evangelien* (München: Kösel-Verlag, 1969), pp. 179–180. Reginald H. Fuller, *The Foundations of New Testament Christology* (New York: Charles Scribner's Sons, 1965), p. 114, said that if the parable is accepted as authentic, the son must not be allegorized into a direct self-designation, but rather "simply stands for God's final eschatological mission." However, this distinction is of little value, and Fuller went on to add that this attempt to eliminate the allegorical element is not very successful.

[35] This is Tim Schramm's basis for saying that there is no reference to Jesus in the parable. (*Der Markus-Stoff bei Lukas,* Cambridge: Cambridge University Press, 1971, p. 168.) Note for example the Parable of the Prodigal Son, but it is also worth noting that the Parable of the Two Sons in Matthew 21,28f. uses τέκνα and that the reference to the son in the Parable of the Wedding Feast (Matthew 22,2) does bear metaphorical significance.

[36] Arthur Gray, "The Parable of the Wicked Husbandmen," *The Hibbert Journal,* XIX (1920–1921), 42–52.

[37] *Scripture and Parable: A Study of the Biblical Features in the Parable of the Wicked Husbandmen and Their Place in the History of the Tradition.* Unpublished Ph. D. Dissertation, Columbia University, 1974, pp. 377–409. Miller did posit the alternative that Jesus spoke the parable as a warning to the tenants to avoid murdering the son (pp. 424–426). The son was apparently also equated with John the Baptist by P.

with the previous pericope where Jesus asked whether John's baptism was from heaven or from men, a connection many would not want to press. The gospels show no evidence that the religious authorities had anything to do with the murder of John[38], and the verb tenses are determined by the Old Testament and not by events in Jesus' time. If the details of the story do not correspond to John's death and if John is not referred to as son as Miller admits[39], there is nothing to show that John was in mind. Certainly John the Baptist was not the one for whom the vineyard was intended. The attempt to interpret the son as John the Baptist is abortive, and therefore, the son in the parable must be an allusion to Jesus.

This raises the question of the filial consciousness of Jesus. While a full analysis of this subject is beyond our scope, the New Testament evidence indicates that Jesus did consider himself to be in a special Son – Father relationship to God. As J. Jeremias has shown[40], this is seen particularly in Jesus' use of אבא as his normal address to God. There is no evidence as yet in the extensive prayer literature of Judaism of the use of this address. It was deliberately avoided since it expressed a familiarity that would have been disrespectful to a Jew if used for God. Jeremias concluded from his study of the prayers and sayings that Jesus' use of the title expressed intimacy, surrender, and a claim to revelation. While Jesus introduced his disciples into this special relationship with the

---

D. van Royen, *Jezus en Johannes de Doper*, unpublished Ph. D. Dissertation, University of Leiden, 1953, but this work was not available to me. Recently Malcolm Lowe, "From the Parable of the Vineyard to a Pre-Synoptic Source," NTS, XXVIII (1982), 257–263, likewise argued that the original reference was to John the Baptist. He went so far as to suggest that there was originally a "Baptist – sequence" which was essentially like Matthew's account and extended, from the cleansing of the temple to the Parable of the Great Banquet. This suggestion has little basis in fact, however, and is extremely hypothetical.

[38] Gray's attempt to counter this by pointing to the use of παραδιδόναι in Matthew 4,12∥ and to Mark 9,13 carries little weight.

[39] Miller, pp. 395f.

[40] Joachim Jeremias, "Abba," *The Prayers of Jesus* (London: SCM Press, 1967), 11–65; and his *New Testament Theology* (New York: Charles Scribner's Sons, 1971), pp. 61–68; Cf. I. Howard Marshall, "The Divine Sonship of Jesus," *Interpretation,* XXI (1967), 87–103; and his *The Origins of New Testament Christology* (Leicester: Inter-Varsity Press, 1977), pp. 45f. and 114f.; van Iersel, pp. 100–110; Klaus Berger, "Zum traditionsgeschichtlichen Hintergrund christologischer Hoheitstitel," NTS, XVII (1970–1971), 422–423; and Martin Hengel, *The Son of God* (Philadelphia: Fortress Press, 1976), p. 63; and James D. G. Dunn, *Jesus and the Spirit* (London: SCM Press, 1975), pp. 21–26.

Father, he did not align himself with them in praying or speaking of "our Father." This consistent distinction suggests a difference between Jesus' relationship to God and that of the disciples[41]. Apparently it is this evidence from the use of אבא that forced F. Hahn to make his artificial and unacceptable dichotomy between the titles "Son of God" and "Son."[42] According to Hahn, the former is due to the work of the Church, but "the Son" points to Jesus' use of אבא and the juxtaposition of "the Father" – "the Son" and indicates his unique status and authority. For much the same reason R. Fuller likewise accepted that Jesus was conscious of his unique Sonship[43]. In addition to the use of אבא, certain passages of the Gospels which indicate Jesus' Sonship, as Matthew 11,27 || and Mark 13,32 ||, although much debated, can be explained as secondary only with difficulty[44]. Thus one may conclude that Jesus

---

[41] "Abba," pp. 52–53 and 62–63; and Marshall, "The Divine Sonship of Jesus," pp. 89–90.

[42] *The Titles of Jesus in Christology* (London: Lutterworth Press, 1969), pp. 279–333, particularly pp. 307–317. He felt that "Son of God" was originally applied by the Palestinian Church to Jesus' eschatological function and then by the Hellenistic Church to his earthly work. With regard to "the Son," he argued that this title came from an independent stratum of tradition and was only secondarily associated with the title "Son of God." That the dichotomy cannot be accepted, see Marshall, "The Divine Sonship of Jesus," p. 88; and R. N. Longenecker, *The Christology of Early Jewish Christianity* (London: SCM Press, 1970), pp. 94–99.

[43] Fuller, pp. 115 and 136 n. 54. J. C. G. Greig, "Abba and Amen: Their Relevance to Christology," *SE*, V (1968), 3–13, attempted to deny the validity of Jeremias' argument from אבא, but he did not deal with Jeremias' textual analysis, nor with the distinction preserved between Jesus and the disciples, nor did he give suffucent weight to the fact that the title is too familiar for and does not occur in Jewish prayer. In addition, he misrepresented Jeremias' position by viewing אבא as a babbling sound of an infant to point to the intimacy of Jesus with God. Jeremias explained that the word was used by fully grown people for their fathers and for older men as everyday language of a family. See Jeremias, "Abba," pp. 60–63.

[44] Jeremias, "Abba," pp. 45–52; and his *New Testament Theology*, pp. 56–61; van Iersel, pp. 117–122 and 146–184; Marshall, "The Divine Sonship of Jesus," *passim;* A. M. Hunter, "Crux Criticorum – Matt. XI.25–30 – A Re-appraisal," *NTS*, VIII (1961–1962), 241–249; Oscar Cullmann, *The Christology of the New Testament* (London: SCM Press, 1963), pp. 286–288; A. Feuillet, "Jesus et la sagesse divine d'après les Evangiles synoptiques," *RB*, LXII (1955), 169–196; and Joachim Bieneck, *Sohn Gottes als Christusbezeichnung der Synoptiker* (Zürich: Zwingli-Verlag, 1951), pp. 75–87. Fuller, pp. 114–115, took Matthew 11,27 as secondary, but accepted that it provides an indirect witness to Jesus' self-understanding. Cf. his *The Mission and Achievement of Jesus* (Chicago; Alec R. Allenson, 1954), pp. 89–95. Dunn, pp. 26–34, remained undecided about the origin of Matthew 11,27 formally, but most of his argument seems to lean toward seeing the verse as reflecting Jesus' own conscious-

considered himself to be in a special Son – Father relationship with God. Evidently it was Jesus' conviction of his filial relation to God that served as the motivating factor for his ministry[45]. One may conclude that the occurrence of "the son" in the parable refers to Jesus regardless of the origin of the parable.

It is at this point that W. G. Kümmel's two objections to the authenticity of the parable must be considered since both objections center on the son. His first objection was that the punishment of the Jews and the transfer of the promise is depicted as a direct result of the murder of the son, whereas Jesus' other teachings do not present the thought that his death should unleash such punishment[46]. Kümmel recognized that Jesus did teach that the punishment of the Jews and the transfer of the promise would follow the rejection of his own person (Matthew 8,11f.; 12,41–42; 19,28f.; 21,43; 23,29f. and 37f.), but found offence in the fact that his death is nowhere else mentioned. According to the picture the Gospels draw, however, the rejection of Jesus by the Jewish leaders was never just a rejection of his "person.". Almost from the first they sought to destroy him. In Matthew 23,31–33 it is implied that the Jews' judgment will result from their duplicating their fathers' sin of killing the prophets. Also, one should not expect the precision that Kümmel required. As far as is known, Jesus spoke explicitly of his death only three or four times, and these announcements were always confined to his disciples. If they could not understand the significance of Jesus' death for their own circle, certainly they could not have understood the ramifications for the Jews. Therefore, Kümmel's first objection is not valid[47].

---

ness. See also Hahn, pp. 309–314; W. D. Davies, "'Knowledge' in the Dead Sea Scrolls and Matthew 11,25–30," *HTR*, XLVI (1953), 113–139; Paul Winter, "Matthew XI 27 and Luke X 22 from the First to the Fifth Century," *NovT*, I (1956), 112–148; and M. Jack Suggs, *Wisdom, Christology, and Law in Matthew's Gospel* (Cambridge, Mass.: Harvard University Press, 1970), pp. 71–97.

[45] Marshall, "The Divine Sonship of Jesus," p. 93; and Longenecker, p. 96; and John A. T. Robinson, "The Use of the Fourth Gospel for Christology Today," *Christ and Spirit*, ed. Barnabas Lindars and Stephen S. Smalley (Cambridge: Cambridge University Press, 1973), p. 70. After indicating that the son clearly stands for Jesus, Robinson stated, "Indeed I believe it is inconceivable that Jesus did not intend it to be taken thus – the story having no point unless in some sense it is a picture of God's dealings with Israel through the prophets and now through himself."

[46] Kümmel, p. 129.

[47] See van Iersel, pp. 128–129; Weiser, pp. 50–51; and Leonhard Goppelt, *Christentum und Judentum* (Gütersloh: C. Bertelsmann Verlag, 1954), pp. 67–68.

Kümmel's other objection relates to the question of what the listeners would understand. He objected that the parable presupposes that the hearers will see in the son a reference to the eschatological bringer of salvation and that they could do this only if they knew the title "Son of God" as a messianic title. Against the claims that "Son of God" was a messianic title, he countered that no certain proof of the title from pre-Christian or early Tannaitic times exists and concluded that no Jew on hearing of the sending and death of the son in the parable would have thought of the Messiah[48].

This charge that "Son of God" was not known as a messianic title in pre-Christian Judaism has lost its force. Until recently the New Testament usage of "Son of God" as the logical implication of messiahship was without convicing attestation from external sources[49]. Some were willing to accept that "Son of God" was sometimes transferred as a royal attribute to messiahship because of the connection between messianic expectation and the idea of a king[50]. Others were content to withhold judgment[51]. The situation has changed with the publication of the Qumran Scrolls, as several studies have shown[52]. II Samuel 7,14 is quoted in 4Q Florilegium ("I will be to him as a father, and he will be to me as a son"), and it is explained that the "he" in question is the Branch (צמח) of David who will arise with the interpreter of the law in the last days. This is further explained by the quotation of Amos 9,11. It would appear from IQSa 2.11–22 that Psalm 2,7 ("Thou art my son; this day I

---

[48] Kümmel, pp. 129–131.
[49] Ethiopic Enoch 105,2 is an interpolation; in IV Ezra 7,28; 13,32, 37, 52; and 14,9 the Latin *filius meus* goes back to παῖς Θεοῦ. Cf. Jeremias, *The Parables of Jesus*, p. 73. See also Erminie Huntress, "'Son of God' in Jewish Writings Prior to the Christian Era," *JBL*, LIV (1935), 117–123. Psalm of Solomon 17,23–31 is apparently dependent on Psalm 2 even though the assertion of sonship is omitted.
[50] As Schniewind, pp. 46–48; Cullmann, p. 274; and Evald Lövestam, *Son and Savior* (Lund: C. W. K. Gleerup, 1961), pp. 89–90. Lövestam did make use of the Qumran evidence.
[51] Rudolf Bultmann, *Theology of the New Testament*, trans. Kendrick Grobel (London: SCM Press, 1952), I, 50; and P. Volz, *Die Eschatologie der jüdischen Gemeinde* (Tübingen: J. C. B. Mohr, Paul Siebeck, 1934), p. 134.
[52] Lövestam, pp. 23 and 89–90; Marshall, "The Divine Sonship of Jesus," p. 92; Fuller, p. 32; Hahn, pp. 282–284; Eduard Lohse, "υἱός, υἱοθεσία," *TDNT*, VIII, 361; Longenecker, p. 95; Geza Vermes, *Jesus the Jew* (New York: Macmillan Publishing Co., 1973), pp. 197–199; and Hengel, pp. 43–44. Cf. Eduard Schweizer, "The Concept of the Davidic 'Son of God' in Acts and its Old Testament Background," *Studies in Luke-Acts*, ed. Leander E. Keck and J. Louis Martyn (Nashville: Abingdon Press, 1966), 186–193.

have begotten you") was also interpreted messianically by the Qumran community[53]. R. H. Fuller concluded from this evidence that "'Son of God' *was just coming into use* as a messianic title in pre-Christian Judaism."[54]

The above evidence points only to the use of the concept "Son of God" expressed by Old Testament citations and does not show a titular use. E. Lohse suggested that this may be due to the fear that the term would be misunderstood as relating to physical Sonship[55]. F. Hahn added to the Qumran and New Testament evidence part of the rabbinic material which indicates the divine sonship of the Messiah and concluded that it is extremely probable that the titular use of "Son of the Blessed" and similar terms had come to be common in pre-Christian Judaism[56]. Hahn appeared to be running ahead of the evidence, but his opinion seems to have been confirmed. The recent publication of a long-awaited Aramaic text from Qumran does indeed refer to "the Son of God" and "the Son of the Most High."[57] No doubt the debate about the meaning of the text will continue[58], but certainly the title "Son of God" was not foreign in Palestinian Judaism. It may be uncertain how widespread the use of the title was and how many of the hearers would have understood to whom reference was made, but Kümmel's main objection to the authenticity of the parable has been proven wrong[59]. Neither of Kümmel's objections is valid, and there is still no feature in the story that specifies its origin.

---

[53] Lohse, p. 361; Matthew Black, *The Scrolls and Christian Origins* (London: Thomas Nelson and Sons, 1961), p. 149; Hahn, p. 283; Lövestam, p. 23. The eschatological relevance of Psalm 2 for the community can be seen in 4Q Flor. Psalm 2,7 may have been included, but the manuscript breaks off after v. 2.

[54] Fuller, p. 32. (Italics his)

[55] Lohse, p. 360.

[56] Hahn, pp. 283–284. See Mekh Ex 15.9 (48b) (S–B,III, 676), and the Targum of Psalm 80,16 (*supra*, p. 75 n. 14). Hahn did not include the evidence for the messianic interpretation of Psalm 2,7, but this too is significant. Cf. Lövestam, pp. 15–23.

[57] Joseph A. Fitzmyer, "The Contribution of Qumran Aramaic to the Study of the New Testament," *NTS*, XX (1973–1974), 391–394; and "The Aramaic Language and the Study of the NT," *JBL*, XCIX (1980), 14–15. Cf. Hengel, pp. 44–45.

[58] Fitzmyer understood the reference to be to a Jewish ruler while J. T. Milik reportedly thought Alexander Balas is referred to by the expression "Son of God."

[59] Both Hahn, pp. 304 and 329 n. 152; and Fuller, pp. 114 and 136 n. 52, followed Kümmel in rejecting the authenticity of the parable even though both argued against his main objection. Fuller listed three objections from Kümmel, but only one was actually an objection for Kümmel (that judgment came because of Jesus' death rather than the rejection of his message).

If one accepts the parable as authentic, it is difficult to know to what extent the reference to the son was comprehended by the hearers[60]. As we have seen, the son of the vineyard owner appears in rabbinic parables with no messianic connotations, and although we now know that the concept "Son of God" was present in pre-Christian Judaism, we do not know how widespread its use was. It is possible to see in the use of the term "son" a reference to Jesus' unique relation to the Father without associating the word with the technical title "Messiah."[61] At this point in the story, the identity of the son may not have been certain.

Whether the story was from Jesus or originated in the Church, the son designated the final emissary from God, one who was in a unique relationship with God and to whom the vineyard rightly belonged. It is implied that he was on a different level than the prophets, but it does not imply the pre-existence of the Son, as Fuller suggested[62], any more than it implies the pre-existence of the prophets. Nor is there any validity to Fuller's suggestion that υἱός in Mark 12,6 represents an original עבד [63]. Nothing in the parable would point in that direction, and the אבן–בן wordplay rules it out completely. One should note with Lohmeyer that scarcely more is said of the death of the son than of the deaths of the prophets[64].

The Judgment Pronouncement

This part of the parable is, in my opinion, the most difficult section. Part of the difficulty arises from the use of the future in Matthew 21,41 ‖ and 43 while 21,42‖ uses the aorist (except for the last line of Psalm 118,23 which is in the present tense). While the tenses of the quotation are determined by the Old Testament text, the use of the future is ambiguous enough to allow for several possibilities. Difficulty also arises in the attempt to determine who is intended by those punished on

---

[60] Flusser, p. 75, stated that the hearers could suspect that Jesus referred to himself as the only son, but he did not provide a basis for the statement. For him, the Parable of the Wicked Tenants is unique because it is the only parable in which Jesus spoke about himself (p. 123).

[61] See Weiser, p. 51.

[62] Fuller, p. 194. See Ernest Best, *The Temptation and the Passion* (Cambridge: Cambridge University Press, 1965), p. 129.

[63] Fuller, p. 172.

[64] Lohmeyer, *Das Evangelium des Markus*, p. 248.

the one hand and who by the new recipients of the vineyard on the other.

How one views the origin of the parable (and this section) is determinative for interpretation. If the parable is from the early Church, the transfer of the vineyard will probably be seen as indicating the destruction of Jerusalem (or at least the defeat of the Jews in the Jewish War) and the transfer of God's election to the Church. S. G. F. Brandon, for example, saw in the owner's destruction of the tenants a reference to the destruction of Jerusalem as divine retribution for the death of Jesus. He also thought that the Matthean account is at pains to underline the application of the parable to the events of 70 A. D.[65] Such a late origin of the parable, and indeed, this judgment saying seems to me almost impossible. The parable as analyzed above, particularly with the בן– אבן wordplay, would seem to call for a much earlier date. The statement about destruction is too vague and imperfectly fulfilled to be a *vaticinium ex eventu*[66], and Matthew 21,43 alters the judgment of destruction to withdrawal of the kingdom[67]. Nothing in the judgment pronouncement suggests such a late origin or such a specific reference to the destruction of Jerusalem. It is much more likely, as Lohmeyer suggested, that the parable at this point bends back toward the original story in Isaiah 5, as can be seen in the question τί ποιήσει[68]. The judgment on the tenants here is paralleled by the judgment on the vineyard there. The destruction of the sinful nation was always a common theme of the prophets (see II Chron. 36,15–16), and there are parallels to the thought expressed in the replacement of the tenants (Jer. 3,15; 23,1–4).

---

[65] *Jesus and the Zealots* (Manchester: Manchester University Press, 1967), pp. 250 and 304. See also Dino Merli, "La parabola dei vignaioli infedeli (Mc. 12,1–12)," *Bibbia e Oriente*, XV (1973), 97–108.

[66] F. C. Burkitt, "The Parable of the Wicked Husbandmen," *Transactions of the Third International Congress for the History of Religions* (Oxford: Clarendon Press, 1908), II, 323; Cranfield, p. 366; and Alfred Suhl, *Die Funktion der alttestamentlichen Zitate und Anspielungen im Markusevangelium* (Gütersloh: Gütersloher Verlagshaus Gerd Mohn, 1965), p. 140. Suhl, and Gaston, p. 82, both thought that the parable looks forward to the Jewish war, but there is no basis for this either.

[67] Trilling, *Das wahre Israel*, p. 65. The change from destruction (the hearers' judgment) to taking away the vineyard (the judgment expressed in Matthew 21,43) is paralleled in II Samuel 12,5 and 10–13 where David announces a judgment of death for the offender, and Nathan changes it to the taking away of David's wives and the death of the child.

[68] Lohmeyer, *Das Evangelium des Markus*, p. 246. Lohmeyer, and Taylor, p. 476, both pointed to the fundamentally Jewish idea of God himself coming in judgment.

If the parable is from Jesus, the futures would be understandable and should be interpreted as a warning to his hearers. Even so, one must still ask if the events that were future and imprecise for Jesus are past (and specific) for the evangelists[69]. The issue of the transfer of the kingdom will be discussed separately, but with regard to the destruction of the tenants (or the taking away of the vineyard) there is nothing in the text of any of the evangelists to show that they thought of the destruction of Jerusalem. If such a position is held, it will have to be supported by other considerations, rather than by the wording of the parable.

Usually such other considerations include dating Matthew about 85 A.D. and seeing allusions to the destruction of Jerusalem in verses like 22,7 or 27,25. M. Hubaut, however, has made a suggestion that is more directly related to our parable. In his view, 21,43 comes from a Palestinian community which was opposed to Judaism and saw the end of Judaism in the destruction of Jerusalem and the temple. His basis for this suggestion is a somewhat complicated theory for the origin of v. 43 which sees the verse as composed from elements from the Targum on Isaiah 5,5 and from Daniel 7,27. On this view, Kingdom of God is an expression to denote God himself or the Shekinah. Jesus is then viewed as the Shekinah which is removed from Judaism and given to a new people[70]. This hypothesis has some attraction because of the use of Isaiah 5 in the parable and the word פלס ("take away") in the targum. On the other hand, there is little else to commend it and the hypothesis seems to go way beyond the evidence. One has to assume the presence of this targum in the first century, which is not impossible. However, the targum at this point seems to presuppose the destruction of Jerusalem[71], which makes dependence by Matthew or his tradition more difficult because of the limited amount of time available. Even more damaging to the suggestion is that one would have to assume that a Christian read the phrase "I will break down their sanctuaries" in the targum as a

---

[69] This view is fairly common. See Hubert Frankemölle, *Jahwebund und Kirche Christi* (Münster: Verlag Aschendorff, 1973), pp. 250–252; Strecker, p. 169; Trilling, *Das wahre Israel*, p. 61; Klauck, pp. 312–313. Michael Hubaut, *La parabole des vignerons homicides*, Cahiers de la Revue Biblique 16 (Paris: Gabalda, 1976), pp. 52f.; and 71f., suggested various stages of interpretation with the destruction of Jerusalem being assumed after 70 A.D.

[70] Hubaut, pp. 67–84. Cf. Juel, pp. 136–137, who also pointed to the similarity of the Targum on Isaiah 5, but recognized that the targum presupposes the destruction of Jerusalem.

[71] See the discussion in Juel, pp. 137, 184–195, and 195.

reference to the destruction of Jerusalem and then read Jesus' parable in a similar light and commented upon it. However, 21,43 says nothing of destruction and any similarity to the Targum on Isaiah 5 seems due to the fact that both are expressions of judgment[72]. If 21,43 is a comment on the destruction of Jerusalem, why is it so vague and why is it milder than 21,41?

With regard to the time referred to in the judgment pronouncement then, I would say that the tenses and wording in Matthew 21,41 ‖ and 21,43 are not specific enough for one to determine the time or type of punishment[73]. Any attempt to see an allusion to the destruction of Jerusalem or the parousia in any of the accounts is unwarranted, and especially is this the case in Matthew, since 21,43 is so much milder than 21,41.

The other issue in the judgment pronouncement that requires consideration and which also relates to the question of the tenses is the transfer of the vineyard. As explained above, what is transferred is the election of God and its privileges, or more specifically as in Matthew, the Kingdom of God with its fulfillment of the promises given to Israel[74]. It is easy to jump to the conclusion that the privileges of Israel were taken from her and given to the Church, or more particularly to the Gentiles, and there is evidence in the Gospels that helps to make such a view plausible[75]. On such a view ἔθνει in 21,43 must be understood as a collective singular referring to the Church[76]. However, I do not believe that this is the message of this parable. In Mark and Luke there is no

---

[72] Hubaut's assumption that the Son of Man was a messianic title and parallel to Son of David because of the בן- אב wordplay (p. 92) also goes beyond the evidence.

[73] Weder, p. 149, recognized that the futures in Mark 12,9b are legitimate only if the punishment of the tenants still has not arrived. Regardless of this, however, he viewed 12,9b as secondary.

[74] *Supra*, pp. 75–76. That Matthew 21,43 interprets the vineyard as the Kingdom of God does not necessarily indicate that the Kingdom was a reality already present in Israel. It may mean that those who were destined to receive the Kingdom lose their opportunity because of their wickedness. The same thought with regard to the future is expressed in Matthew 8,12. Cf. Rudolf Schnackenburg, *God's Rule and God's Kingdom*, trans. John Murray (London: Nelson, 1963), p. 241; and Lohmeyer and Schmauch, p. 315.

[75] Matthew 8,11f. ‖; 12,18, 21; 24,14; 26,13; Mark 4,30–32 ‖; 11,12f. ‖; 14,9. Most of these verses stress only the inclusion of the Gentiles and do not have to be interpreted of the rejection of Israel in favor of the Gentiles. See Werner Georg Kümmel, *Promise and Fulfilment* (London: SCM Press, 1957), pp. 75–81; and N. A. Dahl, "The Parables of Growth," *ST*, V (1951), p. 166.

[76] See Gundry, *Matthew, A Commentary on his Literary and Theological Art*, p. 430.

indication as to whom reference is made by "the others,"[77] but the logical inference in all three Gospel accounts is that the vineyard is taken from the *leaders* of the Jews. When one sees in Matthew 21,41 ‖ a reference to the rejection of Israel as a whole, he or she must assume that the parable is not consistent in that the tenants are partly the people and partly the leaders[78], or that the leaders are merely representatives of the people[79]. There are passages that castigate the people (Matthew 21,18f. ‖ apparently; and 27,25), but there are also numerous texts where Jesus limited his attack to the religious leaders (e.g., Matthew 15,1–20 ‖; 16,5–12 ‖; 23,1–36 ‖). If the Evangelists wanted to direct this parable against the Jewish people, why would all three of them counteract this intention immediately by saying that the religious authorities knew that Jesus spoke about them but could not seize him for fear of the *people*[80]? In all three Gospels the judgment is pronounced against the religious leaders and we will find further confirmation of this in the quotation from Psalm 118,22[81].

Some have suggested that the Matthean account is different from Mark and Luke because of the addition of v. 43[82], but this verse is even

---

[77] Lohmeyer, *Das Evangelium des Markus*, p. 246; and Taylor, p. 476.

[78] As C. Montefiore did (I, 275). Blinzler, p. 200, had to conclude that the parable recognizes the joint guilt of the people. Notice the difficulty that Beare had (pp. 430–431) on recognizing that 21,43 refers to the leaders while still trying to view the tenants in the parable as all the people. Hubaut's treatment of the judgment pronouncement is just as forced. He viewed Jesus' original addressees as all the people (p. 140), but the first stage in the tradition restricted the story to the Jewish authorities (pp. 63, 97, and 144). A later stage refers it again to all of Judaism (p. 63).

[79] Steck, p. 270; Frankemölle, p. 255; Kretzer, p. 151; and Charles W. F. Smith, *The Jesus of the Parables* (Rev. ed., Philadelphia: United Church Press, 1975), p. 135.

[80] Note Trilling's admission (*Das wahre Israel*, p. 45 n. 54) that one must infer that the people are meant and that this does not correspond to the framework of 21,43 and 45.

[81] It seems hardly a coincidence that IVQ Is^b II.11f. interprets Isaiah 5 of the men of scoffing in Jerusalem or that the rabbinic version of our parable in SDt. 32.9 is in the context of spiritual obduracy.

[82] Douglas R. A. Hare, *The Theme of Jewish Persecution of Christians in the Gospel According to St. Matthew* (Cambridge: Cambridge University Press, 1967), p. 151, thought that the vineyard in Mark represents Israel and that only the religious leaders are indicted, but that since the Kingdom of God is taken away in Matthew all the Jewish people are indicted. See also Ruager, p. 144. Against this see W. D. Davies, *The Setting of the Sermon on the Mount* (Cambridge: Cambridge University Press, 1964). pp. 328 and 331–332. Günther Bornkamm, Gerhard Barth, and Heinz Joachim Held, *Tradition and Interpretation in Matthew* (London: SCM Press, 1963), p. 43, thought that Mark refers to the rejection of Israel as a past event, but that in

less harsh than Mark 12,9 and Luke 20,16[83]. If ἔθνος in Matthew 21,43 designated the Gentiles, the "you" in the first part of the verse would mean the Jews as a whole, and the meaning of v. 43 would be different from v. 41b. This seems very unlikely. If the Gentiles had been intended, instead of the singular ἔθνει the almost technical plural form would have been used[84]. (Of the fourteen times ἔθνος is used in Matthew, it is always used in the plural except for 24,7, which uses words from II Chron. 15,6, and the passage here.) The "you" in v. 43 is the same group of people who responded in v. 41, i.e., the religious leaders of Israel. With Franz Mussner, this parable is not anti-Semitic, but anti-Pharisaic[85]; or more accurately, the parable is directed against the religious authorities.

P. Bonnard and W. G. Kümmel objected to the idea that the Jewish people have only to change leaders to become the recipients of the

---

Matthew the giving over of the vineyard is translated into the future so that the disciples themselves are drawn into judgment to determine whether they are the nation that delivers the fruit (cf. p. 20). While the judgment theme is pertinent for Christians, all the gospels use the future and speak from the same perspective. The thought expressed in Matthew 21,41b and 43 is only that the vineyard will be given to a people who will deliver the fruits; i.e., to people who will be faithful to their agreement. Richard J. Dillon, "Towards a Tradition-History of the Parables of the True Israel (Matthew 21,33–22,14)," Bib, XLVII (1966), 20–42, placed the Matthean account in the context of baptismal instruction (primarily because of the fruit bearing), but his assumptions are questionable, and the features of the story may be explained by a much less elaborate hypothesis. We might add here that Ernst Haenchen's attempt (Der Weg Jesu, Berlin: Alfred Töpelmann, 1966, p. 402) to interpret the fruit in Mark as the recognition of Jesus as the son is unjustified since the fruit receives no emphasis in the Markan story and since the tenants recognize the son but reject him anyway.

[83] Beare, pp. 430–431, noted that 21,43 is much milder than the parable.

[84] Lohmeyer and Schmauch, p. 314; Kenzo Tagawa, "People and Community in the Gospel of Matthew," NTS, XVI (1960–1970), 161; and Trilling. Das wahre Israel, p. 61. While Trilling made this observation, on p. 63 he reverted to the Israel-Church antithesis because he felt that the withdrawal of the kingdom only from the leaders is insufficient. However, neither the message of Jesus nor that of the Church was against the whole nation. Jesus preached against the corruption of the established religion, and the Church taught that only some of the Jews were set aside so that the Gentiles might become part of the true Israel (Acts 2,39f.; 3,17f.; 7,1–60; Romans 9,6f.; 11,1–24; Ephesians 2,11–22; and I Peter 2,7).

[85] "Die bösen Winzer nach Matthäus 21,33–46," Antijudaismus im Neuen Testament? ed. Willehad Paul Eckert, Nathan Peter Levinson, and Martin Stöhr (München: Chr. Kaiser Verlag, 1967), 129–134. Cf. Juel, pp. 131 and 212–213. His intention with regard to our parable on p. 213 is not clear.

kingdom[86], but this is not what the parable teaches. The purpose of the statement is to exclude the Jewish leaders rather than to point the way to participation in the Kingdom. In this passage ἔθνος can only have a religious sense which is independent of a reference to a nation as a whole and should be understood as indicating the true people of God (as in I Peter 2,9)[87]. Trilling was correct in saying that the new ἔθνος must be thought of as a counterpart to the old, but he was incorrect in saying that the parable finds this counterpart in the entire Church[88]. The parable is not that explicit. That the "you" in the first half of the sentence refers to a group within the historical people suggests that the "new people" should be understood in a similiar way[89]. At this point, attention should be paid to the surrounding context in Matthew[90]. There is a perfectly analogous case in the preceding Parable of the Two Sons (again using βασιλεία τοῦ Θεοῦ). The same religious leaders were castigated for not believing John the Baptist who came in the way of righteousness, and were told that the publicans and harlots who did believe him would go into the Kingdom of God before them[91]. In a sense the Gospels do teach that the people should change leaders, but, of course, not in just an external alignment. Rather than follow the leaders of established Judaism in their hypocrisy and defilement of the cultus, they should have heeded the messages of John and Jesus and should live in true repentance a life properly oriented to God. The people who do are the true Israel and will replace those who are bound up in the hypocritical established religion and are Israel in name only. Matthew and his readers may well

---

[86] Bonnard, p. 317; Kümmel, "Das Gleichnis von den bösen Weingärtnern," p. 127.

[87] Lohmeyer and Schmauch, p. 314; Trilling, *Das wahre Israel*, p. 61. Cf. Müssner, p. 131; and Frankemölle, p. 247.

[88] Trilling, *Das wahre Israel*, p. 63.

[89] Lohmeyer and Schmauch, p. 314.

[90] The trilogy of parables in Matthew 21,28–22,14 all relate to the rejection of God's requests or invitations and the subsequent judgement. The third parable is not addressed as explicitly as the other two toward the religious leaders. On the trilogy see Akira Ogawa, "Paraboles de l'Israel Véritable? Reconsidération Critique de Mt. XXI 28 – XXII 14," *NovT*, XXI (1979), 121–149; Frankemölle, pp. 248f.; and Kretzer, pp. 150f.

[91] Lohmeyer and Schmauch, p. 314; Mussner, pp. 130–131; and A. Jülicher, *Die Gleichnisreden Jesu* (Freiburg i. B.: Akademische Verlagsbuchhandlung von J. C. B. Mohr, Vol. I, 1888; Vol. II, 1889), II, 404. Cf. Gaston, p. 476. See EsR I.13 where the sovereignty of Israel is taken away because of her sin, and see Schnackenburg, pp. 240–241.

have understood that the "new people" made up the Church, but nothing in the text makes this explicit; the identification of this new group is left imprecise[92]. The parable is a caustic attack on the authorities of established religion and not an argument for the replacement of Israel by the Church[93].

If Swaeles was right in seeing an allusion to Daniel 2,44–45[94], v. 43 of the Matthean account suggests that those who believe they will make up the fifth and enduring Kingdom will forfeit this privilege because of their sin, and the Kingdom will be given to another people who will obey God. Whether the allusion to Daniel is present or not, the sting of the parable is that those who considered themselves as the elite among the elect are described as behaving like illegitimate criminals who have no place in God's ultimate purposes[95]. The emphasis is similar to the saying of John the Baptist that God can raise children to Abraham from the stones, but it goes much further by the addition of the transfer of the Kingdom.

With regard to the origin of the judgment pronouncements, theoretically they could have emerged either from Jesus or the early Church. The direction of the saying against the leaders, with apparently a more positive attitude toward the people, could indicate a dominical origin, especially with the parallel to the positive attitude toward publicans and harlots in 21,32. Hostility toward the religious leaders is more characteristic of the ministry of Jesus than that of the early Church, but the early chapters of Acts indicate a similar attitude on the part of the Church for a short period. The origin of the saying is at least very early[96].

The same may be said concerning Matthew 21,43. The wording of this verse could derive either from Jesus or from the early Church.

---

[92] Mussner, pp. 131–132. As in the discussion of the tenses before, the use of the future in 21,43 does not permit one to pinpoint the time of the transfer. The issue is compounded by the term Kingdom of God since focus may be placed on either the present or future aspects of the Kingdom. There is a good possibility that both aspects are in view here.

[93] Ogawa, p. 149.

[94] R. Swaeles, "L'Arrière-fond scripturaire de Matt. XXI.43 et son lien avec Matt. XXI.44." NTS, VI (1959–1960), 312.

[95] Prof. Otto Betz suggested in a private discussion that there might be an implicit wordplay in the parable between אריסים and עריצים. The ones who are supposed to be tenants (אריסים) have become oppressors or violent men (עריצים).

[96] Cf. Hubaut, pp. 127–128.

Despite the fact that Lohmeyer and Schmauch understood ἔθνος in this verse as referring to a portion of the historical people, they thought that the interpretation in v. 43 stems from a community which lived among the Jewish people and knew itself as the true eschatological Israel[97]. This is possible, but the origin of the saying would have to be very early.

The Stone

The significance of the stone has often been ignored since it has been considered a secondary addition to the parable[98], but we have shown that the stone quotation and the whole parable go back at least to the Aramaic speaking Church and that it is improbable that the parable ever existed without the Old Testament quotation.

With regard to the first stone saying in Matthew 21,42 ||, the objection has often been made that the quotation of Psalm 118,22-23 changes the point of the parable[99], but it would be more accurate to say that the first part of the quotation (Psalm 118,22a) emphasizes the rejection of the son by the Jewish leaders, while the second part (vs. 22b-23) is an advancement on the thought of the parable[100]. The first century listener probably would not have been distracted by the transition from the vineyard

---

[97] Lohmeyer and Schmauch, p. 315. Cf. Hubaut, pp. 67 and 76f. H. D. A. Major, T. W. Manson, and C. J. Wright, *The Mission and Message of Jesus* (London: Ivor Nicholson and Watson, 1937), p. 516, assumed that v. 43 is an editorial comment and that it renders v. 45 superfluous (which states that the priests and Pharisees knew that the parable was directed against them). Verse 45 may have been superfluous from the standpoint of the Jewish leaders, but it is necessary for the reader as one can see if he or she attempts to read the passage without it.

[98] It is still surprising that neither F. Hahn nor R. Fuller gave this title any consideration in their studies of Christology and that L. Gaston *(No Stone on Another)* and Barnabas Lindars *(New Testament Apologetic,* London: SCM Press, 1961), who did provide discussions of the stone imagery, paid little attention to the parable. The use of ἐν παραβολαῖς in Mark 12,1 probably should be understood adverbially, rather than as an introduction to two "allegories," that of the vine and that of the stone (as Seraphinus M. Gozzo suggested in his *Disquisitio critico-exegetica in parabolam N. Testamenti de perfidis vinitoribus,* Romae: Pontificium Athenaeum Anatonianum, 1949, pp. 35 and 82f.). Some have seen an indication here of dependence on Matthew. Hubaut suggested a pre-Markan collection of parables on the vine (p. 117), and saw the vine over the entrance to the temple as the "trigger" that brought the parable into being (p. 139). The support for both suggestions is inadequate.

[99] Jülicher, II, 405; Schmid, p. 218; Suhl, p. 141.

[100] Other parables that include an advancement of thought are the Parable of the Prodigal Son, the Rich Man and Lazarus, and in its present form the Marriage Feast of Matthew 22.

imagery to the building imagery since this transition appears to have been common and is present in Isaiah 5,7[101]. It is clear that the wordplay and the logical equation of the rejected son and the rejected stone tie the quotation and parable together, but one should not overlook that this connection is strengthened by the equation of the tenants and the builders. In fact, the term "builders" is a key word in the quotation since it was a frequent and favorable rabbinic designation for the religious leaders of the people[102]. As suggested earlier[103], the intent of this parable (like the preceding one in Matthew 21,28–32 and the Old Testament parable of Nathan) is not clear until after the question is answered and a reply is given. The reply brings the key for understanding the intent of the parable as is usual with "juridical" parables[104].

Such clarifications or interpretations are not necessarily later additions as some critics suggest, for Old Testament and rabbinic parables always or nearly always have some statement to make the meaning clear[105].

---

[101] See IQS VIII.5; and I Cor. 3,9. Is the parable at this point again bending back to Isaiah 5?

[102] b Shab 114a; b Berak 64a; SSR I.5.3 (ExR XXIII.10); and the Targum on Psalm 118,22–29 (S–B, I, 876). See *infra*, p. 114, and J. Duncan M. Derrett, "The Stone that the Builders Rejected," *SE*, IV (1965), pp. 184f.

[103] *Supra*, pp. 77–78.

[104] On this designation see Uriel Simon, "The Poor Man's Ewe-Lamb: An Example of a Juridical Parable," *Bib*, XLVIII (1967), 220–224. His description on pp. 220–221 merits quotation:
The juridical parable constitutes a realistic story about a violation of the law, related to someone who had committed a similar offence with the purpose of leading the unsuspecting hearer to pass judgment on himself. The offender will only be caught in the trap set for him if he truly believes that the story told him actually happened, and only if he does not detect prematurely the similarity between the offence in the story and the one he himself has commited. Tree and animal parables are intrinsically intended to arouse comparisons. The realistic dress of the juridical parable, on the other hand, is intended to conceal the very fact that it is a parable. The narrator has to strike a careful balance between getting too close to the parable's application and being too remote from it. In both cases, he is liable to undermine the force of the analogy. Once the narrator has succeeded in completely concealing his intentions, he drops the veil and usually points the moral by identifying the villian of the parable with the hearer: "Thou art the man." The juridical parable is a disguised parable designed to overcome man's own closeness to himself, enabling him to judge himself by the same yardstick that he applies to others.

[105] All OT parables include an "interpretation" or explanation, before or after, so that the meaning is clear. (See Judges 9,7–20; II Samuel 12,1–14; 14,1–17; I Kings 20,35–43; II Kings 14,8–10; Isaiah 5,1–7; Ezekiel 17,3–21; 19,1–14; 21,1–5; and 24,3–14.) A perusal of rabbinic parables will show that interpretations there are

David Flusser is correct, at least in general terms, in arguing against Jeremias that interpretations of the parables are not later additions, but belong to the original accounts given by Jesus[106]. In the Parable of the Wicked Tenants, the quotation of Psalm 118,22 functions like Nathan's "You are the man!" in his parable to David and would have almost stated the meaning explicitly[107]. The son (via the wordplay), the special envoy from God to his people, was rejected by the religious authorities. Only at this point would the religious authorities know that they were being depicted as illegitimate abusers of the privileges from God. The quotation then confirms that the parable is directed against the religious authorities rather than the nation. It is not true that the quotation disturbs the ending of the parable. The second part of the quotation is an advancement on the parable, but the first part serves as scriptural attestation for the climax of the story.

Nearly everyone has agreed that the quotation refers to the son, but A. Suhl attempted to interpret the quotation of Psalm 118,22-23 in Mark as free from christological connotations[108]. He suggested that Matthew and Luke both misunderstood Mark by interpreting the stone christologically. For Suhl, the Psalm quotation was needlessly reproduced in Matthew since it serves no purpose and since it is ignored by the connection of v. 43 to v. 41. In Luke the stone has been made a meaningful subject by the addition of v. 18 and as a result of seeing it in light of the resurrection. The original use in Mark was not christological, however, but was an application of the Psalm to the reversal of fortunes described in v. 9, which for Suhl expresses Mark's view of the Jewish War as judgment for the death of Jesus. The emphasis is on the change of circumstances brought about by God. ($αὕτη$ of Psalm 118,23 was understood as referring to this event.)

There are several points which exclude this interpretation:

1. Suhl's placing of the parable in the context of the Jewish War has no basis in the parable itself[109].

---

common as well. See Asher Feldman, *The Parables and Similes of the Rabbis* (Cambridge: Cambridge University Press, 1924), *passim;* and see *supra*, pp. 23-26.

[106] Flusser, pp. 20, 63f., 119f.

[107] Lohmeyer and Schmauch, p. 314; and Miller, p. 355. Tullio Aurelio, *Disclosures in den Gleichnissen Jesu* (Frankfurt: Peter Lang, 1977), p. 199, rightly compared Jesus' parable to Nathan's, but said that while disclosure was told to David, Jesus' hearers needed no help. He did not explain how they would have understood.

[108] Suhl, pp. 140-142.

[109] Martin Hengel, "Das Gleichnis von den Weingärtnern Mc 12,1-12 im Lichte der Zenonpapyri und der rabbinischen Gleichnisse," *ZNW*, LIX (1968), 33f.

2. He is incorrect in saying that Mark is least allegorical. The indications of the identity of the son and the prophets are stronger in Mark than in Matthew and Luke.
3. The application of Psalm 118,23 to the events described in Mark 12,9 would cause Psalm 118,23 to work against the sequence in Psalm 118,22, which speaks of one who was rejected and then exalted. The situation in Mark 12,9 is rather of a group who have tried to exalt themselves and will be punished and rejected by God. Obviously Psalm 118,23 refers to the events of Psalm 118,22 and states that this reversal of fortunes is from God and is pleasing to his people.
4. His interpretation emphasizes Psalm 118,23 to the neglect of Psalm 118,22.
5. The wordplay makes the application of the quotation to the son definite.

Consequently, the parable must be seen as referring to Jesus, and he is presented as making a forceful charge against, and a warning to, the religious authorities.

The force of this warning is strengthened when one realizes the eschatological implications in the story. The Qumran writings have revealed the significance of the concept Son of God (if not the title itself) with respect to the end time for some circles at least[110]. An analysis of the stone testimonia will show that Daniel 2,45 and Isaiah 28,16 were understood eschatologically, if not more specifically messianically, in pre-Christian Judaism and that Isaiah 28,16 and 8,14 had already been connected[111]. This may seem irrelevant at first glance, but if there are allusions to Daniel 2,45 and Isaiah 8,14 in Matthew 21,44 ||[112], then the eschatological tone of the end of the parable is important. The background of Psalm 118,22 is obviously more significant, but the evidence here is not as precise as one would like. In the rabbinic writings this

---

[110] *Supra*, pp. 85–86.
[111] On Dan. 2,45 see Josephus, *Antiq.* X.210; Tanch B תרומה 6 (Cf. תולדות 20 and עקב 8); PRE. 32; NmR XIII.14; and Yalkut Shimoni on Zech. 4,7. On Isaiah 28,16 see the LXX translation, the targum, IQS V.5; VIII.5f.; IQH VI.25–27; and VII.8b–9; cf. LvR XVII.7; DtR III.13; and EcclR III.8.2. On the connection between Isaiah 8,14 and 28,16, note the similarity between Isaiah 8,8 and 28,15 and 18 and between Isaiah 8,15 and 28,13, and note the reframing of Isaiah 8,14 with material from 28,16 in the LXX. In J. D. Eisenstein's *Ozar Midrashim: A Library of Two Hundred Minor Midrashim* (New York: Reznick, Menschel & Co., 1928), p. 216b, there are allusions to both Isaiah texts in the same context. See also my "I Peter II.1–10: Its Formation and Literary Affinities," *NTS*, XXIV (1978), 99–100. On Isaiah 8,14, cf. b Sanh 38a. The Targum of Zechariah also interprets the cornerstone of the Messiah in 4,7 and 10,4. Obviously, not all of this material is early enough for our purposes, but the material from the LXX, Qumran, and Josephus will provide firm evidence. The later witnesses may be viewed as providing corroboration.
[112] *Supra*, p. 68.

verse is understood variously as referring to Abraham[113], Jacob[114], Israel[115], an anonymous individual[116], and David[117]. Raschi, the medieval Jewish scholar, interpreted the verse of the Messiah[118], and some would argue on the basis of the Targum of Psalm 118 that this understanding is pre-Christian[119]. While one might suspect that this understanding is pre-Christian, it cannot be satisfactorily demonstrated. One can safely say that Psalm 118, as indeed the rest of the Hallel psalms, was understood eschatologically in rabbinic and pre-Christian Judaism[120]. One can easily see, therefore, that both stone sayings would have heightened the eschatological flavor of the parable.

If this is the case, then the parable and quotations provide a pointed, but indirect claim that Jesus is the eschatological Deliverer from God[121]. The reasons for the anger of the Jewish authorities are obvious, and if authentic, the parable and quotation could easily serve as the basis of the question of the high priest in Mark 14,61 as to whether or not Jesus was the Christ, the Son of the Blessed.

The quotation of Psalm 118,22 is important as well because of its

---

[113] PRE 24.

[114] MPs 118.20 and Eisenstein, *Ozar Midrashim*, p. 137a (although the interpretation is a bit muddled). It is surprising to find an adaptation of the parable in which the descendants of Abraham and Isaac were rejected, which is similar to our parable, used in connection with Psalm 118,22! See *supra*, p. 25.

[115] EsR VII.10 and MPs 118.21.

[116] MPs 118.21.

[117] b Pes 119a; MPs 118.21; and ExR XXXVII.1.

[118] In his comment on Micah 5,1. Cf. S-B, I, 876.

[119] E. g., Bertil Gärtner, "שילא als Messiasbezeichnung," *SEA*, XVIII–XIX (1953–1954), 98–108; cf. Eisentein, *Ozar Midrashim*, p. 217a. Gärtner argued that the Targum on Psalm 118,22 should be understood messianically because אבן was changed to שליא, but one cannot be certain.

The attempt by Michael Giesler (*Christ the Rejected Stone*, Pamplona; Ediciones Universidad de Navarra, 1974, pp. 34–47 and 96) to find several items or persons to which Psalm 118 and the stone refer is unacceptable. While there are reasons to suggest that Psalm 118 may have arisen in the context of rebuilding the temple in the post-exilic time (Cf. Ezra 3,1–13), the attempts to see references in the stone to Nehemiah, the law, or the restored walls have no basis. The way in which various texts are connected is methodologically suspect.

[120] Joachim Jeremias, *The Eucharistic Words of Jesus* (London: SCM Press, 1966), pp. 256–261; S-B, I, 849–850. Note especially b Pes 119a and MPs 118.22. In the antiphonal chant of the latter, Psalm 118,24 is understood as referring to the day of redemption which ends all enslavement.

[121] Klauck, *Allegorie und Allegorese*, p. 309; Hubaut, pp. 136–140; Pesch, p. 221; Weiser, pp. 51–52; and Xavier Léon-Dufour, "La parabole des vignerons homicides," *Sciences Ecclésiastiques*, XVII (1965), 378–379.

similarity to the rejection-exaltation theme in Jesus' passion predictions (especially Mark 8,31 || and 9,12||; but also 9,31 || and 10,33||), and one's assessment of this theme is to some extent involved in an evaluation of these sayings. It is beyond our scope to go into a discussion of the passion predictions[122], but it should be said that even apart from them it is probable that Jesus did expect a violent death[123]. The death of John the Baptist and the continued hostilities with the religious authorities would have indicated the result of his opposition to the established religion. The prediction of death in Mark 8,31 has a special claim to validity in that the saying is inseparably bound to the context of the rebuke of Peter as Satan, a description which would hardly have been placed on the lips of Jesus later[124]. The argument has frequently been made that the basis of these passion predictions is Isaiah 53[125], but recently it has been recognized that at least the sayings in Mark and Luke show dependence on Psalm 118,22[126]. This may be a case of "both . . . and" rather than "either . . . or" since both Old Testament passages may have influenced these sayings[127]. Both Old Testament texts play an important role in the Gospels and the thinking of the early Church, and some scholars have

---

[122] See especially Morna D. Hooker, *The Son of Man in Mark* (Montreal: McGill University Press, 1967), pp. 103–140; Frederick Houk Borsch, *The Son of Man in Myth and History* (London: SCM Press, 1967), pp. 329–353; H. E. Todt, *The Son of Man in the Synoptic Tradition* (London: SCM Press, 1965), pp. 141–221; Georg Strecker, "The Passion and Resurrection Predictions in Mark's Gospel," *Interpretation*, XXII (1968), 421–444; and Norman Perrin, "Towards an Interpretation of the Gospel of Mark," *Christology and a Modern Pilgrimage*, ed. Hans Dieter Betz (Claremont: New Testament Colloquium, 1971), 14–30.

[123] Joachim Jeremias and Walther Zimmerli, "παῖς Θεοῦ," *TDNT*, V, 713; Hubert Frankemölle, "Hat Jesus sich selbst verkündet?" *Bibel und Leben*, XIII (1972), 202–204; Hans Schürmann, "Wie hat Jesus seinen Tod bestanden und verstanden?" *Orientierung an Jesus*, ed. Paul Hoffmann (Freiburg: Herder, 1973), 325–363; Jeremias, *New Testament Theology*, pp. 277–286; Hans Kessler, *Die theologische Bedeutung des Todes Jesu* (Düsseldorf: Patmos-Verlag, 1970), pp. 229–235; and Virgil Howard, "Did Jesus Speak About his own Death?" *CBQ*, XXXIX (1973), 515–527.

[124] Jeremias and Zimmerli, p. 715; Hooker, p. 104; and Taylor, pp. 374–380.

[125] Jeremias and Zimmerli, *passim*. See the argument against this possibility in Morna D. Hooker's *Jesus and the Servant* (London: SPCK, 1959), pp. 92–97.

[126] Tödt, pp. 162–170; Fuller, p. 118; Hooker, *The Son of Man in Mark*, p. 114. The synonymous use of ἀποδοκιμασθῆναι in Mark 8,31 and ἐξουδενηθῆναι in 9,12 is paralleled by the use of both words to translate מאס in Psalm 118,22 (Luke 20,17 and Acts 4,11).

[127] Matthew Black, "The 'Son of Man' Passion Sayings in the Gospel Tradition," *ZNW*, LX (1969), 4.

drawn connections between the stone and servant imageries[128]. Certainly both contain the themes of rejection and exaltation. Whatever else is said, however, the dominant role in the formation of the passion predictions belongs to Psalm 118,22, especially as these sayings are framed in the accounts of Mark and Luke. For example, Mark 8,31 is almost a *paraphrase* of Psalm 118,22: *The stone which the builders rejected* – i. e., "It is necessary for the Son of Man to suffer and be rejected by the religious authorities and to be killed;" – *This has become the head of the corner* – i. e., ". . . To arise after three days."

The reason for the use of the psalm quotation with the parable is plain enough in that it emphasizes the climax of the parable, but no suggestion has been given to account for its use in the passion predictions and with the Son of Man concept[129]. Without getting into the complex questions of the latter, it appears that the bridge between Psalm 118,22 and the Son of Man was the stone of Daniel 2, which corresponds to the Son of Man in the parallel chapter 7. Psalm 118 was frequently used in Jewish festivals, and if one had made the obvious identification of the two chapters in Daniel, the adaptation of the language of Psalm 118,22 to speak of the Son of Man would have been easy[130]. The discussion in scripture of the rejected stone provided the means for speaking of the rejection of the Son of Man and thus may help explain the use of δεῖ and γέγραπται with the Son of Man in Mark 8,31[131]. Quite apart from the

---

[128] See *supra*, p. 64 n. 85. Ellis, *The Gospel of Luke*, p. 233; and Gärtner, pp. 101–108, used the Targum on Psalm 118,22–29, but even if this targum is understood as referring to David, it does offer a basis for the connection between the two images. Of special importance is Zech. 3,8–9 where the stone in question is physical proof that Yahweh's Servant, the Branch, (צמח) would come. The targum interprets this as "my Servant the Messiah." At least one must admit that the two imageries are parallel. See also Borsch, pp. 333–334.

[129] Gaston, p. 400, spoke of the great importance of Psalm 118,22 for the understanding of Jesus' death, but asserted that the verse has nothing to do with the Son of Man.

[130] Philip Carrington, *According to Mark* (Cambridge: Cambridge University Press, 1960), pp. 249–250, did note the connection between Dan. 2 and 7. With Hooker, *The Son of Man*, pp. 114f., Jesus did not derive the idea of rejection from the psalm since it was inherent in the Son of Man concept. On the connection of Dan. 2 and 7 in the ministry of Jesus, see R. T. France, *Jesus and the Old Testament* (London: The Tyndale Press, 1971), pp. 98–99.

[131] See Borsch, pp. 333f. and cf. Tödt, pp. 187f. The latter traced the use of δεῖ to Dan. 2,28. The attempt of W. J. Bennett, Jr. ("The Son of Man Must . . .," *NovT*, XVII, 1975, 119–129) to reject Psalm 118,22 as the basis of δεῖ fails because he

passion predictions, if Jesus used the stone imagery of himself, the identification of the stone and the Son of Man in Daniel is probably the reason. The use of the proverb based on Daniel 2 in Matthew 21,44 ‖ provides a further confirmation of this connection. If this suggestion is correct, it shows how fundamentally important the stone of Psalm 118,22 was for Jesus and why it was used so frequently by the Church. In fact, Psalm 118,22 with its rejection-exaltation theme may be the basic form of the passion prediction.

If Jesus anticipated his death, the fact that the parable speaks of the killing of the son (and the rejection of the stone) could have its origin in Jesus or in the early Church. The second part of the quotation adds that God has made the rejected stone the head of the corner and that this is pleasing to his people. It is often said that this is the missing reference to the resurrection and that this feature has its origin in the Church. Two points should be mentioned. First of all, it is by no means clear that the resurrection is meant. Certainly it was understood in this way later by the Church (Acts 4,11; I Peter 2,7), but in the context of Jesus, all that the quotation says is that God will make (or has made) the rejected stone the most important part of the building. Nothing more may be meant than the rejection-exaltation theme which occurs frequently in both testaments to express God's vindication of the righteous oppressed[132]. Certainly this is all that is explicit. Jeremias went so far as to interpret the exaltation of the stone as the parousia[133], but this has little basis. It is

---

ignored the rabbinic understanding of "builders" as the religious leaders of the community. See *supra*, p. 96 n. 102.

[132] See C. F. D. Moule, "From Defendant to Judge – and Deliverer: An Inquiry into the Use and Limitations of the Theme of Vindication in the New Testament," *Bulletin of Studiorum Novi Testamenti Societas*, III, (1952), 40–53 (reprinted in his *The Phenomenon of the New Testament*, Naperville: Alec R. Allenson, 1967, pp. 82–99).

[133] Joachim Jeremias, "λίθος, λίθινος," *TDNT*, IV, 274f. Is the building in this context the house of Israel in Isaiah 5,7? Donahue, p. 127, viewed the quotation as saying that Jesus is the cornerstone of the new temple and that the new temple is the ἄλλοις who are the nucleus of the new community. The conclusion for him of this whole section of Mark is that the role of the temple has been brought to a close. While the theme of the replacement of the temple by Jesus is legitimate, it seems that Donahue's treatment is much more explicit than the wording of Mark warrants. Rather than a reference to the new temple, it seems that a general reference to the people of God as the building of God is all that is intended. Cf. Isaiah 54,11f. and I Cor. 3,9. Often with this imagery, however, the idea of a spiritual temple is not far behind.

Derrett, "The Stone that the Builders Rejected," interpreted Matthew 21,42 ‖ as referring to the stone which binds the two walls of a house together, serves as an

dependent on his acceptance of the stone as the keystone and the building as the future temple, neither of which is certain. There is no indication that the position of the stone is of significance for the interpretation. It is sufficient to stress that the stone is the most important part of God's building. I would add parenthetically that the evidence used to interpret a cornerstone in the Bible as a top stone or keystone is weak and late[134].

Secondly, it should not be excluded that Jesus spoke of vindication and/or resurrection. M. Black mentioned that there may well be a pre-Easter "exaltation-resurrection" *didache* traceable to the mind of the Lord himself[135], and M. Hooker pointed out that it would be strange if Jesus spoke of his death without reference to resurrection since this would indicate the defeat of God's purposes[136]. The Synoptists and their readers no doubt understood the quotation as referring to the resurrection, but regardless of whether the quotation was used first by Jesus or the Church, this meaning is only implicit in this context.

In our study thus far we have seen that none of the features of the parable indicates its origin, and this is true of the stone quotation as well. There are slight considerations here that may show that the parable goes back to Jesus. If there is validity to the explanation of the

---

ornament, a shelter, and a part of the parapet which every house must have. To him this explains Matthew 21,44 ||. If one trips on the stone he would fall off the roof; if one leans on the stone (and it were too light) it would fall on passers-by. This interpretation is fanciful and has little in its favor: 1) it is extremely doubtful that κεφαλὴ γωνίας refers to a stone on top of the wall (see the next note); 2) the OT texts adduced do not prove what Derrett claimed for them (p. 181 n. 2) – in fact they militate against the view proposed; 3) the identification of the stone in Matthew 21,42|| with that in 21,44|| in the structural plan of a building is unwarranted; 4) the destruction caused by the stone in 21,44|| cannot refer to one falling off a building or one pushing stones on passersby.

[134] See R. J. McKelvey, *The New Temple* (Oxford: Oxford University Press, 1969), pp. 195–204; and my unpublished Ph. D. dissertation, *The Christological Stone Testimonia in the New Testament,* University of St. Andrews, 1973, pp. 290–300.

[135] Black, "The 'Son of Man' Passion Sayings in the Gospel Tradition," 4–8. He drew attention particularly to the Isaianic theme of the final triumph of the servant, the Targum of Hosea 6,1–2, and the Johannine "Son of Man" sayings. Jeremias and Zimmerli, p. 715, also thought that the core of the predictions of glorification are from a pre-Easter tradition. If ἐγενήθη is not simply due to the use of the LXX, it may be the equivalent of the prophetic perfect. (See Matthew Black, "The Christological Use of the Old Testament in the New Testament," *NTS*, XVIII, 1971–1972, 13, n. 3.)

[136] Hooker, *The Son of Man,* p. 115; see also Taylor, p. 378; Borsch, pp. 350f; and Léon-Dufour, p. 389.

connection between Psalm 118,22 and the Son of Man, the presumption is that this connection was made by Jesus because he is virtually the only one who uses "Son of Man" as a title[137]. Further indicatons are that the introductory formula to the quotation (ἀνέγνωτε) also occurs only on the lips of Jesus[138] and that the claims put forward are veiled and indirect.

With regard to the other stone saying, our discussion above showed that Matthew 21,44 is not an interpolation from Luke. The failure to include this verse in the text of Matthew leads to a misunderstanding of the Matthean account of the parable as can be seen in the studies of W. Trilling and A. Suhl where it was suggested that Matthew is not concerned with christology[139]. Matthew has not, however, shifted the focus from christology to ecclesiology. With the inclusion of 21,44, the Matthean account turns on two directly related foci just as the accounts of Mark and Luke[140]. These two foci are rejection and accountability (or judgment). Stated differently, the parable warns that the Kingdom will be transferred because of the rejection of God's final and special envoy. Matthew 21,43 emphasizes the transferral, and 21,44 emphasizes the importance of the rejected son/stone in that he will bring destruction on those who work against him. These two verses could stem from the tradition as an attempt to underline the meaning of the parable, but nothing prohibits viewing them as explications of Jesus and in fact such explications could have been used effectively in the original telling of the parable. If one compares the Matthean form of the parable with the juridical parable in II Samuel 12,1–12, one will find that they are quite similar from first to last: the parable itself, the judgment expressed by

---

[137] See the discussions of the Son of Man in C. F. D. Moule, *The Origin of Christology* (Cambridge: Cambridge University Press, 1977), pp. 11–22; Longenecker, pp. 82–93; Ragnar Leivestad, "Exit the Apocalyptic Son of Man," *NTS*, (1971–1972), 243–267; and Barnabas Lindars, "Re-Enter the Apocalyptic Son of Man," *NTS*, XXII (1976), 52–72.

[138] See E. Earle Ellis, "Midrash, Targum and New Testament Quotations," *Neotestamentica et Semitica*, ed. E. Earle Ellis and Max Wilcox (Edinburgh: T. & T. Clark, 1969), p. 67. Possibly this shows a rabbinic distinction between "reading" and "understanding." See David Daube, *The New Testament and Rabbinic Judaism* (London: Athlone Press, 1956), pp. 432 and 435. The introductory formula is non-Markan (cf. Taylor, p. 476), and one can only wonder at Trilling's statement that it conforms to the literary style of Christian scribes (*Christusverkündigung in den synoptischen Evangelien*, p. 178).

[139] Trilling, *Christusverkündigung in den synoptischen Evangelien*, pp. 181–182; Suhl, pp. 141–142.

[140] Cf. Kazmierski, p. 133.

the hearers, the reversal so that the hearers are accused, and a different judgment by the author of the parable[141].

B. Lindars proposed that the reference to the stone in Daniel 2 (which stands for the Jewish nation) suggests that in this second quotation, Christian exegetes have transferred the image to the Church as the new people of God[142]. His basis for this theory is not at all clear since he did not include the verse in the Matthean account and in Luke this saying follows the christological use of Psalm 118,22. Whether one follows the account of Matthew or Luke makes little difference. If the author of either account intended that the second stone saying should be understood differently from the first, he gave no indication that would convey this to the reader.

The second stone saying is, therefore, a statement emphasizing the importance of the one referred to as a stone. Opposition to him will lead to destruction. For both Matthew and Luke, the saying is a broader christological saying[143]. It is not an interpretation of the quotation of Psalm 118,22[144], nor is it even primarily a change of emphasis[145]. While Psalm 118,22 underscores the importance of the son/stone and the rejection by the builders, the proverb continues these thoughts by illustrating the fate of those who are at odds with the son/stone. The messianic associations of Daniel 2 placed in this context would have altered the meaning of the rabbinic proverb. The latter spoke of the destruction that Israel will bring upon the other nations. In the New

---

[141] Cf. Flusser, p. 147, and on the pattern of the juridical parable, see Yee, p. 34.

[142] Lindars, *New Testament Apologetic*, p. 184. The Jewish proverb in EsR VII.10 understands the stone as Israel too and is likely the origin of the saying, but there still is no reason to interpret the stone in the parable context as the Church.

[143] Jeremias, "λίθος, λίθινος," p. 276. Jeremias' interpretation (*Golgotha*, Heft I, *Angellos*, Leipzig: Eduard Pfeiffer, 1926, pp. 79–80) of this saying as an allusion to the "holy rock" imagery is without foundation. His further understandings of Luke 20,18b as a stone that falls referred to in the Testament of Solomon and of Luke 20,18a as an attack against the stone (*πίπτειν ἐπί*) are also without foundation and are the result of his forcing the meaning "keystone" upon these verses. Discussions of the "holy rock" imagery and the location of the cornerstone may be found in my unpublished Ph. D. dissertation, pp. 207–211 and 290–300.

[144] *Contra* Traugott Holtz, *Untersuchungen über die alttestamentlichen Zitate bei Lukas* (Berlin: Akademie-Verlag, 1968), p. 161.

[145] *Contra* Martin Rese, *Alttestamentliche Motive in der Christologie des Lukas* (Gütersloh: Gütersloher Verlagshaus Gerd Mohn, 1969), p. 172. With Rese, the proverb is part of the citation, but it does not evidence the freedom of Luke in the application of scripture as he suggested. His omission of Matthew 21,44 did not permit a proper analysis.

Testament, the proverb still speaks of destruction for those who arrange themselves against God's chosen, but in this case, the chosen one is the Messiah. While this is stated as a general maxim, the allusion to Daniel 2 probably indicates that the destruction envisaged is the final judgment[146]. As the son in the parable and the stone in the quotation of Psalm 118,22, the stone in this saying occupies a position of unparalleled importance in the purposes of God. The implicit message of the parable and both quotations is that one's success depends on his or her response to the person intended by the son and stone images.

The parable as a unit

We have considered the individual features of the parable, but it remains to look at the parable as a whole. It is not precise to describe the parable as a graphic presentation of the course of salvation-history since this would require a much fuller treatment similar to that in Acts 7. The content of the parable is basically a prophetic message. Attention is focused on the prophetic era and the refusal of the leaders to respond to God's message is indicated[147].

As several others have pointed out, the message of the parable is the same as that of the lament over Jerusalem (Matthew 23,37–38/Luke 13,34–35)[148]. The context of the lament and the exact time meant when Jesus would be greeted with Psalm 118,26 are uncertain. It is also ambiguous as to who was meant by "Jerusalem," but the reference may have been to Jerusalem as the official seat of the Jewish hierarchy[149]. The important features of the lament are clear however. The prophets have been rejected and killed, and now one with the authority to gather the "children" under his own keeping is being rejected as well. Judgment will follow (Jer. 12,7 and 22,5), and the rejected one will in some way be restored. This restoration is expressed through Psalm 118,26, a verse which had messianic connotations in pre-Christian Judaism[150]. The

---

[146] Jeremias, "λίθος, λίθινος," p. 276.

[147] See *supra*, pp. 77–80.

[148] Dodd, p. 131; Geraint Vaughan Jones, *The Art and Truth of the Parables* (London: SPCK, 1964), p. 95; Josef Blank, "Die Sendung des Sohnes," *Neues Testament und Kirche*, ed. Joachim Gnilka (Freiburg: Herder, 1974), 24.

[149] See Charles W. F. Smith, *The Jesus of the Parables* (rev. ed.; Philadelphia: United Church Press, 1975), p. 135.

[150] MPs 118.22. See Jeremias, *The Eucharistic Words of Jesus*, pp. 256–261; S–B, I, 849–850; and *supra*, p. 99. See also Daube, pp. 20–23; Gundry, *The Use of the*

parable says in pictorial form what the lament says more expressly. It seems that this similarity is intentional and that the lament and the parable both have the same origin[151]. The use of Psalm 118 at the end of both can hardly be due to coincidence; rather, it reflects the opinion that the last of Psalm 118 was associated with the end time and was formative for the one who spoke these words.

As we have seen, no feature of the parable serves as the key which designates the origin. The usual objections to the authenticity of the parable have lost their force. The rabbinic evidence has verified both the form and the details, and the Qumran evidence has obviated Kümmel's objections about the title "Son of God". One's evaluation of the authenticity of this parable depends to some extent upon his or her whole approach to the Gospel tradition, and particularly to the passion predictions and the lament over Jerusalem. If the passion predictions and the lament over Jerusalem are rejected, the parable probably will be too. If one does decide that the parable stems from the post-resurrection community, he or she must see it as going back at least to the primitive stages of the Palestinian Church[152]. The wordplay, the Semitisms, the rabbinic parallels, and the whole tenor of the parable make this unquestionable[153]. Every indication of the parable and the Gospel tradition is that we are dealing with the very basic strata of Christianity. If this parable comes from the early Church, it comes from the very earliest days when the Church was condemning only the Jewish leaders. It should be clear, however, that if one rejects the dominical origin of this

---

Old Testament in St. Matthew's Gospel pp. 40–43; and Eduard Lohse, "Hosiana," *NovT*, VI (1963), 113–119. Lindars' attempted reconstruction (*New Testament Apologetic*, pp. 172–173) of the use of Psalm 118 in Christian apologetic is subject to several questions and his interpretation of Luke 13,35 is very doubtful. He assumed that ὁ ἐρχόμενος refers to someone other than the speaker because of the introduction to the psalm quotation (οὐ μὴ ἴδητέ με ἕως ἥξει ὅτε εἴπητε). This view requires that ἥξει be understood as referring to the coming of another, but every indication is that this is an impersonal designation of time (cf. B–A–G, p. 344). The parallel account in Matthew confirms this interpretation. Certainly this is what Luke intended since he considered that Jesus was referring to himself.

[151] Trilling, *Das wahre Israel*, p. 56 n. 9, assumed that the wording of the lament has influenced the wording of the parable in Matthew, but that the wording of the two passages is similar does not prove that one saying has been derived from the other.

[152] *Contra* Steck, pp. 269–272, who attempted to view the parable as from the Hellenistic Christian tradition.

[153] Henry J. Cadbury, *The Making of Luke-Acts* (London: SPCK, 1961), p. 152; and Hengel, "Das Gleichnis von den Weingärtnern Mc 12,1–12 im Lichte der Zenonpapyri und der rabbinischen Gleichnisse," 34.

parable, he or she does so because of presuppositions about the nature of the Gospels or because of the results from studies elsewhere and not because of any element in the parable itself. There is nothing in the parable that is not in keeping with the ministry of Jesus.

One may read the parable as from the *Sitz im Leben der Kirche*, but for me there is little question that the parable stems from the *Sitz im Leben Jesu*. With a significant number of other scholars, I would say that the grounds for denying the parable to Jesus are insufficient[154]. More important are several factors that I would view as pointing to Jesus as the author:

1) In the New Testament the method of teaching in parables is confined to the earthly Jesus. The early Church dropped the parabolic form and spoke openly and propositionally[155].
2) This parable is hardly the work of a group. While there have been later additions, the basic form of the parable stems from an expert in parable construction[156]. Indeed, it is one of the most artistic of the parables with its reversal and the force with which it makes its point. In the context of Jesus' life, the parable is as forceful and powerful as any. Placed, however, in the later context of the early Church after the events of the cross and resurrection, it is rather limp and without force. The speech of Peter in Acts 4,10–12 reveals how the Church used Psalm 118,22 with force.
3) The introductory formula to the quotation uses ἀνέγνωτε which occurs only on the lips of Jesus.
4) The images of the son and judgment, particularly in the Matthean account, are too imprecise to be *vaticinia ex eventu*. Even with the citation of Psalm

---

[154] Besides Dodd, Jeremias, and van Iersel, see Lohmeyer, *Das Evangelium des Markus*, p. 249; Hengel, "Das Gleichnis von den Weingärtnern Mc 12,1–12 im Lichte der Zenonpapyri und der rabbinischen Gleichnisse," pp. 31f.; Hubaut, pp. 11 and 127f.; and his "La parabole des vignerons homicides: son authenticité, sa visée première," *Revue Theologique de Louvain*, VI (1975), 51–61; Pesch, p. 221; Klauck, pp. 309f.; Weder, pp. 150f.; Mussner, p. 132; Weiser, pp. 50f.; Léon-Dufour, *passim;* Frankemölle, "Hat Jesus sich selbst verkündet?" pp. 196f.; Rafael Silva, "La parábola de los renteros homicidas," *Compostellanum*, XV (1970), pp. 349f.; and Anton Fridrichsen, "Til Lignelsen om de onde Vingartnere," *Svensk Teologisk Kvartalskrift*, IV (1928), 355–361. Of course numerous other scholars have accepted the authenticity of the parable as well. Of the detailed studies that have been done on this parable, where people have expressed themselves on the subject, only Jülicher, Kümmel, Blank, Merli, Carlston, and Gnilka (*Das Evangelium nach Markus*, Zürich: Benzinger Verlag, 1979, II, 148) have assigned the parable completely to the early Church.

[155] Anselm Schulz, *Nachfolgen und Nachahmen* (München: Kösel-Verlag, 1962), p. 43; and Hengel, "Gleichnis von den Weingärtnern Mc 12,1–12 im Lichte der Zenonpapyri und der rabbinischen Gleichnisse," 36.

[156] Hengel, "Das Gleichnis von den Weingärtnern Mc 12,1–12 im Lichte der Zenonpapyri und der rabbinischen Gleichnisse," 35; and Burkitt, p. 321.

118,22, there is nothing on the significance of the death of Jesus and the all important reference to the resurrection is missing. If this were an early Church product, some reference to both would have been included[157].
5) The slant of the parable against the Jewish leaders rather than the nation as a whole (or the unbelieving element) is more in keeping with Jesus' message than that of the Church.
6) Most important is that the message of the parable, the wordplay, and the place of Psalm 118,22 in the passion predictions and the lament over Jerusalem and its connections with the title "Son of Man" are much too complex and subtle to be accidental or the work of a "creative community." One would have to assume a rather deliberate and highly sophisticated endeavor to accept that these nuances are the work of the community.

The message of the parable is the same in all three accounts. It is first and foremost a judgment parable similar to the message of the Old Testament prophets, but it has christological implications. One should not seek to find more in this christological element than is there, but nor can one neglect the implicit υἱὸς τοῦ Θεοῦ christology, the rejection-exaltation theme, or the place of importance accorded the son and stone. At least to a certain extent it is correct to say that this is not so much the Parable of the Wicked Tenants as it is the Parable of the Rejected Son[158]. The parable is an accusation and a threat against the Jewish leaders, but at the same time it is a veiled claim of Jesus to be the authoritative and decisive representative from God. More than likely, the Jewish leaders knew to whom reference was made by the son and the stone, but a parable would hardly have served as grounds for a political charge.

If the parable is from Jesus, there is a significant corollary that should be mentioned. The Church's use of the stone testimonia, which are among the most important Old Testament passages in the New Testament, has its origin in Jesus' application of Psalm 118,22 to himself. While Isaiah 28,16 and Daniel 2,45 were already popular in Judaism, the church adopted Psalm 118,22 as a resurrection apologetic because Jesus

---

[157] J. A. T. Robinson, "The Parable of the Wicked Husbandmen: A Test of Synoptic Relationships," *NTS*, XXI (1974–1975), 445, pointed out that this parable is not applied to Christians awaiting the parousia as other parables of responsibility. One can only wonder at the suggestion of Marie-Louise Gubler (*Die frühesten Deutungen des Todes Jesu*, Freiburg: Universitätsverlag, 1977, pp. 83–84) that the parable provides explicit reflection on the death of Jesus as an event in the past. If the parable provided such reflection, surely some mention would be made of the soteriological effect of the death.

[158] As suggested by Black, "The Christological Use of the Old Testament in the New Testament," 13; and Frankemölle, "Hat Jesus sich selbst verkündet," 201.

had already attracted attention to it. Subsequently, and with the help of the allusions to Daniel 2,45 and Isaiah 8,14, the Isaiah stone texts were joined to Psalm 118,22 by the Church and applied in a variety of ways theologically (Romans 9,32–33; Ephesians 2,20; and I Peter 2,4–8[159]).

---

[159] *Contra* Donahue, p. 125, who suggested that Mark's use of Psalm 118,22–23 stood half-way between the apologetic use in Acts 4,11 and the ecclesiological use in Peter. Note that Barnabas Lindars (*New Testament Apologetic*, p. 174) said Psalm 118,22 hardly warranted its role as a classic text on rejection, but if Jesus used the text first, that would explain its importance for the church. A full discussion of the stone testimonia is available in my unpublished Ph. D. dissertation, *The Christological Stone Testimonia in the New Testament*.

Conclusions

As one can easily see, the Parable of the Wicked Tenants has caused considerable debate. The positions adopted in this study are at several points contrary to what has frequently been suggested for the parable, but the eagerness with which this parable has been read from a post-resurrection perspective has prevented our *hearing* this story as Jesus' audience would have. The alleged difficulties of the form of the story, of the improbability of the events, and of the connection of the stone quotation fade when one views the parable in its Palestinian context. In particular, the stone quotation is integrally related to the parable and shows that the parable stems from an Aramaic-speaking context. There is no reason to doubt and good reason to believe that the parable was told originally by Jesus toward the end of his ministry in the context of his conflict with the Jewish authorities. The artistry and force of the parable make it one of the most important and effective of all of Jesus' parables.

The numerous studies on this parable have led to quite an array of views and certainly one cannot speak of agreement among scholars on many aspects of the discussion. However, it is possible to observe several trends that have emerged in recent years, all of which I think are correct. First, there is increasingly a rejection of the opinion that the Gospel of Thomas account is the original form of the parable. Second, since the studies of Martin Hengel and J. Duncan M. Derrett, objections to the logic or realism of the story in its basic components have disappeared. Third, a significant number of scholars have recognized that the Matthean account is earlier than Mark or Luke or at least that Matthew used a parallel tradition. Fourth, the presence of the wordplay between בן and אבן is regularly accepted now. However, no one, so far as I know, has recognized the importance of the wordplay in the context of Jesus' original hearers. There are several recent studies that have argued that the quotation belonged with the parable originally, but one must also realize the force the quotation would have had with those who saw themselves as part of the vineyard rather than its illegitimate occupants. Fifth, the tendency toward viewing the parable (or some form of it) as an authentic parable of Jesus seems to be the regularly accepted position.

There are also some other lessons to be learned from the study of this parable which should be mentioned. The discussions on parable and allegory and on methodology should underscore that one cannot lay down a hermeneutical grid or a concept of the "form" of a parable to which the parables must be forced to conform. Rather, each of the parables must be approached on its own grounds and in the context of Jesus' original hearers. That is not easy to do, but to hear the parables merely with the meanings that we "know" they have deprives them of much of their force and significance. In addition, the use of Psalm 118 with the parable, with the lament over Jerusalem, and with "Son of Man" in the passion predictions should show how formative Psalm 118 was in Jesus' own thinking. It seems to me that Psalm 118 should rank along with Isaiah 61 and Daniel 7 as providing the framework for his mission.

If our explanation is correct, this parable is of the utmost significance for understanding Jesus and his mission. The parable stands as a threat to the Jewish authorities, but in doing so it stresses the authority of the son, who like the prophets, brings a message from God, but who, unlike the prophets, stands in a unique relation to God and is the final messenger. Rejection of him is disasterous in that one loses participation in God's Kingdom and faces judgment.

There is one other item that is important in the parable. In focusing on the stone quotation and the earliest account, one should not neglect the message of the parable, which, indeed, is the message of much of the Bible, but which many today seem to ignore. The emphasis on responsibility in the context of covenant seems to be the assumption of the parable. The privilege of having the vineyard belongs only to those who produce its fruits.

Appendix

The Wordplay Between בן and אבן

Were it not for the importance of this wordplay in the Parable of the Wicked Tenants, the marshalling of evidence on its behalf would be unnecessary since it is frequently accepted as "traditional."[1] There is evidence from various strata of Judaism that substantiates the label.

In the Old Testament one finds several instances of the wordplay in Exodus 28,9f. (and the parallel passage in Exodus 39) where in the description of the priest's garments stones represent the children of Israel. Two stones on the shoulder-pieces of the ephod were engraved with the names of the children of Israel (the names of six tribes on each stone), and twelve stones on the breastplate represented the twelve tribes as well. Even if the writer had not intended a wordplay, the readers (or listeners) could not have missed the assonance in אבני זכרן לבני ישראל ("stones of remembrance for the children of Israel") in 28,12. See also 28,17, 21; and 39,6, 7, and 14. Similarly in Joshua 4 one again finds that stones are representative of the children of Israel. A man from each of the twelve tribes was to take a stone from the Jordan as a sign to the coming generations. The wordplay is evident in 4,6–7: בניכם ... האבנים ... והיו האבנים האלה לזכרון לבני יראל ("your children ... the stones ... and these stones will be for a memorial to the children of Israel")[2]. Again one finds the wordplay in Lamentations 4,1–2 where אבני־קדש ("Precious stones" or the more traditional "stones of the sanctuary"[3]) is understood figuratively as בני ציון ("the sons of Zion")[4], and it is present also in Zechariah 9,16. Finally, one should note the

---

[1] J. Massingberd Ford, "The Jewel of Discernment," *BZ*, XI (1967), 109.

[2] It is implied that the stones have a double significance. Each stone represented one tribe of Israel, and collectively the stones were a memorial to the coming generations.

[3] J. A. Emerton, "The Meaning of אבני־קדש in Lamentations 4,1," *ZAW*, LXXIX (1967), 233.

[4] *Ibid.*

wordplay in Isaiah 54,11–13 between אבניך and the double occurrence of בניך where the Israelites are viewed as stones in a building. If for the double occurrence of בניך one reads בֹּנָיִךְ ("your builders") for the first and בָּנָיִךְ ("your children") for the second as Christopher North suggested[5], there is a three-way wordplay which shows just how traditional the connection between these words was.

Since אבן is usually retained in the targums, the wordplay between בן and אבן in Exodus 28; 39; Joshua 4; and Isaiah 54 would have been evident to readers of the targums. At times, however, the wordplay has been lost because of the change of אבן to מרגלי ("jewel") as in the Targum on Lamentations 4,1 and in Pseudo-Jonathan on Exodus 28; 39,6 and 14, but the retention of אבנא in Pseudo-Jonathan on Exodus 39,7 was probably due to the wordplay. (In Onkelos, the Fragment Targum, and Neofiti, אבנא is used throughout Exodus 28 and 29.) In several other places the targumists have interpreted אבן as referring to individuals. At Genesis 49,24, Onkelos, the Fragment Targum and Neofiti have understood אבן ישראל ("the stone of Israel") as a reference to the children (or tribes) of Israel. The Targum on Ezekiel 28,14 and 16 understood "stones of fire" as "holy people," and most importantly, the Targum of Psalm 118,22 changed אבן to טליא ("young man, servant or lamb")[6].

The talmudic literature, likewise, verifies the connection between בן and אבן. The wordplay occurs twice in b Semahoth 47b–48a:

> This is an argument from minor to major: if with the stones (אבני) of the altar which do not see and speak, eat or drink because they make peace between Israel and their Father in heaven the Torah declared, "Thou shalt lift no iron tool upon them" (Deut. 27,5), the children (בני) of the Torah, who are an atonement for the world, how much more [should they not lift up an iron tool against each other!] Similarly Scripture declares "Thou shalt build the altar of the Lord thy

---

[5] *The Second Isaiah* (Oxford: Clarendon Press, 1964), pp. 193–195 and 251. North cited IQIs[a] as having this reading, but apparently there has been some mistake. For the first occurrence IQIs[a] has בניך instead of the reported בוניכי but it does have the second occurrence corrected to "builders" by a *waw* written above the word.

[6] The Qumran material has not yielded, as far as I am aware, an example of the wordplay, but there is evidence that בן and אבן were closely related. In IQH f II.8 there is apparently an occurrence of אבן with an apocopated *aleph*. The text reads על חבנים תבחננני (the triple *nun* is the result of dittography) and should be translated "Over the stones you prove me." See Svend Holm-Nielsen, *Hodayot: Psalms from Qumran* (Aarhus: Universitetsforlaget, 1960), p. 262. There are several instances in the scrolls where stones in a building are representative of individuals. See IQH VI.26f.; VII.8f.; IQS VIII.5–9; and IV QpIs[d] (on Isaiah 54,11f.).

God of unhewn stones" (Deut. 27,6) . . . if with stones which do not see or hear, speak or eat or drink . . . must be "whole" before [the Holy One, blessed be He], how much more the children of the Torah . . . must be "whole" before the Holy One, blessed be He.

The rabbinic literature also interprets the mention of stones in several contexts as referring to individuals. See LmR IV.1; ExR XX.9; XLVI.2: and EsR VII.10.

The most illustrative instance of the wordplay, however, is found in Josephus' account of the Jewish War. During the seige of Jerusalem, the Romans used war machines to toss large stones at the Jews on the walls of the city. To counter the effect of this tactic, the Jews placed watchmen on the towers to shout a warning when the stone was in flight. Josephus described this counter-tactic in Bell. V.272:

Watchmen were accordingly posted by them on the towers, who gave warning whenever the engine was fired and the stone in transit, by shouting in their native tongue, "The son is coming" (ὁ υἱὸς ἔρχεται); whereupon those in the line of fire promptly made way and lay down, owing to which precautions the stone passed harmlessly through and fell behind them.

The phrase ὁ υἱὸς ἔρχεται in the "native tongue" has prompted some discussion, but regardless of whether Hebrew or Aramaic was meant, the warning obviously contained a corruption of אבן to בן [7]. If Hebrew were used, the corruption is easily understood[8]. If Aramaic were used, one need only ask if בן would have been a meaningful word to an Aramaic-speaking populace (for whom בר would be the word for "son"). It is doubtful that any Aramaic-speaking person in first century Palestine would have been unaware of the meaning of בן. In the plural forms, the *resh* of בר changes to a *nun*. Even more important, the use of בן in proper names such as שמעון בן כוסבא would have made the word so familiar that all would have known it. The name Simeon ben Kosiba also appears as Simeon bar Kosiba, usually depending upon which language was being used at the time. At both Murabba'at and the Cave

---

[7] H. St. J. Thackeray and others (eds. and trans.), *Josephus, The Loeb Classical Library* (London: William Heineman, 1926–65), III, 285. For a full discussion of the passage, see my unpublished Ph. D. dissertation, *The Christological Stone Testimonia in the New Testament*, University of St. Andrews, 1973, pp. 88–93.

[8] In connection with the wordplay in Matthew 21,42‖, one should remember that all the rabbinic parables are preserved in Hebrew. See David Flusser, *Die rabbinischen Gleichnisse und der Gleichniserzähler Jesus. 1. Teil: Das Wesen der Gleichnisse* (Bern: Peter Lang, 1981), p. 18.

of Letters, however, בר occurs in Hebrew texts[9] and בן occurs in Aramaic texts[10]. At times בן and בר stand beside each other in the same document[11]. Therefore, in trying to cry out "the stone is coming," the *aleph* of אבן would not have been given sufficient stress and the people would have heard בן or something very similar. בן probably became a nickname for the stones so that later there was no attempt to pronounce אבן. Through repetition the cry became so common that it was written down. Josephus has given us a certain example of the wordplay[12].

Not surprisingly, the wordplay between בן and אבן is also reflected in the New Testament. The occurrence of the words for "stone" and "son" in close proximity may be due to coincidence in some cases (Matthew 4,3 ||; 7,9 ||), but the wordplay probably lies behind Luke 19,39–40 ("If these should keep silent, the stones would cry out"), since the parallel account in Matthew 21,15 refers to the ones proclaiming Jesus in the temple as "children."[13] A more definite instance of the wordplay occurs in Matthew 3,9 || in the saying of John the Baptist that "God is able from these stones to raise up children to Abraham" (Matthew 3,9 ||)[14].

The explanation that the wordplay occurs in Matthew 3,9 has been challenged by J. Jeremias. He argued that the Aramaic equivalent of λίθος could be either אבנא or כיפא since λίθος is used in Matthew 3,9 and Mark 15,46 with the meaning "rock" and since the Syriac Gospels

---

[9] Y. Yadin, "The Expedition to the Judean Desert, 1960: Expedition D," *IEJ* (1961), 47. Cf. *DJD*, II, nos. *22, 29, 30*, and *36*.

[10] Y. Yadin, "The Expedition to the Judean Desert, 1961: Expedition D – The Cave of Letters," *IEJ*, XII (1962), 243. Cf. *DJD*, II, nos. *23* verso 1 and 74, 3.

[11] Y. Yadin, "The Expedition to the Judean Desert, 1961: Expedition D – The Cave of Letters," 255. Cf. *DJD*, II, *30*, 32–35.

[12] Matthew Black suggested in private conversation that the connection between בן and אבן may have been even closer since בן may have occurred with a prosthetic *aleph*. See James A. Montgomery, "Notes on Early Aramaic Inscriptions," *JAOS*, LIV (1934), 423; H. A. Brongers and A. S. van der Woude, "Wat is de Betekenis van 'abnayim in Exodus 1,16?" *Nederlandsch Theologisch Tijdschrift*, XX (1966), 250f.; J. Levy, *Chaldäisches Wörterbuch über die Targumim* (Leipzig: Verlag von Baumgartner's Buchhandlung, 1867), p. 6; and Johannis Buxtorfii, *Lexicon Chaldaicum, Talmudicum et Rabbinicum*, ed. Johanne Buxtorfio Filio (Basileae: Ludovici König, 1640), p. 319.

[13] Alan Hugh M'Neile, *The Gospel According to St. Matthew* (London: Macmillan and Co., 1915), p. 301; and Philip Carrington, *According to Mark* (Cambridge: Cambridge University Press, 1960), p. 249.

[14] M'Neile, p. 28; Carrington, p. 249; and Matthew Black, *An Aramaic Approach to the Gospels and Acts* (3d. ed.; Oxford: Clarendon Press, 1967), p. 145 and also pp. 12f. and 194, where mention is made of a possible wordplay between בן and בנה in Matthew 23,31 and Luke 11,48.

always have כיפא (כאפא) for λίθος. He therefore interpreted the saying of the Baptist as a reference to Isaiah 51,1–2 where Abraham is referred to as a rock from which Israelites were hewn[15]. Jeremias' challenge, however, will not stand up under examination. It is doubtful that Isaiah 51,1–2 forms the background of the New Testament saying. Both Matthew and Luke have λίθων τούτων while the LXX in Isaiah 51,1 has στερεὰν πέτραν, and the targum has טינרא instead of כיפא. Even if the passage in Isaiah does underlie the New Testament saying in the sense that Abraham is a quarry from which stones, i. e., Israelites, were dug[16], the stones would be designated by אבניא rather than כיפיא. It is only in Syriac and sometimes the talmudic literature that כיפא is used to designate stones detached from a natural rock formation. In the Hebrew Old Testament, the targums, and the LXX a distinction is maintained between צור / סלע, טינרא / כיפא, and πέτρα on the one hand and אבן, אבנא, and λίθος on the other. Λίθος was used in Matthew 3,9 ‖ and Mark 15,46 ‖ in the normal way to designate stone detached from a natural rock formation, and its only Aramaic equivalent is אבנא. Accordingly, in the Targum on Joshua 4,3–4, אבניא is used of the stones along the Jordan (cf. Matthew 3,9), and in Daniel 6,18 the Aramaic אבנא is used to refer to the stone placed over the opening to the lion's den (cf. Mark 15,46). Thus λίθος is not used with the meaning "rock".

Jeremias' main basis for arguing that כיפא is a possible equivalent of λίθος is that the Syriac New Testament regularly has kyp' (k'p') for λίθος, but this assumes that the Aramaic כיפא and the Syriac kyp' are equivalents. A. F. J. Klijn has pointed out that one cannot use Syriac to reconstruct the Palestinian Aramaic in this instance since a semantic shift has taken place in Syriac[17]. אבנא dropped out of use in Syriac and was replaced by kyp'[18]. The only Aramaic equivalent of λίθος is אבנא, and

---

[15] J. Jeremias, "λίθος, λίθινος," TDNT, IV, 268–270. On the question of the meaning of the OT passage, see N. A. van Uchelen, "Abraham als Felsen (Jes. 51,1)," ZAW, LXXX (1968), 183–191; contra P. A. H. De Boer, "The Rock," Second-Isaiah's Message, Vol. II, Oudtestamentische Studien (Leiden: E. J. Brill, 1956), 58–67, who understood the rock as a reference to God.

[16] Cf. Yalkut Shimoni I, 716 (S–B I, 733).

[17] A. F. J. Klijn, "Die Wörter 'Stein' und 'Felsen' in der syrischen Übersetzung des Neuen Testaments," ZNW, L (1959), 99–105.

[18] 'bn' is used in the Syriac NT only at I Peter 2,8 (for πέτρα!) and in two manuscripts of the Palestinian Syriac Lectionary at Matthew 21,42. kyp' is used for πέτρα in a few passages in the NT and sometimes for צור/ סלע in the Peshitta OT. šw'' is usually used for πέτρα in the Syriac NT. See Klijn, passim.

Matthew 3,9 is a good example of the wordplay between בן and אבן.

With this evidence, one can easily see that the quotation at the end of the Parable of the Wicked Tenants is not illogical and disruptive; rather, it is bound inextricably to the parable through the wordplay.

Bibliography

Monographs and Commentaries

Almeida, Yvan, *L'Opérativité semantique des récits-paraboles*. Louvain: Editions Peeters, 1978.
Aurelio, Tullio, *Disclosures in den Gleichnissen Jesu*. Frankfurt: Peter Lang, 1977.
Beare, Francis Wright, *The Gospel According to Matthew*. New York: Harper & Row, Publishers, 1981.
Black, Matthew, *An Aramaic Approach to the Gospels and Acts*. 3d ed. Oxford: Clarendon Press, 1967.
–, *The Scrolls and Christian Origins*. London: Charles Scribner's Sons, 1961.
Bonnard, Pierre, *L'Evangile selon Saint Matthieu*. Neuchatel: Editions Delachaux & Niestle, 1963.
Bornkamm, Günther, Barth, Gerhard, and Held, Heinz Joachim, *Tradition and Interpretation in Matthew*. London: SCM Press, 1963.
Boucher, Madeleine, *The Mysterious Parable*. Washington: The Catholic Biblical Association of America, 1977.
Brandon, S. G. F., *The Fall of Jerusalem and the Christian Church*. London: SPCK, 1951.
–, *Jesus and the Zealots*. Manchester: Manchester University Press, 1967.
Bruce, Alexander Balmain, *The Parabolic Teaching of Christ*. London: Hodder and Stoughton, 1882.
Bultmann, Rudolf, *The History of the Synoptic Tradition*. Translated by John Marsh. Oxford: Basil Blackwell, 1963.
Burkitt, F. Crawford (ed.), *Evangelion Da-Mepharreshe*. 2 vols. Cambridge: Cambridge University Press, 1904.
Cadoux, A. T., *The Parables of Jesus*. London: James Clarke & Co., n. d.
Carlston, Charles E., *The Parables of the Triple Tradition*. Philadelphia: Fortress Press, 1975.
Carrington, Philip, *According to Mark*. Cambridge: Cambridge University Press, 1960.
Crossan, John Dominic. *Cliffs of Fall*. New York: The Seabury Press, 1980.
–, *In Parables*. New York: Harper & Row, Publishers, 1973.
Daube, David. *The New Testament and Rabbinic Judaism*. London: The Athlone Press, 1956.
Dodd, C. H., *The Parables of the Kingdom*. London: Nisbet & Co., 1936.
Donahue, John R., *Are You the Christ?* Missoula, Montana: Society of Biblical Literature, 1973.
Ellis, E. Earle, *The Gospel of Luke*. London: Nelson, 1966.

Farmer, William R., *The Synoptic Problem*. New York: The Macmillan Company, 1964.
Feldman, Asher, *The Parables and Similes of the Rabbis*. Cambridge: Cambridge University Press, 1904.
Fiebig, Paul, *Altjüdische Gleichnisse und die Gleichnisse Jesu*. Tübingen: Verlag von J. C. B. Mohr (Paul Siebeck), 1904.
–, *Die Gleichnisreden Jesu im Lichte der rabbinischen Gleichnisse des neutestamentlichen Zeitalters*. Tübingen: Verlag von J. C. B. Mohr (Paul Siebeck), 1912.
Findlay, J. Alexander, *Jesus and his Parables*. London: The Epworth Press, 1950.
Flusser, David, *Die rabbinischen Gleichnisse und der Gleichniserzähler Jesus*. 1. Teil: *Das Wesen der Gleichnisse*. Bern: Peter Lang, 1981.
Frankemölle, Hubert, *Jahwebund und Kirche Christi*. Münster: Verlag Aschendorff, 1973.
Fuller, Reginald H., *The Foundations of New Testament Christology*. New York: Charles Scribner's Sons, 1965.
Funk, Robert W., *Language, Hermeneutic, and Word of God*. New York: Harper & Row, Publishers, 1966.
Gaston, Lloyd, *No Stone on Another*. Leiden: E. J. Brill, 1970.
Giesler, Michael, *Christ the Rejected Stone*. Pamplona: Ediciones Universidad de Navarra, 1974.
Gnilka, Joachim, *Das Evangelium nach Markus*. 2 vols. Zürich: Benzinger Verlag, 1979.
Gozzo, Seraphinus M., *Disquisitio critico-exegetica in parabolam N. Testamenti de perfidis vinitoribus*. Romae: Pontificium Athenaeum Anatonianum, 1949.
Gundry, Robert Horton, *Matthew: A Commentary on his Literary and Theological Art*. Grand Rapids: William B. Eerdmans Publishing Company, 1982.
–, *The Use of the Old Testament in St. Matthew's Gospel*. Leiden: E. J. Brill, 1967.
Haenchen, Ernst, *Der Weg Jesu*. Berlin: Alfred Töpelmann, 1966.
Hahn, Ferdinand, *The Titles of Jesus in Christology*. London: Lutterworth Press, 1969.
Hengel, Martin, *The Son of God*. Philadelphia: Fortress Press, 1976.
Hermaniuk, Maxime, *La parabole évangélique*. Louvain: Bibliotheca Alfonsiana, 1947.
Holtz, Traugott, *Untersuchungen über die alttestamentlichen Zitate bei Lukas*. Berlin: Akademie-Verlag, 1968.
Hooker, Morna D., *The Son of Man in Mark*. Montreal: McGill University Press, 1967.
Hubaut, Michel, *La parabole des vignerons homicides*. Cahiers de la *Revue Biblique* 16. Paris: Gabalda, 1976.
Hunter, A. M., *Interpreting the Parables*. London: SCM Press, 1964.
Iersel, B. M. F. van, *"Der Sohn" in den synoptischen Jesusworten*. Leiden: E. J. Brill, 1961.
Jeremias, Joachim, *The Eucharistic Words of Jesus*. London: SCM Press, 1964.
–, *Golgotha*. Heft I, *Angellos*. Leipzig: Eduard Pfeiffer, 1926.
–, *New Testament Theology*. New York: Charles Scribner's Sons, 1971.
–, *The Parables of Jesus*. London: SCM Press, 1963.

Jones, Geraint Vaughan, *The Art and Truth of the Parables*. London: SPCK, 1964.
Juel, Donald, *Messiah and Temple*. Missoula, Montana: Scholars Press, 1973.
Jülicher, A., *Die Gleichnisreden Jesu*. Freiburg i. B.: Akademische Verlagsbuchhandlung von J. C. B. Mohr. Vol. I, 1888; Vol. II, 1889.
Kahlefeld, Heinrich, *Gleichnisse und Lehrstücke im Evangelium*. Frankfurt: Josef Knecht, 1964.
Kazmierski, Carl R., *Jesus the Son of God*. Echter Verlag, 1979.
Kissinger, Warren S., *The Parables of Jesus*. Meteuchen, N.J.: The Scarecrow Press, 1979.
Klauck, Hans-Josef, *Allegorie und Allegorese in synoptischen Gleichnistexten*. Münster: Aschendorff, 1978.
Kretzer, Armin, *Die Herrschaft der Himmel und die Söhne des Reiches*. Stuttgart: Katholisches Bibelwerk, 1971.
Kümmel, Werner Georg, *Promise and Fulfilment*. London: SCM Press, 1957.
Lindars, Barnabas, *New Testament Apologetic*. London: SCM Press, 1961.
Linnemann, Eta, *Parables of Jesus*. Translated by John Sturdy. London: SPCK, 1966.
Lohmeyer, Ernst, *Das Evangelium des Markus*. Göttingen: Vandenhoeck & Ruprecht, 1967.
Lohmeyer, Ernst, and Schmauch, Werner. *Das Evangelium des Matthäus*. Göttingen: Vandenhoeck & Ruprecht, 1967.
Longenecker, R. N., *The Christology of Early Jewish Christianity*. London: SCM Press, 1970.
Lövestam, Evald, *Son and Saviour*. Lund: C. W. K. Gleerup, 1961.
Manson, T. W., *The Teaching of Jesus*. Cambridge: Cambridge University Press, 1935.
McKelvey, R. J., *The New Temple*. Oxford: Oxford University Press, 1969.
North, Christopher R., *The Second Isaiah*. Oxford: Clarendon Press, 1964.
Oesterley, W. O. E., *The Gospel Parables in the Light of their Jewish Backgrounds*. London: SPCK, 1936.
Perkins, Pheme, *Hearing the Parables of Jesus*. New York: Paulist Press, 1981.
Perrin, Norman, *Jesus and the Language of the Kingdom*. Philadelphia: Fortress Press, 1976.
—, *Rediscovering the Teaching of Jesus*. London: SCM Press, 1967.
Pesch, Rudolph, *Das Markusevangelium*. 2 vols. Freiburg: Herder, 1977.
Quispel, G., *Makarius, das Thomasevangelium und das Lied von der Perle*. Leiden: E. J. Brill, 1967.
Rese, Martin, *Alttestamentliche Motive in der Christologie des Lukas*. Gütersloh: Gütersloher Verlagshaus Gerd Mohn, 1969.
Ruager, Sören, *Das Reich Gottes und die Person Jesu*. Frankfurt: Verlag Peter Lang, 1979.
Sanders, E. P., *The Tendencies of the Synoptic Tradition*. Cambridge: Cambridge University Press, 1969.
Schnackenburg, Rudolf, *God's Rule and Kingdom*. Translated by John Murray. London: Nelson, 1963.
Schrage, Wolfgang, *Das Verhältnis des Thomas-Evangeliums zur synoptischen*

Tradition und zu den koptischen Evangelienübersetzungen. Berlin: Verlag Alfred Töpelmann, 1964.

Schramm, Tim, *Der Markus-Stoff bei Lukas*. Cambridge: Cambridge University Press, 1971.

Sciascia, Pius, *Lapis Reprobatus*. Rome: Pontificium Athenaeum Antonianum, 1959.

Smith, B. T. D., *The Parables of the Synoptic Gospels*. Cambridge: Cambridge University Press, 1937.

Smith, Charles W. F., *The Jesus of the Parables*. Rev. ed. Philadelphia: United Church Press, 1975.

Steck, Odil Hannes, *Israel und das gewaltsame Geschick der Propheten*. Neukirchen-Vluyn: Neukirchener Verlag des Erziehungsvereins, 1967.

Stendahl, Krister, *The School of St. Matthew*. Lund: C. W. K. Gleerup, 1954.

Strack, Hermann, and Billerbeck, Paul, *Kommentar zum Neuen Testament aus Talmud und Midrasch*. 6 vols. 4th ed. München: C. H. Beck'sche Verlagsbuchhandlung, 1965.

Strecker, Georg, *Der Weg der Gerechtigkeit*. Göttingen: Vandenhoeck & Ruprecht, 1962.

Suhl, Alfred, *Die Funktion der alttestamentlichen Zitate und Anspielungen im Markusevangelium*. Gütersloh: Gütersloher Verlagshaus Gerd Mohn, 1965.

Taylor, Vincent, *The Gospel According to St. Mark*. London: Macmillan & Co., 1952.

TeSelle, Sallie McFague, *Speaking in Parables: A Study in Metaphor and Theology*. Philadelphia: Fortress Press, 1975.

Tödt, H. E., *The Son of Man in the Synoptic Tradition*. London: SCM Press, 1965.

Trilling, Wolfgang, *Christusverkündigung in den synoptischen Evangelien*. München: Kösel-Verlag, 1969.

–, *Das wahre Israel*. 3d ed. München: Kösel-Verlag, 1964.

Via, Dan Otto, Jr., *The Parables*. Philadelphia: Fortress Press, 1967.

Weder, Hans, *Die Gleichnisse Jesu als Metaphern*. Göttingen: Vandenhoeck & Ruprecht, 1978.

Weiser, Alfons, *Die Knechtsgleichnisse der synoptischen Evangelien*. München: Kösel-Verlag, 1971.

Wilson, R. McL., *Studies in the Gospel of Thomas*. London: A. R. Mowbray & Co., 1960.

Articles

Aland, Kurt, "Neue neutestamentliche Papyri II," NTS, XII (1965–1966), 193–210.

–, "The Significance of the Papyri for Progress in New Testament Research," *The Bible in Modern Scholarship*. Edited by J. Philip Hyatt. Nashville: Abingdon Press, 1965, 325–346.

Bammel, Ernst, "Das Gleichnis von den bösen Winzern (Mc 12,1–9) und das jüdische Erbrecht," *Revue International des Droits de L'Antiquité*, 3me série, VI (1959), 11–17.

Bauer, Johannes B., "Gleichnisse Jesu und Gleichnisse der Rabbinen," *Theologisch-praktische Quartalsschrift,* CXIX (1971), 297–307.

Björck, Gudmund, "Drei Markus-Stellen," *Coniectanea Neotestamentica* I (1936), 1–7.

Black, Matthew, "The Christological Use of the Old Testament in the New Testament," NTS, XVIII (1971–1972), 1–14.

–, "The Parables as Allegory," BJRL, XLII (1959–1960), 273–287.

–, "The 'Son of Man' Passion Sayings in the Gospel Tradition," ZNW, LX (1969), 1–8.

Blank, Josef, "Die Sendung des Sohnes," *Neues Testament und Kirche.* Edited by Joachim Gnilka. Freiburg: Herder, 1974, 11–41.

Brown, Raymond E., "Parable and Allegory Reconsidered," NovT, V (1962), 36–45.

Burkitt, F. C., "The Parable of the Wicked Husbandmen," *Transactions of the Third International Congress for the History of Religions.* Oxford: Clarendon Press, 1908, II, 321–328.

Crossan, John Dominic. "Parable, Allegory, and Paradox," *Semiology and the Parables.* Edited by Daniel Patte. Pittsburgh: The Pickwick Press, 1975, 247–281.

–, "The Parable of the Wicked Husbandmen," JBL, XC (1971) 451–465.

–, "The Servant Parables of Jesus," *Semeia,* I (1974), 17–55.

–, "Structuralist Analysis and the Parables of Jesus," *Semeia,* I (1974), 192–221.

Dehandschutter, B., "La parabole des vignerons homicides (Mc., XII, 1–12) et l'evangile selon Thomas," *Bibliotheca Ephemeridum Theologicarum Lovaniensium,* XXXIV (1974), 203–219.

Derrett, J. Duncan M., "Allegory and the Wicked Vinedressers," JTSns, XXV (1974), 426–432.

–, "Fresh Light on the Parable of the Wicked Vinedressers," *Revue Internationale des Droits de L'Antiquité,* 3me série, X (1963), 11–42.

–, "The Stone that the Builders Rejected," SE, IV. Edited by F. L. Cross. Berlin: Akademie-Verlag, 1965, 180–186.

Dillon, Richard J., "Towards a Tradition-History of the Parables of the True Israel (Matthew 21, 33–22,14)," Bib, XLVII (1966), 1–42.

Doherty, J., "The Murder of the Good Will Ambassadors," *Liguorian,* LI (1963), 48–52.

Dombois, Hans, "Juristische Bemerkungen zum Gleichnis von den bösen Weingärtnern (Mk 12,1–12)," *Neue Zeitschrift für Systematische Theologie und Religionsphilosophie,* VIII (1966), 361–373.

Drury, John, "The Sower, the Vineyard, and the Place of Allegory in the Interpretation of Mark's Parables," JTSns, XXIV (1973), 367–379.

Durand, A., "Life by Death," *Sponsa Regis,* XXXV (1963), 10–17.

Ellis, E. Earle, "Midrash, Targum and New Testament Quotations," *Neotestamentica et Semitica.* Edited by E. Earle Ellis and Max Wilcox. Edinburgh: T. & T. Clark, 1969, 61–69.

Fitzmyer, Joseph A., "The Aramaic Language and the Study of the NT," JBL, XCIX (1980), 5–21.

–, "The Contribution of Qumran Aramaic to the Study of the New Testament," NTS, XX (1973–1974), 382–407.
Flemmig, G., "Die Sünde der bösen Weingärtner (Mc. 12,1–12; Mt. 23,13–33)," *Christentum und Wirklichkeit*, XI (1933), 70–75.
Frankemölle, Hubert. "Hat Jesus sich selbst verkündet?" *Bibel und Leben*, XIII (1972), 184–207.
Fridrischsen, Anton, "Til Lignelsen om de onde Vingartnere," *Svensk Teologisk Kvartalskrift*, IV (1928), 355–361.
Funk, Robert W., "The Parables: A Fragmentary Agenda," *Jesus and Man's Hope II*. Pittsburgh: Pittsburgh Theological Seminary, 1971, pp. 287–303.
–, "Structure in the Narrative Parables of Jesus." *Semeia*, II (1974), 51–73.
Gärtner, Bertil, "טליא als Messiasbezeichnung," SEA, XVIII–XIX (1953–1954), 98–108.
Ginneken, P. van, "Au-dela de l'oedipe? La parabole des vignerons homicides d'un point de vue psychanalytique," *La Foi et le Temps*, IX (1979), 360–383.
Gray, Arthur, "The Parable of the Wicked Husbandmen," *The Hibbert Journal*, XIX (1920–1921), 42–52.
Hauck, Friedrich, "παραβολή," TDNT, V, 744–761.
Hengel, Martin, "Das Gleichnis von den Weingärtnern Mc 12,1–12 im Lichte der Zenonpapyri und der rabbinischen Gleichnisse," ZNW, LIX (1968), 1–39.
Hubaut, Michel, "La parabole des vignerons homicides: son authenticité, sa visée première," *Revue Theologique de Louvain*, VI (1975), 51–61.
Jeremias, Joachim, "Abba," *The Prayers of Jesus*. London: SCM Press, 1967, 11–65.
–, "λίθος, λίθινος," TDNT, IV, 268–280.
Jeremias, Joachim and Zimmerli, Walther, "παῖς Θεοῦ," TDNT, V, 654–717.
Klauck, Hans-Josef, "Das Gleichnis vom Mord im Weinberg (Mk 12,1–12; Mt 21,33–46; Lk 20,9–19)," *Bibel und Leben*, XI (1970), 118–145.
Klijn, A. F. J., "Die Wörter 'Stein' und 'Felsen' in der syrischen Übersetzung des Neuen Testaments," ZNW, L (1959), 99–105.
Kümmel, Werner Georg, "Das Gleichnis von den bösen Weingärtnern (Mark 12,1–9)," *Aux sources de la tradition chrétienne. Mélanges offerts à M. Goguel*. Neuchatel: Delachaux & Niestle S. A., 1950, 120–131.
Léon-Dufour, Xavier, "La parabole des vignerons homicides," *Sciences Ecclésiastiques*, XVII (1965), 365–396.
Lindemann, Andreas, "Zur Gleichnisinterpretation im Thomas-Evangelium," ZNW, LXXI (1980), 214–243.
Lohmeyer, Ernst, "Das Gleichnis von den bösen Weingärtnern (Mark 12,1–12)," ZST, XVIII (1941), 243–259.
Lohse, Eduard, "υἱός, υἱοθεσία," TDNT, VIII, 357–362.
Lowe, Malcolm, "From the Parable of the Vineyard to a Pre-Synoptic Source," NTS, XXVIII (1982), 257–263.
Marshall, I. Howard, "The Divine Sonship of Jesus," *Interpretation*, XXI (1967), 87–103.

Merli, Dino, "La parabola dei vignaioli infedeli," *Bibbia e Oriente*, XV (1973), 97–108.
Mihaly, Eugene, "A Rabbinic Defense of the Election of Israel," HUCA, XXXV (1964), 103–143.
Montefiore, Hugh, "A Comparison of the Parables of the Gospel According to Thomas and of the Synoptic Gospels," NTS, VII (1960–1961), 220–248.
Moule, C. F. D., "From Defendant to Judge –and Deliverer: An Inquiry into the Use and Limitations of the Theme of Vindication in the New Testament," *Bulletin of Studiorum Novi Testamenti Societas*, III (1952), 40–53.
Mussner, Franz, "Die bösen Winzer nach Matthäus 21,33–46." *Antijudaismus im Neuen Testament?* Edited by Willehad Paul Eckert, Nathan Peter Levinson and Martin Stöhr. München: Chr. Kaiser Verlag, 1967, 129–134.
Newell, Jane E. and Raymond R., "The Parable of the Wicked Tenants," NovT, XIV (1972), 226–237.
Ogawa, Akira, "Paraboles de l'Israel Véritable? Reconsideration Critique de Mt. XXI 28–XXII 14," NovT, XXI (1979), 121–149.
Oort, H., "Lucas 20,18b," *Theologisch Tijdschrift*, XLIII (1909), 138–140.
Orchard, Bernard, "J. A. T. Robinson and the Synoptic Problem," NTS, XXII (1976), 346–352.
"Parabola de perfidis vinitoribus," *Collationes Diocesis Tornacensis*, XXXII (1937), 510–514.
Pedersen, Sigfred, "Zum Problem der vaticinia ex eventu (Eine Analyse von Mt. 21,33–46 par; 22,1–10 par.)," ST, XIX (1965), 167–188.
Ricoeur, Paul, "The Bible and the Imagination," *The Bible as a Document of the University*. Edited by Hans Dieter Betz. Chico, California: Scholars Press, 1981, 49–74.
Robinson, J. A. T., "The Parable of the Wicked Husbandmen: A Test of Synoptic Relationships," NTS, XXI (1975), 443–461.
–, "The Use of the Fourth Gospel for Christology Today," *Christ and Spirit*. Edited by Barnabas Lindars and Stephen S. Smalley. Cambridge: Cambridge University Press, 1973, 61–78.
Schoedel, William R., "Parables in the Gospel of Thomas: Oral Tradition or Gnostic Exegesis?" CTM, XLII (1972), 548–560.
Sellin, Gerhard, "Allegorie und 'Gleichnis'," *Zeitschrift für Theologie und Kirche*, LXXV, 1978, 281–335.
Simon, Uriel. "The Poor Man's Ewe-Lamb: An Example of a Juridical Parable," Bib, XLVIII (1967), 207–242.
Silva, Rafael, "La parabola de los renteros homicidas," *Compostellanum*, XV (1970), 319–353.
Snodgrass, Klyne, The Parable of the Wicked Husbandmen: Is the Gospel of Thomas Version the Original?" NTS, XXI (1974), 142–144.
–, "I Peter II. 1–10: Its Formation and Literary Affinities," NTS, XXIV (1978), 97–106.
–, "Western Non-Interpolations," JBL, XCI (1972), 369–379.
Swaeles, R., "L'Arrière-fond scripturaire de Matt. XXI.43 et son lien avec Matt. XXI.44," NTS, VI (1959–1960), 310–313.

Tinsley, E. J., "Parable and Allegory: Some Literary Criteria for the Interpretation of the Parables of Christ," *The Church Quarterly*, III (1970), 32–39.
Trilling, W., "Le Jugement sur le faux Israël (Matthieu 21, 33–46)," *Lectio Divina*, LXIX (1971), 165–189.
Vincent, J. J., "The Parables of Jesus as Self-Revelation," SE, I (1959), 79–99.
Yee, Gale, "A Form Critical Study of Isaiah 5,1–7 as a Song and a Juridical Parable," CBQ, XLIII (1981), 30–40.

Dissertations

Miller, Merrill, *Scripture and Parable: A Study of the Biblical Features in the Parable of the Wicked Husbandmen and Their Place in the History of Tradition*. Unpublished Ph. D. Dissertation, Columbia University, 1974.
Snodgrass, Klyne, *The Christological Stone Testimonia in the New Testament*. Unpublished Ph. D. Dissertation, University of St. Andrews, 1973.

Index of Passages Cited

1. Old Testament

Genesis
31,42	38 n.33
37,20	51
49,24	69 n.106, 114

Exodus
3,10	24
28	114
28,9f.	113
28,12	113
28,17	113
28,21	113
39	113, 114
39,6	113
39,7	113
39,14	113

Leviticus
19,23	34 n.6

Numbers
23,9	69 n.106

Deuteronomy
15,13	38 n.33
27,5	114
27,6	115

Joshua
4	113, 114
4,6–7	113

Judges
3,13	39 n.36
9,7–20	96 n.105

II Samuel
7,14	85
12,1f.	20, 24, 61
12,1–7	17, 22 n.46
12,1–12	104
12,1–14	96 n.105
12,5	88 n.67
12,10–13	88 n.67
14,1–17	96 n.105

I Kings
14,18	78 n.25
14,22	80 n.31
14,27	80 n.31
15,29	78 n.25
18,13	80 n.31
19,10	80 n.31
20,15f. (LXX)	39
20,35–43	96 n.105
21,13	61 n.66

II Kings
9,7	78 n.25
9,36	78 n.25
10,10	78 n.25
14,8–10	96 n.105
14,24	78 n.25
17,13	78 n.25
17,23	78 n.25
19,30	75
21,10	78 n.25
24,2	78 n.25

II Chronicles
15,6	92
16,10	80 n.31
24,20f.	79
24,41	79 n.27
26,10	33 n.4
36,15–16	80 n.31, 88

Ezra		20,3	78 n.25
3,1–13	99 n.119	27,2f.	75
9,11	78 n.25	28,13	98 n.111
Nehemiah		28,14	77 n.20
9,24–25	39 n.36	28,15	98 n.111
9,26	80 n.31	28,16	98, 109
Job		28,18	98 n.111
22,9	38 n.33	30,14	69 n.106
Psalms		37,31	75
1,3	62	42,1	58
2,7	85, 86 n.53	44,26	78 n.25
80,9–20	75	50,10	78 n.25
80,16	75 n.14	51,1–2	117
80,18	75 n.14	51,5	69 n.106
118	65, 99, 107, 112	53	100
118,22	4, 6, 51, 62, 63, 69 n.106, 70, 91, 95, 97, 98, 99, 100, 101, 102, 104, 105, 106, 108, 109, 110	54	114
		54,11f.	102 n.133, 114, 114 n.6
		61	112
118,22–23	81, 95, 97, 110 n.159	**Jeremiah**	
118,23	51, 55, 62 n.75, 87, 97, 98	2,21	75
		2,30	80 n.31
118,24	99 n.120	3,15	88
118,26	106	5,31	77 n.20
Song of Solomon		6,9	75
8,11f.	33 n.4	7,25	78 n.25
Isaiah		12,7	106
3,14	75, 77 n.20	12,10	76, 77 n.20
3,14–15	76	14,13f.	77 n.20
5	6, 11 n.30, 17,, 47f., 52, 53 n.35, 55, 71, 74, 75, 76, 78, 88	22,5	106
		23,1–4	88
		25,4	78 n.25
5,1	47, 48, 59 n.56	26,5	78 n.25
5,1–7	64 n.85, 76 n.17, 96 n.105	26,20	79
		29,19	78 n.25
5,2	47, 76	35,15	78 n.25
5,4	48, 61	37,15	80 n.31
5,5	61	44,4	78 n.25
5,7	75 n.14, 96, 102 n.133	**Lamentations**	
8,8	98 n.111	4,1–2	113
8,14	68, 98, 110	**Ezekiel**	
8,15	68, 98 n.111	11,2	77 n.20
19,1	24	13,2	77 n.20
		17,3–21	96 n.105
		19,1–14	96 n.105

21,1–5	96 n.105	7,27	68 n.101
22,23f.	77 n.20	9,6	78 n.25
24,3–14	96 n.105	9,10	78 n.25
34,2f.	77 n.20	**Hosea**	
38,17	78 n.25	10,1	75
Daniel		14,6–9	75
2	68, 70, 101, 102, 105, 106	**Amos**	
		3,7	78 n.25
2,28	101 n.131	9,11	85
2,44	68, 69	**Micah**	
2,44–45	68, 69, 70, 71, 94	3,9–12	77 n.20
2,45	69, 70 n.106, 98, 109, 110	5,1	99 n.118
6,18	117	**Zechariah**	
7	68, 101, 112	1,6	78 n.25
7,12–14	68 n.101	3,8–9	101 n.128
7,13f.	68 n.102	9,16	113

2. New Testament

Matthew

3,9	116, 117, 118	20,1–16	74
3,12	22 n.46	21,18f.	91
4,3	116	21,23	46 n.6
4,12	82 n.38	21,26	46 n.6
5,12	79	21,28–32	73, 74 n.9, 81 n.35, 96
6,33	66 n.91	21,28–22,14	93 n.90
7,9	116	21,31	66 n.91
7,16–20	66 n.90	21,32	94
8,11f.	84, 90 n.75	21,33	26 n.59, 46, 56
8,12	90 n.74	21,33–45	1, 39 n.37, 50 n.22
11,27	83	21,33–22,14	58 n.53
12,15	116	21,34	75 n.13
12,18	58, 90 n.75	21,34–37	49, 58 n.53
12,21	90 n.75	21,38–39	51
12,28	66 n.91	21,39	60 n.62, 75 n.13
12,41–42	84	21,40–44	51
13,11	68	21,41	40 n.38, 65, 66, 87, 90, 91, 92
13,11–12	68		
13,22	65	21,42	70, 87, 95, 102 n.133, 103 n.133, 115 n.8, 117
15,1–20	91		
16,5–12	91		
18,34	39 n.37	21,43	4, 6, 65, 66, 68, 69, 70, 75 n.13, 76, 84, 87, 88, 89, 90, 91, 92,
19,24	66 n.91		
19,28f.	84		

	94, 95, 104	12,2–6	49, 53
21,43–44	68, 70,, 71	12,4	53
21,44	65, 66, 67, 68, 71, 102, 103, 104, 105 n.145	12,5	5, 6, 8, 58
		12,6	87
		12,7	8
21,46	46 n.6	12,7–8	51
22	95 n.100	12,9	5, 7, 11, 90 n.73, 92, 97, 98
22,2	81 n.35		
22,3–4	58 n.53	12,9–11	51
22,7	89	12,10	4, 7
23,1–36	91	12,12	46 n.6
23,29–37	79, 84	12,21	64 n.85
23,31	116 n.14	12,27	64 n.85
23,31 f.	79 n.28	12,37	46 n.6
23,31–32	79 n.30	12,41–44	73
23,31–33	84	13,22	83
23,34	50 n.21	14,14	46 n.8
23,37	50 n.21	14,61	99
23,37–39	73, 84, 106	15,6–15	37
24,7	92	15,46	116, 117
24,14	90 n.75	**Luke**	
26,13	90 n.75	4,29	60 n.62, 61 n.66
27,5	89	8,27	49 n.17
27,25	91	9,22	63
27,32	60 n.62	10,29–37	20 n.41
		11,48	116 n.14
Mark		11,49–51	50 n.21
3,23–30	72	12,46	39 n.37
4	72	13,6	34 n.7
4,1–12	20 n.39	13,6–9	74
4,26–29	20	13,34	50 n.21
4,30–32	90 n.75	13,34–35	73, 106
8,31	63, 100, 101	13,35	107 n.150
9,12	100	14,17 f.	58 n.53
9,13	82 n.38	15,19	50 n.24
9,31	100	16,19–31	20 n.41
10,33	100	17,25	63
11,12 f.	90 n.75	18,1–8	37
11,17	73	19,27	39 n.37
11,23	64 n.85	19,28–24,53	46 n.7
11,27–33	81	19,37–40	116
11,32	46 n.6	20,1	46 n.6
12,1	46, 95 n.98	20,6	46 n.6
12,1–9	4, 8 n.21, 31 n.2	20,9	46, 46 n.6, 47, 55
12,1–12	1, 17 n.24, 23 n.49, 39 n.37, 40 n.39, 50 n.22, 59 n.59, 61	20,9–19	1, 39 n.37, 50 n.22
		20,10	52, 55

20,10–13	49, 53	8,11	49 n.17
20,11	53 n.35	12,3	50 n.26
20,12	53 n.35	14,19	61 n.66
20,13	48, 52, 55	24, 26 f.	37
20,14–15a	51		
20,15–18	51	**Romans**	
20,16	70, 92	9,6 f.	92 n.84
20,17	55, 100 n.126	9,32–33	110
20,18	4, 65, 68, 70, 97, 105 n.143	11,1–24	92 n.84
20,19	46 n.6	**I Corinthians**	
22,11	46 n.8	3,9	96 n.101, 102 n.133
23,8	49 n.17	**Ephesians**	
John		2,11–22	92 n.84
3,21–32	67	2,20	110
8,35	50 n.24	**I Thessalonians**	
8,59	61 n.66	2,14–16	79 n.30
Acts		2,15	79 n.28
2,39 f.	92 n.84	2,15–16	79
3,17 f.	92 n.84	**Hebrews**	
4,10–12	108	11,36–38	79 n.28
4,11	100 n.126, 102, 110 n.159	**I Peter**	
7	106	2,4–8	110
7,1–60	92 n.84	2,7	92 n.84, 102
7,52	79 n.28	2,8	63 n.82, 117 n.18
7,58	61 n.66	2,9	93

3. Dead Sea Scrolls

IQS VIII. 5	96 n.101, 98 n.111	8–9	98 n.111
5–9	114 n.6	IQH f II. 8	114 n.6
IQSa 2. 11–22	85	4Q Florilegium	85, 86 n.53
IQH VI. 25–27	98 n.111	IQIs^a	114 n.5
26 f.	114 n.6	IVQpIs^d	114 n.6
VII. 8 f.	114 n.6		

4. Apocrypha and Pseudepigrapha

Enoch		**Psalms of Solomon**	
89	79 n.27	17,23–31	85 n.49
105,2	85 n.49	**IV Ezra**	
Jubilees		7,28	85 n.49
1,12–13	79	13,32	85 n.49

13,37	85 n.49	14,9	85 n.49
13,52	85 n.49		

5. Josephus

Antiquities
VII 11.8	61 n.71	XIV 432f.	40 n.38
X 210	98 n.111	XIV 450	40 n.38
XI 5.4	61 n.72	Jewish War	
XIV 415f.	40 n.38	V 272	115

6. Philo

De Specialibus Legibus

III. 159–162	40 n.38

7. Mishnah

Kilaim		Baba Bathra	
IV.1–V.8	34 n.7	III.1–6	38 n.29
Shebuoth		III.2	33 n.4
IV.12	37 n.24	III.2–3	38 n.30
		III.3	38 n.28
Rosh Ha-Shanah		VII.8	36 n.20
I.8	37 n.24	X.4	36 n.20
Baba Metzia		Pirke Aboth	
V.8	36 n.20	I.3	22 n.46
VIII.6–X.5	36 n.20	II.19	15 n.14
		III.25	15 n.14

8. Babylonian Talmud

b Berakoth		Baba Kamma	
5b	36 n.18	27b	39
64a	96 n.102	66a–70a	38 n.32
b Shabbath		68b	34 n.6
114a	96 n.102	70a	37 n.25
153a	22 n.46	114a	38 n.32
b Pesahim		b Baba Metzia	
119a	99 n.117, 99 n.120	21a–22a	38 n.32
		103b–110b	36 n.20
b Gittin		110a	38 n.31
39a	38 n.28	112b	36 n.20

b Baba Bathra		91a	23 n.49, 36 n.18, 39 n.37
28a	38 n.29	91b	23 n.49, 36 n.18, 39 n.37
28a–36b	38 n.31		
34b	38 n.33	b Gerim	
35b	38 n.29	61a	38 n.28
36a	38 n.33		
38–39a	37 n.24	b Semahoth	
47a	39 n.34	47b–48a	114
53a–55a	38 n.28		

b Sanhedrin	
38a	98 n.111

9. Palestinian Talmud

p Bikkurim	1, 64^b, 55	38 n.31

10. Targums

Fragment Targum		Targum on Psalms	
on Genesis		80,16	86 n.56
49,24	114	118	99
on Exodus		118,22	99 n.119
28 & 39	114	118,22–29	96 n.102, 114

Neofiti		Targum on Isaiah	
on Genesis		5	74 n.11, 90
49,24	114	5,5	89
on Exodus		28,16	98 n.111
28 & 39	114	51,1	117

Onkelos		Targum on Lamentations	
on Genesis		4,1	114
49,24	114		
on Exodus		Targum on Daniel	
28 & 39	114	7,27	89

Pseudo Jonathan		Targum on Hosea	
on Exodus		6,1–2	103 n.135
28	114		
39,6	114	Targum on Zechariah	
39,7	114	4,7	98 n.111
39,14	114	10,4	98 n.111

Targum on Joshua	
4,3–4	117

11. Midrashim

Midrash Rabbah
Exodus Rabbah
XV.19	24 n.52, 36 n.18
XX.9	115
XXIII.10	96 n.102
XXX.17	23 n.51, 39 n.37, 77 n.19
XXXVII.1	99 n.117
XLVI.2	115

Leviticus Rabbah
V.8	36 n.18
XI.7	36 n.19, 39 n.37
XIII.5	39 n.37
XVII.7	98 n.111
XXIII.10	96 n.102
XXV.8	34 n.6

Numbers Rabbah
XIII.14	98 n.111

Deuteronomy Rabbah
III.13	98 n.111
VII.4	36 n.18

Ecclesiastes Rabbah
III.8.2	98 n.111
V.10.2	36 n.18

Song of Songs Rabbah
I.5.3	96 n.102

Esther Rabbah
I.13	93 n.91
VII.10	69 n.106, 99 n.115, 105 n.142, 115

Lamentations Rabbah
IV.1	115

Mekilta on Exodus
15.9 (48b)	86 n.56

Midrash on Psalms
118.20	99 n.114
118.21	99 n.115
118.22	99 n.120, 106 n.150

Pesiqta
99^a	33 n.5

Pesiqta Rabbati
26	79 n.29

Pirqe de Rabbi Eliezer
24	98 n.111, 99 n.115

Sifre Deuteronomy
32, 9 § 312 (134b)	25 n.55, 36 n.18, 91 n.81

Shoḥer Tob
Psalm 2,12	15 n.16

Tanchuma
Tanchuma (Buber, p. 38a, 57)	קדושים 23 n.50, 33 n.4
Tanchuma B 7(29^a)	בשלח 26 n.56, 36 n.18
תרומה 6	98 n.111
תולדות 20	98 n.111
עקב 8	98 n.111

Yalkut Shimoni
on Zech 4,7	98 n.111

Yalkut Shimoni
I, 716	117 n.16

12. Maimonides (YJS)

XIII.I.8	36 n.20	XIII.IV.13	38 n.30, 39 n.34
XIII.IV.11–16	38 n.31		

13. Other Ancient Literature

Papyri
B.G.U. 1121   40 n.38, 61 n.72
P. Columbia
VI.270   61 n.72
   270   40 n.38
P. Oxy. 1631   33 n.3
Zenon papyri
(PCZ 50915)   37 n.22

Quintilian
Instit. Orat.
VIII, VI.4   18 n.29
VIII, VI.58   21 n.42

Tatian's Diatessaron 54 n.37

Gospel of Thomas
52   54 n.38
65   46
65–67   1
66   51
67   51

Testament of Solomon   105 n.143

Patristic Writers
Chrysostom   3 n.1
Origen   3 n.1

Index of Persons

Abrahams, I. 22 n.45
Aland, Kurt 67
Almeida, Yvan 10 n.24, 11 n.30, 72 n.1
Aurelio, Tullio 50 n.23, 97 n.107

Baird, J. Arthur 16 n.17
Balas, Alexander 86 n.58
Bammel, Ernst 37, 38 n.29, 54 n.39
Barth, Gerhard 65 n.87, 91 n.82
Bauer, Johannes B. 22 n.44, 23 n.47
Beare, Francis Wright 75 n.13, 91 n.78, 92 n.83
Bennett, W. J., Jr. 101 n.131
Berger, Klaus 50 n.24, 64 n.85, 82 n.40
Bertram, Georg 69 n.104
Best, Ernest 87 n.62
Betz, Hans Dieter 11 n.30
Betz, Otto 94 n.95
Bieneck, Joachim 83 n.44
Black, Matthew 6, 13 n.6, 63 n.79 and n.80, 64, 78 n.26, 86 n.53, 100 n.127, 103, 109 n.158, 116 n.12
Blank, Josef 59 n.59, 106 n.148
Blinzler, Josef 75 n.15, 91 n.78
Bonnard, Pierre 75 n.15, 77 n.19, 92, 93 n.86
Bornkamm, Gunther 65 n.87, 68 n.99, 91 n.82
Borsch, Frederick Houk 100 n.122, 101 n.128, 103 n.136
Boucher, Madeleine 16 n.17, 19, 20
Bowman, John 64 n.85
Brandon, S. G. F. 66 n.93, 69 n.103, 88
Brongers, H. A. 116 n.12
Brown, Raymond E. 16 n.17
Bruce, Alexander Balmain 62 n.76
Bultmann, Rudolf 15, 16, 17. 85 n.51

Burkitt, F. C. 53, 54 n.37, 67 n.94, 88 n.66, 108 n.156
Buxtorfii, Johannis 116 n.12

Cadbury, Henry J. 107 n.153
Cadoux, A. T. 14 n.11, 60 n.64
Caird, G. B. 19, 29
Calvert, D. G. A. 27 n.60
Carlston, Charles E. 10 n.22, 39 n.35, 57 n.51, 59 n.54, 64 n.85
Carrington, Philip 63 n.79, 74 n.10, 101 n.130, 116 n.13
Cerfaux, L. 68 n.101
Conzelmann, Hans 46 n.7
Cranfield, C. E. B. 63 n.77, 64 n.85, 78 n.26, 88 n.66
Creed, John Martin 50 n.26
Crossan, John Dominic 10, 13, 19, 20 n.39, 22 n.46, 29, 52 n.28
Cullmann, Oscar 83 n.44, 85 n.50

Dahl, N. A. 90 n.75
Daube, David 60,, 104 n.138, 106 n.150
Davey, Noel 20 n.41
Davies, W. D. 84 n.44, 91 n.82
DeBoer, P. A. H. 117 n.15
Dehandschutter, B. 54 n.40
Derrett, J. Duncan M. 18, 34 n.7, 36 n.17, 38 n.29 and n.32 and n.33, 48 n.16, 60, 60 n.64, 74 n.10, 96 n.102, 102 n.133, 103 n.133, 111
Dibelius, Martin 23 n.47
Dillon, Richard J. 58 n.53, 66 n.91, 68 n.102, 92 n.82
Dodd, C. H. 5 f., 14 n.11, 20 n.41, 26, 34, 35 n.10, 52, 60 n.60, 61 n.69,

Index of Persons

62 n.76, 65 n.88, 78 n.23, 81 n.34, 106 n.148
Dombois, Hans 40 n.39
Donahue, John R. 73 n.4, 74 n.10, 102 n.133, 110 n.159
Drury, John 19 n.33
Dunn, James D. G. 82 n.40, 83 n.44

Edgar, C. C. 33 n.3, 35 n.13
Ehlers, Barbara 53 n.36
Eisenstein, J. D. 98 n.111, 99 n.114, 99 n.119
Ellis, E. Earle 60 n.60, 64 n.85, 65 n.88, 78 n.26, 101 n.128, 104 n.138
Emerton, J. A. 113 n.3

Farmer, William R. 26, 56, 58
Farrer, Austin 74 n.10
Feldman, Asher 15 n.16, 22 n.24, 23 n.50, 33 n.4 and n.5, 73 n.7, 97 n.105
Feuillet, A. 83 n.44
Fiebig, Paul 14f., 22 n.44, 23 n.47, 62
Findlay, J. Alexander 38 n.8
Finkel, A. 63 n.79
Fitzmyer, Joseph A. 86 n.57 and n.58
Fletcher, Angus 19 n.36
Flusser, David 19, 20 n.37, 22, 26, 28, 34, 46 n.5, 55, 74 n.9, 87 n.60, 97, 105 n.141, 115 n.8
Foerster, Werner 39 n.35
Ford, J. Massingberd 113 n.1
France, R. T. 101 n.130
Frankemölle, Hubert 89 n.69, 91 n.79, 93 n.87, 93 n.90, 100 n.123, 108 n.154, 109 n.158
Freedman, David Noel 54 n.37
Fridrichsen, Anton 108 n.154
Fuller, Reginald H. 63 n.78, 81 n.34, 83, 85 n.52, 86, 87, 95 n.98, 100 n.126
Funk, Robert W. 10 n.24, 20 n.41, 25 n.54, 34 n.8

Gärtner, Bertil 54 n.38, 64 n.85, 99 n.119, 101 n.128

Gaston, Lloyd 74 n.10, 88 n.66, 93 n.91, 95 n.98, 101 n.129
Gibson, Margaret Dunlop 63 n.83
Giesler, Michael 64 n.85, 99 n.119
Gnilka, Joachim 3 n.1, 59 n.59
Goppelt, Leonhard 84 n.47
Goulder, M. D. 26 n.59
Gozzo, Seraphinus M. 2, 64 n.85, 95 n.98
Grant, Robert M. 54 n.37
Gray, Arthur 11, 45 n.2, 81, 82 n.38
Greig, J. C. G. 83 n.43
Grenfell, Bernard P. 33 n.3
Grundmann, Walter 32 n.2, 45 n.4, 65 n.88, 77 n.19
Gubler, Marie-Louise 109 n.157
Gundry, Robert Horton 47 n.11, 62 n.75, 64 n.85, 66 n.93, 69 n.103, 74 n.10, 75 n.13, 90 n.75, 106 n.150

Haenchen, Ernst 32 n.2, 35, 50 n.24, 54 n.39, 92 n.82
Hahn, Ferdinand 63 n.78, 83, 84 n.44, 86, 95 n.98
Hare, Douglas R. A. 91 n.82
Hauck, Friedrich 16 n.17, 22 n.44, 23 n.47
Held, Heinz Joachim 65 n.87, 91 n.82
Hengel, Martin 2 n.4, 27, 33 n.5, 35, 36, 38 n.29, 40 n.39, 46 n.5 and n.8, 46, 47 n.11, 51 n.27, 60 n.60, 62 n.76, 82 n.40, 85 n.52, 86 n.57, 97 n.109, 107 n.153, 108 n.154 and n.155 and n.156, 111
Hennecke, E. 53 n.36, 54 n.37
Hermaniuk, Maxime 16 n.17, 18, 21 n.42, 22 n.44, 23 n.47
Hermann, J. 39 n.35
Hirsch, E. D., Jr. 29
Hoffmann, Paul 27 n.60
Holtz, Traugott 62 n.75, 105 n.144
Holm-Nielsen, Svend 114 n.6
Honig, E. 19 n.36
Hooker, Morna 27 n.61, 62 n.76, 100 n.122 and n.124 and n.126, 101 n.130, 103
Hort, Fenton John Anthony 66, 67

Hoskyns, Edwyn 20 n.41
Hough, Graham 21 n.43
Howard, George 54 n.37
Howard, Virgil 100 n.123
Hubaut, Michel 2, 7 n.19, 54 n.40, 59, 60 n.62, 61 n.67, 64 n.84, 68 n.101, 89, 89 n.69, 90 n.72, 91 n.78, 94 n.96, 95 n.97 and n.98, 99 n.121, 108
Hunt, Arthur S. 33 n.3
Hunter, A. M. 25 n.53, 83 n.44
Huntress, Erminie 85 n.49

Iersel, B. M. F. van 8, 12, 26, 41, 46 n.8, 50 n.24, 60 n.60, 62 n.76, 78 n.23, 80, 82 n.40, 83 n.44, 84 n.47

Jastrow, M. 47 n.11
Jellicoe, Sidney 73 n.5, 74 n.11, 89 n.70, 92 n.85
Jeremias, Joachim 5 f., 12, 14 n.11, 23 n.47, 26, 28, 34, 35 n.10, 47 n.10 and n.11, 50 n.25, 52, 55 n.44, 56, 57 n.51, 60 n.60, 61, 62 n.74, 62 n.76, 63 n.77, 65 n.87, 67 n.97, 69 n.103, 73 n.7, 81 n.34, 82, 83 n.43, 85 n.49, 97, 99 n.120, 100 n.123, 102, 103 n.135, 105 n.143, 106 n.146, 116, 117
Johnson, Sherman E. 32 n.2
Jones, Geraint Vaughan 1 n.1, 16 n.17, 17 n.25, 20 n.41, 23 n.47 and n.49, 25 n.53, 32 n.2, 41 n.1, 106 n.148
Juel, Donald 73 n.5, 74 n.11, 89 n.70, 92 n.85
Jülicher, Adolf 3 f., 9, 12, 13 f., 16, 17, 18, 56 n.45, 62 n.76, 63, 65 n.88, 93 n.91, 95 n.99

Kahlefeld, Heinrich 56 n.49
Kazmierski, C. R. 72 n.2, 104 n.140
Kertelge, Karl 27 n.60
Kessler, Hans 100 n.123
Kissinger, Warren S. 1 n.1
Klauck, Hans-Josef 13 n.7, 19, 39 n.37, 50 n.22, 54 n.40, 59 n.54, 60 n.62, 61, 74 n.8, 89 n.69, 99 n.121, 108 n.154
Klijn, A. F. J. 54 n.36 and n.37, 63, 117
Klostermann, Erich 32 n.2, 45 n.2, 76 n.19
Kodell, Jerome 46 n.7
Kretzer, Armin 76 n.18, 91 n.79, 93 n.90
deKruijf, Th. 58 n.54
Kümmel, Werner Georg 8 f., 17 n.25, 31 n.2, 55 n.44, 56 n.45, 78 n.26, 84, 85 n.48, 86 n.59, 90 n.75, 92, 93 n.86, 107

Lagrange, M.-J. 45 n.3, 48 n.13, 49 n.17, 50 n.21, 56 n.45, 57 n.51, 60 n.60, 75 n.15, 77 n.20, 78 n.26, 79 n.27
Lambrecht, Jan 72 n.3
Lauterbach, J. Z. 22 n.44
Leivestad, Ragnar 104 n.137
Leon-Dufour, Xavier 2 n.4, 55 n.40, 56 n.49, 59, 60 n.62, 66 n.91, 69 n.103, 99 n.121, 103 n.136, 108 n.154
Levy, J. 116 n.12
Lewis, Agnes Smith 63 n.83
Lightfoot, John 63 n.79
Lindars, Barnabas 65 n.87 and n.88, 95 n.98, 104 n.137, 105, 107 n.150, 110 n.159
Lindemann, Andreas 52
Lindsey, Robert Lisle 55, 55 n.41
Linnemann, Eta 14 n.11, 16, 17 n.25, 34
Lohmeyer, Ernst 31 n.2, 45 n.4, 57 n.51, 58 n.54, 61, 62, 64 n.85, 65 n.87, 74, 76 n.18, 78 n.26, 80 n.31, 87, 88, 90 n.74, 91 n.77, 92 n.84, 93 n.87, 95, 97 n.103, 108 n.154
Lohse, Eduard 85 n.52, 86, 107 n.150
Loisy, Alfred 31 n.1, 32 n.2, 45 n.2, 62 n.76
Longenecker, Richard N. 27 n.60, 64 n.85, 83 n.42, 84 n.45, 85 n.52, 104 n.137

Index of Persons

Lövestam, Evald 85 n.50, 86 n.53
Lowe, Malcolm 82 n.37

MacMullen, Ramsey 34 n.5, 37 n.22
Major, H. D. A. 65 n.87 and n.88, 66 n.92, 95 n.97
Manson, T. W. 46 n.5, 65 n.87 and n.88, 66n.92, 95n.97
Marshall, I. Howard 60 n.61 and n.64, 82 n.40, 83 n.41 and n.44, 84 n.45, 85 n.52
McEleney, Neil J. 27 n.60
McKelvey, R. J. 103 n.134
Merli, Dino 10 n.22, 64 n.85, 88 n.65
Michaelis, W. 50 n.21
Mihaly, Eugene 25 n.55
Milik, J. T. 86 n.58
Miller, Merrill 11, 51 n.27, 54 n.40, 59, 64 n.85, 68 n.99, 69 n.103, 81, 82, 97 n.107
M'Neile, Alan Hugh 116 n.13
Montefiore, Hugh 26 n.59, 27 n.62, 47, 49 n.18, 52 n.28, 53 n.36, 54 n.37 and n.38, 60 n.60, 77 n.20, 91 n.78
Montgomery, James A. 116 n.12
Moule, C. F. D. 12 n.3, 102 n.132, 104 n.137

Neirynck, F. 58 n.52
Neusner, Jacob 22 n.46
Newell, Jane E. and Raymond R. 7 n.14, 11, 13, 35 n.16, 52 n.28
North, Christopher 114

Oesterley, W. O. E. 22 n.44, 76 n.18
Ogawa, Akira 93 n.90, 94 n.93
Oort, H. 69 n.105
Orchard, Bernard 28 n.70, 56 n.48, 59

Pallis, Alex 31 n.1
Patte, Daniel 10 n.25, 20 n.39
Pedersen, Sigfred 60 n.61
Perkins, Pheme 11
Perrin, Norman 1 n.1, 14, 27 n.60, 100 n.122
Pesch, Rudolph 39 n.37, 60 n.62, 64 n.84, 77 n.19 and n.20, 78 n.26, 99 n.121, 108 n.154
Plummer, Alfred 60 n.61

Quispel, G. 48, 54 n.37

Raschi 99
Rengstorf, Karl Heinrich 46 n.8
Rese, Martin 65 n.88, 105 n.145
Ricoeur, Paul 11 n.30, 72 n.1
Robinson, John A. T. 7 n.14, 46 n.5, 50 n.24, 52 n.28, 56, 59, 61 n.68, 84 n.45, 109 n.157
Royen, P. D. van 82 n.37
Ruager, Sören 74 n.8, 91 n.82

Sanders, E. P. 27, 28
Schippers, R. 79 n.30
Schmauch, Werner 57 n.51, 58 n.54, 61, 62, 65 n.87, 74 n.12, 90 n.74, 92 n.84, 93 n.87, 95, 97 n.107
Schmid, Josef 32 n.2, 75 n.15, 95 n.99
Schmidt, Karl Ludwig 69 n.104
Schnackenburg, Rudolf 66 n.91, 90 n.74, 93 n.91
Schniewind, Julius 60 n.60, 66 n.92, 75 n.15, 78 n.26, 85 n.50
Schoedel, William R. 54 n.38, 54 n.39
Schoeps, Joachim 79 n.29
Schottroff, Willy 76 n.16
Schrage, Wolfgang 52
Schramm, Tim 10 n.23, 11 n.31, 47 n.10 and n.12, 52 n.28, 59 n.56, 81 n.35
Schulz, Anselm 108 n.155
Schürmann, Heinz 27 n.60, 55 n.40, 100 n.122
Schweizer, Eduard 85 n.52
Sciascia, Pius 64 n.85
Sellin, Gerhard 21 n.43
Sharpe, Eric J. 54 n.38
Sheppard, Gerald T. 76 n.16
Silvia, Rafael 3 n.1, 59 n.59, 108 n.154
Simon, Uriel 96 n.104
Smith, B. T. D. 14 n.11, 15, 17 n.25, 21 n.43, 32 n.2, 50 n.22, 62 n.76

Smith, Charles W. F. 91 n.79, 106 n.149
Snodgrass, Klyne 53 n.33, 67 n.94 and n.98, 68 n.103, 98 n.111, 105 n.143, 110 n.159, 115 n.7
Steck, Odil Hannes 79 n.29, 91 n.79, 107 n.152
Stein, Robert 27 n.60
Stendahl, Krister 47 n.11, 64 n.85, 69 n.103
Strathmann, H. 46 n.7
Stoldt, Hans Herbert 29 n.70
Strecker, Georg 65 n.87, 66 n.92, 69 n.103, 76 n.18, 89 n.69, 100 n.122
Sturdy, John 14 n.11
Suggs, M. Jack 84 n.44
Suhl, Alfred 62 n.76, 88 n.66, 95 n.99, 97, 104
Swaeles, R. 68, 69, 94
Swete, Henry Barclay 51 n.27, 60 n.61, 64 n.85, 78 n.26
Strack-Billerbeck 24 n.52, 25 n.55, 26 n.56, 33 n.5, 34 n.7, 38 n.31, 48 n.16, 70 n.106, 86 n.56, 96 n.102, 99 n.118 and n.120, 106 n.150, 117 n.16

Tagawa, Kenzo 65 n.87, 92 n.84
Taylor, Vincent 32 n.2, 64 n.85, 78 n.23, 88 n.68, 91 n.77, 100 n.124, 103 n.136, 104 n.138
Tcherikover, Victor 33 n.5
TeSelle, Sallie Mc Fague 14 n.11
Thackeray, H. St. J. 115 n.7
Thiselton, Anthony C. 10 n.24
Tinsley, E. J. 20 n.38
Tischendorf, C. 69 n.103

Tödt, H. E. 63 n.78, 100 n.122, 101 n.131
Tolbert, Mary Ann 29 n.71
Trilling, Wolfgang 59 n.54, 65, 66, 78 n.26, 81 n.34, 88 n.67, 89 n.69, 91 n.80, 92 n.84, 93, 104, 104 n.138 and n. 139, 107 n.151
Turner, C. H. 49 n.19
Turner, H. E. W. 53 n.36, 54 n.37

Uchelen, N. A. van 117 n.15

Vermes, Geza 85 n.52
Via, Dan Otto, Jr. 13 n.7, 20 n.41, 23 n.47
Vincent, J. J. 13 n.6, 20 n.41
Volz, P. 85 n.51

Weder, H. 19, 54 n.40, 62 n.76, 78 n.26, 90 n.73, 108 n.154
Weiser, Alfons 78 n.24, 79 n.27, 84 n.47, 87 n.61, 99 n.121, 108 n.154
Westcott, Brooke Foss 66, 67
Wilcox, Max 64 n.85
Wilder, Amos N. 18 n.29, 34 n.8
Wilson, R. McL. 52 n.28 and n.31, 53 n.36, 54 n.37
Winter, Paul 84 n.44
Woude, A. S. van der 116 n.12
Wright, C. J. 65 n.87 and n.88, 66 n.92, 95 n.97

Yadin, Y. 116 n.9 and n.10 and n.11
Yee, Gale 76 n.16, 105 n.141

Zimmerli, Walther 100 n.123, 103 n.135

www.ingramcontent.com/pod-product-compliance
Lightning Source LLC
Chambersburg PA
CBHW071502160426
43195CB00013B/2180